25·7·13

MALVERN CHASE

This pre-publication copy is for Inspection or
Review purposes only and must not be re-sold.

Birtsmorton Court in 1880

MALVERN CHASE

AN EPISODE OF

THE WARS OF THE ROSES

AND

THE BATTLE OF TEWKESBURY

W.S. SYMONDS

Cappella Archive
Book on Demand Limited Editions

First Edition: W. North, Tewkesbury, 1880.
Second Edition: W. North, Tewkesbury, 1881.
Third Edition: W. North, Tewkesbury, 1883.
Fourth Edition: reset: W. North, Tewkesbury, 1885.
Fifth Edition: W. North, Tewkesbury, 1887.
Sixth Edition: W. North, Tewkesbury, 1901.
Seventh Edition: W. North, Tewkesbury, ? 1905.
Eighth Edition: W. North, Tewkesbury, 1913.
Reprinted Edition: Malvern Bookshop, 1974.
Revised Edition: Cappella Archive, Malvern 1999.

This copy was printed on demand · March 1999

Revised Edition © 1999 David Byram-Wigfield
All Rights Reserved

No part of this publication may be reproduced or stored in a retrieval system, nor transmitted in any form or by any means – digital scanning, mechanical, photocopying, recording, or by any other media – without prior permission of the copyright owner.

British Library Cataloguing-in-Publication Data
A catalogue record for this book is
available from the British Library

ISBN 0-9525308-8-0

Cappella Archive
Foley Terrace · Great Malvern · England

Typeset in a Cappella realization of a Baskerville of 1769 and printed on Five Seasons paper from John Purcell of London.

The Author's Preface to the First Edition

THOSE who are acquainted with English literature and MSS between the times of Chaucer and Caxton will be aware of the difficulty of so modernising the spelling, and arranging the sentences, as to render the following biography intelligible to the general reader.

That it is not easy to rewrite the manuscripts of the time of Henry VI and Edward IV in modern English will be apparent to any one who will read the Leet Book of the Corporation of Coventry, how, on the 21st September, 1450:

> 'The meyre and his worthy bredurn arayed in skarlet, and al the comonaltie cladde in grene gownes and redde hodes, met King Henry VI' and 'the meyre and his peeres lyghten on fete, and thries mekeley kneeling on ther knees did ther due obeysaunce'. And how the King, 'herkening the meyres speche in faverabull wyse seyde: "Well seyde, Sire Meyre, take your hers, and Sirs I thank you of youre goode rule and demene, and for the best ruled pepull thenne within my reame, and also I thank you for the p'sent that ye now gave to us." The which p'sent was a tonne wyne and xx^{tie} grete fat oxen.'

Should the reader desire to be informed respecting the MSS which constitute the Autobiography of Sire Hildebrande de Brute, the Editor must refer him to the publications of 'The Royal Society for Investigating the Literature of Ancient Manuscripts' (London, York Street, Lancaster Square, and Rose Alley).

The Editor has ventured to direct attention, in certain foot-notes, to the remarkable correlation of some of the events in the Autobiography with that historic lore which is principally due to researches into Parliamentary Rolls, Swinfield Roll (Camden Soc.), Harleian MS, Paston Letters, Fabyan, Holinshed, &c.

PENDOCK RECTORY
DEC., 1880.

Acknowledgements

I HAVE to thank Jonathan Gibbs for suggesting that this remarkable historical documentary merited being republished, and for providing those illustrations which were only included in the first and second editions. I am also grateful for the assistance given by the staff of the Malvern Library and the St Helen's Record Office in Worcester.

I salute with admiration the shade of William Symonds, as a supreme example of that vanished breed of academic country parson, whose enquiring and cultured minds maintained the lamp of learning in the remotest corners of the kingdom. His many publications are listed in the Bibliography but, in his own words, perhaps his greatest wish would be for everyone to 'maintain an interest in local history and traditions, which have become, like the Dodo, well nigh extinct'.

DB-W

Illustrations

Birtsmorton Court in 1880	Frontispiece
Eastington Court	32
The New Inn, Gloucester	88
The Market House in the Bull Ring, Ledbury	104
The Ruins of Branshill Castle (drawn after Buck, 1731)	148
Kitel Keep (a reconstruction)	189
The Black Bear, Warwick	205
Payne's Place, Bushley	222

End Papers adapted from John Speed's county map of 1611

Contents

Chapter One   1
The Ancient Family of Hildebrande de Brut – Where they lived, and how they came there.

Chapter Two   15
The Meet at the Holly Bush Pass – the Boar Hunt – An Uninvited Visitor.

Chapter Three   33
Lord Edward of March – the Predicament at Wainlode Hill – the Witch of Eldersfield and her Medicaments.

Chapter Four   48
Lord Edward of March at Birtsmereton – Hanley Castle.

Chapter Five   58
The Trials of Archers on the Mere of Longdune – the Stranger Archer – the Miracle Play at Theocsbury.

Chapter Six   74
A Dilemma through Necromancy – Trollop again – Robin of Elsdune and Mary of Eldersfield – the Whispering Gallery

Chapter Seven   89
Master Snakes, the Witchfinder – the Administration of Discipline by Robin of Elsdune – the Earl of March at Gloucester Castle.

Chapter Eight   104
The Ride after Recruits for the White Rose – Bull Baiting at Ledbury – Branskill Castle – the Shadow of the Ragged Stone – News of the Battle of Wakefield.

Chapter Nine   119
On the March – Hereford – the Review at Widemere – Master Vaughan – the Shadow Hound.

Chapter Ten   134
Wigmore Castle and the Duchess of York – the Skirmish at Brampton Brian – the Battle of Mortimer's Cross – A Narrow Escape in Kinsham Dingle.

Chapter Eleven 148
After the Battle – Ivvan Ivvans – Changes at Home – Lord Edward, King of England – Sir John Carfax of Castlemereton – Bessie Kitel and Sir John.

Chapter Twelve 162
Strange Visitors at Birtsmereton – the Sneeze in the Secret Chamber – the Flight to Bristol – Calverley and Bessie.

Chapter Thirteen 173
King Edward at Windsor – Mistress Elizabeth Gray – Grafton Grange – St Fool's Day – Outlaws in Malvern Chase – Calverley in Sore Straits – Mary Bolingbroke after the Herbs on the Malverns.

Chapter Fourteen 189
Castlemereton Lambs – the Attack upon the Keep – Bessie Kitel a Brave Lass – the Rescue – the Tower of London – the Queen – the King-maker – the Coronation Feast – No Tidings of Rosamond.

Chapter Fifteen 205
Master Vaughan's Letter – Hamme Castle – the Castle of Sudeley – Dame Despenser – the Escape from Banbury – Slop's Hole and Lord Rivers – the Last of Sir Andrew Trollop.

Chapter Sixteen 222
The Strange Episodes 1469 – the Battle of Nibley Green – the King-maker at the Abbey of Theocsbury – Master Vaughan at Payne's Place – the Ides of March – the King-Maker – Christmas among the Hollanders – Gladsmore Heath – the March to meet Queen Margaret – the March before the Fight at Theocsbury.

Chapter Seventeen 243
The Battle of Theocsbury – the Bloody Meadow – An Unexpected Meeting at Lincoln's Green – the Scene in the Abbey – Prince Edward – Queen Margaret at Payne's Place – At Worcester – the Wedding – King Edward and Queen Elizabeth at Great Malvern – the Shadow – the End.

Author's Notes x

Bibliography xv

Biography xvi

Editor's Preface

WHEN I first read this book, a series of extraordinary coincidences presented themselves. As a young history student I had written a paper on the Nevilles of Middleham, and later I lived for eight years almost within bowshot of the battlefield of Mortimer's Cross. I was sometimes a guest at Kinsham Court, where lies the Dingle where Hildebrande de Brut was so nearly undone, and, when our children were young, we often explored the castle remains at Ludlow and Wigmore.

To complete the association of chance, I now live on the Malvern Hills, and I can see in the distance the silver curve of the Severn and the site of the Earl of Warwick's disembarkation at Hanley Quay, with Upton-on-Severn and Tewkesbury lying beyond.

Personal feelings apart, I immediately decided that the well-drawn characterisation, breadth of scholarship, lively dialogue, and descriptive writing in themselves deserved the reprinting of this remarkable historical narrative.

I have made few alterations to the text, which is that of the original edition, but I have removed the quotation marks with which William Symonds, or his printer William North, liberally sprinkled the name of every dog, horse, plant, and hostelry. I have similarly discarded some exclamation marks and, where the sense allows, I have divided some very long paragraphs into shorter units. The spelling of place-names has been retained, but I have removed the final letter from the word 'Sire' when used as a title, so that it is read less phonetically.

One characteristic of William Symonds' writing is the occasional delay of a related clause or phrase until the end of a sentence. An example is where he states in a note for the last chapter: 'if this was the spot, there were entrenchments, before Queen Margaret's occupation, of older date'. Most remain as they were written, but in some instances I have re-ordered the sequence where the punctuation became elaborate.

The author's notes are placed at the end of the book and I have resisted the temptation to add to their number.

DAVID BYRAM-WIGFIELD
GREAT MALVERN

Chapter One

I AM ONE of that race which was English before William the Norman conquered our country. One of my ancestors followed Robert of Normandy to the wars of Palestine, and from plain John Birts changed his name to John de Brute. The Roman poet called the great Saxon race from whom we sprang 'sea wolves that live on the pillage of the world', and I fear that this was too true of their earlier history; but when the land was conquered, they soon settled down around the villages of the forest glades, or by the banks of the rivers, each settlement being independent of its fellow settlement.

The Birts who assisted in the Saxon conquest of England were landholders in a land of Birch trees, and land tillers before they crossed the seas. Their first settlement in this country was on the banks of the Severn, below the site of the ancient town of Theocsbury, at a place called Deorhyst. At Deorhyst, the religion of the Cross succeeded the pagan worship of Woden, the War God, earlier than in many parts of Saxon England, and a priory was founded in Saxon times.

Here, on the conversion of the Birts to Christianity, the sacred rite of baptism was performed by immersion in the waters of the Severn, and when they died, our Edwards, or Ealdwulfs, and their Ethelgifas were laid in the grave to the ringing of the passing bell. For many years the Priory of Deorhyst acquired great and deserved celebrity among the early Christian establishments.

It was rich and flourishing when the fires of the Danish invasion wrapped in flames its great wooden structures. Church and Grange were alike destroyed, and the family of the Birts had, like the Prior of Deorhyst himself, to take refuge in the dense forest which then stretched from the Malvern Hills to the Severn, and from beyond Worcester to Gloucester, and which in after times became the Malvern Chase of the haughty Norman conqueror.

From old traditions handed down through long generations of the Birts, it is well nigh certain that at the time of the burning of Deorhyst, a family of Saxons had settled in a glade in the forest near to the old Roman trackway which led from Gloucester across the Malverns to Saxon Hereford. Here, too, an ancient Christian church was built of forest oaks with nothing of stone save mayhap the font, and it was called Pendyke from very early times, the church being built at the head of a dyke or trench, which was once a boundary of British tribes before the Saxons landed in Britain or the Romans either.

The family who dwelt at Pendyke[1] bore the name of Kitel, and in Saxon times the Birts of Deorhyst, and the Kitels of Pendyke, were mighty hunters in the forest, and many a wolf and many a wild boar fell before their spears. It was to the Kitels that the Birts fled for safety at the burning and sacking of Deorhyst by Sweyne, and it was by their aid that our family reclaimed some hides of forest land within a short distance of Pendyke and established a settlement, to which they gave the name of Birtsmereton, or the ton or village where the Birts settled, close upon the borders of a great mere or moorland swamp.

The time came when the Kitels and de Brutes were no longer contented with their wooden granges and barns in the forest glades; moreover, they were always in danger from the troublous Welsh; so they each built their Keep or strong tower, round which the ton or village clustered, one at Pendyke, on Kitel Hill, and the other at Birtsmereton, while close by each was erected a little church, for our gallant ancestors were God-fearing men.

Birtsmereton Keep was small, but strong, surrounded by massive stone walls and a deep trench or moat. A little stream fed this moat and ran through a large upper fish-pool, which answered two purposes, it fed the moat with water and the occupiers of the Keep with fish on fast days. The only entrance to the Keep was by a drawbridge across the deep, dark moat, and a strong portcullis hung from the battlemented gateway, which was loopholed for archers, while from a niche looked down our patron saint, St Gunhilda. It was a forest Keep, and, when the farmer became a knight among Normans, he still followed in the footsteps of our Saxon forefathers. He kept large droves of swine to feed upon the acorns and the beech mast on the Swineyard Hill of the Malverns, which rose above the Norman Chase and forest, but it never was a great stronghold in which a crowd could be banqueted or a numerous retinue summoned to arms.

My grandfather, Giles de Brute, pulled down the Keep, leaving only the basement, and erected the manor house in which I was born. Instead of the tower-like Keep with its round lights for windows, we had a comfortable dwelling with hanging roofs and gables, and my dear mother always pointed with pride to our windows filled with glass. Indeed, neither at Kitel Keep or Castlemereton are there now such lattices which can be opened or shut at pleasure, neither are there such andirons for the burning logs in the winter time, or so fine a vent to carry off the smoke as in our Hall. Then our bedrooms are far larger and more lofty than the little cub-holes which our ancestor Sir Giles and his dame used to occupy, up the winding stone staircase of the Norman Keep. The walls too are painted with the romance of George and the Dragon, and with Noah's Ark and the wild beasts which came out of it.

Our tenants were thirteen in number, and they did service for the land they occupied, which was taken in from the forest, and the gift of the Red Earl of Gloucester, Gilbert de Clare. Besides this, there were two hundred acres of arable and pasturage for the stock of the home farm, which consisted of oxen and heifers, calves and sheep, geese and capons, cocks and hens. These, with the gardens, fish-ponds, rabbit-warren, and pigeon-house, kept us well provided, and right hospitable my father was to poor as well as rich. Then there was the chaplain, an old friend of my mother's family, and the steward who lived in the house, and the forester who lived in the woods, while the plough drivers and swineherds occupied mud cottages outside but near to the Manor for defence.

Our nearest neighbours of gentle blood were Sir John Carfax of Castlemereton, and the Kitels of Pendyke, the Calverleys of Branshill across the Malvern Kills, and the Berews of Berew, the descendants of a Saxon family as ancient as our own, but who had gone down in the world through fines and spoliations, and by offence given the de Clares by appropriations of land from the forest without saying with or by your leave.

Then farther off were the Bromwiches of Broomsbarrow, and the Brydges of Longdune, who lived at an old grange – Eastington – once the homes of the Saxon Eastings. To all these places there were trackways through the Chase so broad that two or three might ride abreast, while there were many portways and paths, known only to those who lived in the neighbourhood, which led to different parts of the forest, sometimes to open glades where the deer would pasture, sometimes to dense thickets, the lair of the wild boar, though boars were becoming scarce to find and difficult to kill.

The south Malverns under which our manor house is built, are very different in their character to the northern hills which rise above the

Priory and little village of Malvern. They are far more wooded up their slopes, and although not so high, the thickets are more dense and the gullets more deeply riven. For ages the forests about Waum's Well, on the flanks of the Herefordshire fire-beacon, have been refuges for those who, like Owen Glendower and Sir John Oldcastle, have had to seek shelter from the wrath of kings and ecclesiastics, or the poacher who had offended against the forest laws and was liable to pains and penalties. The side of the Midsummer Hill, below the camp on its summit, is famous for its hollows and masses of stone, with which the Britons built rude huts and circles, and here we find ever the biggest stag, and sometimes the lair of a boar.

The Ragged Stone, or Rent Hill, with its valleys of the white-leaved oak and holly bush on either Bank, and seamed with gullets both on the northern and southern slopes, is a sunny hill-top on a summer's day, where swallows skim and butterflies haunt the stunted flowers, but below are the densest thickets of our forest, and the little rill which runs through the hawthorn glades. Here grow the earliest primroses of spring and the sweet white violet; and here, in the summer, are the purple foxgloves, and the yellow mullein with its woollen leaves.

Then the last hill of all is the Chase End, or the end of our Malvern Chase, for at Murrell's End, beyond the groves of Hazeldine, begins the great Chase of Gloucester. At the base, towards the south, nestles the little Norman church of Broomsbarrow, and behind is the wildeness of the Howling Heath. But through all the forest, go where you will, the spring time is resonant with the songs of birds, the nightingale and mavis, the storm-cock and the blackbird; and among the hill-tops we listened to the trill of the stone-chat and the whistle of the whin-cock, or the piping of the white dappled wheat-ear.

I was born in the year of grace 1438, just eight years after the Maid of Orleans, Joan of Arc, was bunt to death for witchcraft, and three years before Eleanor Cobham, who was a sort of relation of ours through the Oldcastles, did public penance in three places in London, being accused of the great sin of endeavouring to destroy the king, his majesty Henry VI, by divinations and enchantments. But my dear and learned father was more affected, as I have often heard him say in after years, by the death of his friend the learned astrologer Roger Bolingbroke, who was most falsely accused, with Margery Jourdain, of making a wax figure of his most sacred majesty the King for Eleanor Cobham, and in necromancing it under the light of the stars, so that in proportion as it was sweated and melted before a fire it would, by magical sympathy, cause the flesh and substance of the King to wither and melt away and his marrow to be dried up in his bones.

Roger Bolingbroke was hanged, drawn, and quartered at Tyburn, and Margery Jourdain was burned alive in Smithfield. At this my father was most indignant, for he, like Bolingbroke, was much given to the sciences, and especially to the studies of astronomy and astrology. As indeed was my grandfather before him, he having learned much at the time when the celebrated Owen Glendower, who was himself reputed to be a magician, was accustomed to take refuge in our forest home, and to go to and fro to Kenderchurch, the home of his daughter, Jane Scudamore, where he passed by the name of Jack of Kent.[2]

My dear mother and ever respected father did not agree on these subjects, she never liked my father star-gazing on the Malverns or squaring the circle with Bolingbroke, or watching the moon night after night; while she knew well that her calves once died in the paddocks hard by when Moll Billings went away cursing and blaspheming from the drawbridge. She knew too that the butter would not churn, and the conserves got mouldy when Moll was seen squinting in at the dairy door after a moonlight night, so she kept Moll at a distance and wished my father would let the moon alone also.

My father was a Wycliffite, or as was now termed a Lollard, and our grandfather's dearest friend and cousin, Sir John Oldcastle, after he had been hunted and persecuted for six long years, during which he had often sheltered in our manor house, had been hung in iron chains and roasted over a fire, because he had been found guilty of heresy, as Bolingbroke was of necromancy, and this only a little more than twenty years before I was born.

My father was a powerful man, with large brown eyes and strongly marked forehead, round which clustered thick brown hair. An air of resolute determination expressed somewhat of his character, and a just, true man was he. My sweet mother was of Norman blood, the daughter of Sir Giles and Dame Acton; a family which came originally from France in the time of Edward the Confessor. Mother was ever beautiful, at least to father and me, her only child. Her face was lighted by dark but kindly eyes, her thoughts were ever for others rather than for herself, and she nursed Moll Billings when she was sick with fever well nigh unto death, after she believed the calves had died through her witchments.

My boyhood was passed entirely at home, and to my father I owe that excellent education which has been of such service to me during a somewhat long life. He was a scholar, and had written out with his own hand much of Wycliffe's Bible and the works of Master Chaucer and Boccaccio. While my mother was busy in the long winter nights with her needle or spindle, my father would be engaged with his parchments and grey goose quill, and often would she rise up from by the burning logs, and with beaming eyes look over the writing, and, putting her arms round his neck, ask what it betokened.

Above our manor house, within a two miles' gallop, rises the south end of Malvern Hills, and many a time and oft have I clambered up the Beacon of Herefordshire, or the Swineyard Hill, where the swine do pasture, or the Hill of Midsummer, with its ancient camp, which my father said was occupied, with Danesmoor, by the Danes, some of whom settled around this hill when they had harried all the Saxons they could find. Then there is the Dead Oaks below the Gullet Pass, where many a poacher of deer has been hung in chains as a scare to others who would trespass on the rights of those Norman barons who claimed all animals of the Chase and the falcons of the hills. Here, when a boy, I have passed in fear and trembling, as the bones of the dead clattered in the wind as it whistled down the Gullet, or sighed and sobbed round the Swineyard above.

When I was about twenty years of age, John Hasting, our forester and woodman, became my frequent companion, and after the morning's studies with my father over scrip, parchment, and pen, it was my delight to persuade Hasting to accompany me to the mere of Longdune, where in autumn time we snared snipes and plover in numbers with horse-hair springes, while he would occasionally kill both wild ducks and wild geese with his cross-bow, or the grey goose shaft from the long-bow, in the use of which he had no compeer.

In the summer time the mere was dry in large portions, though much covered by the bullrush and the flag, and John could always find a heron for our falcons; while many a boomer[3] have we brought home from the mere before the summer's sun had risen above the spire of Longdune. In the summer days flags and rushes held wild ducks' eggs and plovers, with which mother loved to make a dainty dish, when our friends and neighbours came to dine, or to pass the day fishing in the moat for the luce,[4] or in the little stream for the silver trouts.

Under the auspices of Hasting I learned a good deal of the noble sport of falconry, and our tercels were taught to fly at herons, while we had hobbies and merlins which would pounce on wild pigeons, snipe, and partridges. I also learnt to reclaim the birds and direct their diet, while, in the spring time, we would search for the young on some rocky shelf among the Malverns, or in a crow's nest from which the owners had been driven, among the tops of the highest oaks. Hasting always made our bows, and he exercised the boys and serfs around us in archery on the great green between our churches of Birtsmereton and Berew.

He knew every yew and ash tree in the forest for miles around, and no arrows were so tapered, or winged with such wild-goose feathers, as those we called the 'Hasting's shaft'. No wonder then that in such company I became a proficient with the 'gallant grey goose shaft', and that before I was twenty I could have transfixed a man at three hundred paces, or a pigeon at fifty.

One evening, in the mid-spring time, Hasting told me he had heard a bittern booming at the moon down among the reeds and willows in the mere; so we were up before the sun, the grey mist still hanging over the vale, I with my cross-bow, and Hasting with his long-bow and sheaf of arrows. The air was, as Hasting said, "filled with a charm of the songs of birds." We could hear the stormcock whistling on the tops of the elms and the blackbird trolling in every thicket; by and by, from a paddock, a lark would rise carolling his welcome to the sun, then a blackcap would whistle with a tune that made us think it was the nightingale until we heard the trill, trill of that songster himself, while the zoo zoo[5] was cooing in every grove.

The sun rose as we neared the mere, and we heard the boom, boom of the bittern, the quack of the mallard, and the shrill cauk, cauk of the heron. The mere possessed a character of its own. It was, if possible, more lonely than the Chase with its scattered villages and granges, and silent as the grave, save the calls of its wild fowl and the croak of the frog. 'Boom, boom', rang out the bittern, and we directed our course towards it, as we knew it would cease to call soon after sunrise, but it was not easy to reach the spot from which the sound emanated. There were mires, tall rushes and sedges, with here and there water lying in deep hollows filled by a spring-time flood, and boggy places which would engulf a man if he slipped in, and cover him up to the day of doom in black peaty slush. So it was agreed that I should try a creep with my cross-bow in order to get a sitting shot at the boomer, which I longed to obtain, for it was the birthday of our neighbour Rosamond Berew.

I then half-scrambled and half-waded through the sedges to within some five hundred yards of the place where the coveted bird sat, offering, in his own way, his hymn to the rising sun. The boomer always feeds by night, not, like the heron, by day, and in the early morning it will often sit close, whereas the heron quickly takes flight on the slightest sound. This was in our favour, and while Hasting went a little to the right, I crawled straight for some thick reeds from which the loud call note seemed to come.

Creeping and creeping, with as little noise as possible, I was at last rewarded by seeing the beautiful bird squatted on a little knoll among the bull-rushes, his head hung well back as it uttered its call, and the sun lighting up its beautiful buff brown and chestnut plumage, while down the breast was a tippet I fervently hoped would soon grace the neck of a turtle dove who nestled under the groves of Berew. But my nerves were unsteady, and though within fifty paces of the bittern I felt that I might miss.

In after years, when my life depended on steadiness of aim, I never felt so unnerved as I did when watching that bittern on that spring morning. At last, placing the bolt of the cross-bow in readiness, and bending on one knee, I took careful aim, but my hand shook, and the bolt sped close above the head of the bird. One sharp boom, a toss, as it were, through the sedges, and the strong bird was high above me, winging its flight to less dangerous quarters. In my chagrin I threw my crossbow on the ground, when suddenly the bittern fell almost at my feet, an arrow having pierced its body from wing to wing. A pang of jealousy shot through me for a moment, as Hasting came splashing through the sedges.

"Never mind, Master Hildebrande," said he, "better luck next time; I have missed more boomers than ever I killed."

Soon recovering, I congratulated him on his success, but I said nothing about the feathers for the tippet, or the birthday present.

By this time we had got well across the mere, and it was determined I should try my luck with the long-bow at a wild duck on the water, and that we would return by Kitel Hill and the trackway to our manor. We had just crossed the brook that ran by Pendyke through the mere, when we heard the whimper of a small dog in the sedges, and coming down the bank towards the brook we saw Bessie Kitel with her red tercel[6] on her wrist, the very red tercel I gave her just a year before.

"Oh, Hildebrande de Brute," she said, "it is too bad of you and Hasting thus early disturbing every hern within a reach of Kitel. You naughty boy, I would fly the tercel at a hern, but you and Hasting never give a poor girl a chance, and we of Kitel must content ourselves with duck or partridge. However, it is your own loss and you will not now have a hern's crest worked by my own fingers to wear in your cap and bring you the luck of falconry."

Hardly had she spoken when a hern rose from the sedges by the brook. In a moment Bessie released the hood, and the tercel made such a dash towards the hern as at once told us it was a bold bird.

"Right well trounced," said Hasting, as the noble bird made his first swoop, and cauk, cauk, cried the hern, as the falcon missed his strike. Again the falcon trounced, again missed, and the hern rose circling in the air. Here the tercel appeared to change its tactics, as it rose higher in great sweeps above the quarry, until both seemed soaring to the clouds. At last down came the swoop with lightning force, and we could hear the air whistle as the tercel descended, when suddenly there seemed a struggle among the clouds and slowly the heron fell fluttering to the ground.

"Spiked! by all that's holy," shouted Hasting, as he rushed towards the mere in which the heron had fallen. Among the rushes lay both birds, dead, the falcon transfixed by the heron's beak, and the neck of the heron so injured by the shock that it too was killed. A tear stood in Bessie's eye as we brought back her dead tercel and the heron's plume.

"Poor Hildebrande," she said, for thus had she named her falcon, "You shall lie under the yew tree on our hill of Kitel, a fitting grave for so bold a bird."

Bessie Kitel was about eighteen years of age, and with her long fair hair and sparkling grey eyes looked the picture of good health and good temper. I did not altogether like her appropriating the bittern which Hasting had slung over his shoulder, saying, "Well, Hildebrande, if I have lost my tercel in endeavouring to obtain a heron's plume for you, you have won the boomer's tippet for me." She then inquired into the circumstances of the capture, and I had the mortification of confessing my miss and the good aim of Hasting. I thought a shade of displeasure passed across her face as I told her I sought the bird for the birthday of Rosamond Berew, but she was far too kindly-hearted to bear enmity, and invited us to take some refreshment at Kitel Keep, which rose immediately above us on the hill-top.

The Keep of Kitel, in the parish of Pendyke, is one of the most curious relics of antiquity in this part of England. It is a single tower, standing on the edge of a plain, and overlooking the mere of Longdune, while in the distance rise the range of the Cotswolds and the hill of Bredon. To the north we see the hills and priory of Malvern, and below the green woodlands of Malvern Chase; while at a short distance to the southward is the little monastery and church of Pendyke. The Keep is said to have been built upon the site of a Saxon grange by a Kitel who turned soldier in the days of William Rufus. In later times, the occupiers surrounded the tower with barns and pleasant cots, so that the stronghold became the residence of the descendants of the founder, who cultivated their land with the aid of their own labourers and cottars, who gathered the grain, sheared the sheep, made the cider, hewed the wood, and malted the barley. The entrance to Kitel Keep is by a flight of stone steps, and the chambers are somewhat small and confined, while the narrow window lights are not filled with glass, but with thin cow's horn, inasmuch as Master Kitel had a great objection to employing any of the modern novelties or new luxuries.

We were greeted by the deep baying of two deerhounds, and John Kitel seeing us approaching up the hill, from the mere below, met us on the steps, followed by his bulldog Holdfast, a brute that would have pinned a lion at his master's signal, but was singularly tractable to the sound of his voice. Kitel gave us a homely greeting and hearty welcome, bidding us to the table, where his serving men were already gathered awaiting the important hour of dinner, for it wanted only two hours of mid-day.

I soon found myself seated between the Master and Bessie, above the massive silver salt cellar, while Hasting placed himself at the lower board with the grieve and hinds. Cups and trenchers of bread were soon supplied to us, and a great collop pasty with salt pork was already on the table. Flagons of cider were passed round, also a small double-handed cup with wine in honour of the guests, which was carried to myself and Hasting by the hands of the fair Bessie. Kitel congratulated me on my prowess with the bow and cross-bow, and expressed a fervent hope that I should never be immersed in parchments, or become a scholar, which was fit only for 'priests and scriveners'. He gave us an invitation to repeat our visit whenever sport took us in that direction, and concluded by an exhortation to "Ware scholarship, which took Sir John Oldcastle to the gallows, and never yet enabled a man to draw a good bow or wield a battle-axe".

We proceeded from Kitel Keep to the Berew, or home of the Berews, in order that I might present Rosamond Berew with the boomer's tippet.

Underhill, as their new manor house is called, from its situation below the round hill of Berew, is a very different place from Kitel Keep, although its site was formerly occupied likewise by a small Saxon grange. Surrounded by a moat it is almost entirely constructed of timber from the forest, with stone foundations and wattle and daub for the walls. It is not nearly so large as our own manor house of Birtsmereton, but far more comfortable than are the ancient keeps, for here there are windows with glass, and a parlour fitted up with beautiful tapestry, also a chimney, a very rare structure in common country houses. This parlour, too, boasted one luxury which we did not then possess, and which old Master Berew is said to have received from the far East. This was a carpet, an article much too valuable to tread upon, and which is only put down for show on rare occasions, the floor being usually occupied by clean rushes, of which the meres of Longdune or Eldersfield furnish abundance. Indeed the parlour itself at Underhill is rarely occupied, the central hall being the chamber usually frequented by the household.

The first person we beheld on our arrival was the youth known to our neighbourhood as Silent John, the only brother of Rosamond, who never spoke save when he was spoken to, and not always then. Clad in a hunting vest with woollen hose, he was engaged in making horse-hair springes for snipes and plover, while his eyes brightened as he beheld the bittern, and he vouchsafed a quiet nod to our salutations. John superintended the farming of the estate, and the ploughing and sowing of autumn and spring. Under him were half-a-dozen churls, and in his quiet way he managed to set an example of industry to the neighbourhood, while, owing to the careful cultivation bestowed on the land, the farming at Berew was conspicuous for its crops at harvest, and the breed of cattle on the pastures. John and his sister Rosamond were orphans, and lived with their grandfather at the grange of Underhill, having lost both their parents in early childhood.

The Berews were of Saxon origin, like ourselves, but, owing to various circumstances, they had yielded less to Norman influences, and therefore were subjected more to Norman despotism. For a long time therefore the family remained churls, under the bondage of Norman lords, until one of them paid forty marks for his manumission, which was obtained by the Sub-Prior of Little Malvern. This was about one hundred years before I was born, but since that time the Berews had accumulated money, and the grandfather of Rosamond was known to possess many broad pieces, in addition to certain hides of land. Master Berew had known Sir John Oldcastle personally, and, himself a Lollard, had witnessed some of the persecutions of that sect. Age did not diminish his hatred of the house of Lancaster, though for years he had lived a life of retirement, varied only by occasional visits from my father, with whom, as a scholar, he was ever delighted to converse.

Master Berew had been tall in his younger days, and his face now a good deal resembled the profile of the tercel or the kite. His hair was long and almost white, and he looked at us as we entered with sharp grey eyes, which seemed to search for information before we were ready to give it. He had a sorrowful expression, and wore a somewhat stern demeanour, as he rose to give his salutations to myself and my companion. He requested us to be seated on the oaken bench opposite the great chair he occupied, and on which Rosamond sat when she was released from her household duties, and listened to the instructions of her grandfather, or when he related the events of his younger days. He heard my account of the morning's sport with some interest, but I said nothing about the destiny of the boomer's tippet, or the crest of the hern. Then he inquired what were my studies, and seemed to think more of scholarship than of the hawk or the hound.

Rosamond Berew would only be pronounced beautiful by those who knew and loved her, for her principal beauty lay in expression, and no face I ever beheld equalled hers in the smiles which lighted it when she was glad, or the look of deep sympathy when she sorrowed with the bereaved. She had a gentle voice, too, which contrasted not a little with the gruff tones of her grandfather, or the shrill loud calls of the country wenches. Her long brown hair hung in clusters down her neck as she advanced with beaming eyes to welcome us as we crossed over the drawbridge, a posie of spring violets in her bodice, and a white dove nestling on her shoulder.

In the chamber where Master Berew was sitting, she had gathered a store of herbs from the woods above the house, which are famous as medicaments and salves. There was the ground ivy and the roots of the daffodil, with maiden's fingers and lords and ladies, all of which awaited the arrival of the celebrated herbalist Mary of Eldersfield, some times called the Witch, when they were to be stewed and compressed for future use, given, as need required, among the house holds of the labourer and the poor. Then there were large branches of primroses and cowslips, and the white wind-flower, all fresh-gathered in the woods, and with these the nest of the blue Isaac,[7] which John had brought in only to receive a scolding from his sister for robbing the poor bird of its bright blue eggs, and an entreaty to spare the nest of the water-hen, which had built its sedgy cradle on the borders of the moat.

The wild flowers were a birthday gift from the children of the cottars, one of whom had brought a young furze pig[8] and another a pair of quice or woodpigeons, for the Rose of Berew, as she was often called, was almost worshipped by the hinds and their children, as she had ever a kind word and friendly greeting for those who are too often regarded as of less consequence than the cattle on the land, and are rarely so well treated.

Hasting meanwhile learnt from John Berew that a wild boar had been seen in the thickets of the Holly Bush hill, and a large stag near the pass of the hill of the Swineyard. It was therefore agreed that we should consult my father and Kitel of Pendyke, and with our combined foresters and others should hold a Chase some early day. Rosamond agreed to accompany us to Birtsmereton, only about a distance of a score of bow-shots, as she wished to convey some flowers from the woods of Berew for the acceptance of my mother. We said good-bye to the venerable Nigel, and set forth together.

Hitherto I had said nothing of the bittern's tippet, but as Rosamond tripped along by my side, and John was deep about potions for sick kine with Hasting, I took the opportunity of requesting her to accept the feathers and wear them for the sake of old acquaintance since we were children, as it was her birthday and I had taken much trouble to obtain them. She turned away her face while I spoke and was engaged in pulling her violets to pieces; then turning cheerily, she said with a smile, "I thank you gratefully, Master Hildebrande." Still, I did not like the 'Master'. We soon arrived in sight of the tower of our church and the gables of the manor-house.

The rooks were cawing from the big elms and the moorhen and coot flitted across the great fish-pond, as we passed towards the drawbridge. My father and mother were seated on the parapet above the moat, in the evening's sunshine, and Rosamond Berew curtsied as she received my mother's kiss and blessing. John soon possessed himself of the big tankard of cider which was brought from the house, and said little save giving some directions as to the most probable place for finding the boar on the day of the proposed chase.

My father willingly gave his consent to the boar hunt, but declined joining us, as he was engaged on business of a pressing nature. It was agreed that the Kitels of Pendyke should be invited, and that we should borrow two boar-hounds from Sir Hugh Calverley of Branshill, in addition to the deer-hounds which would be furnished by the Kitels and ourselves. Bessie Kitel and Rosamond Berew were to join our party, with any of the Calverleys who liked to ride from Branshill, and Sir John Carfax from Castlemereton. The meeting place was to be the summit of the pass between the Ragged Stone and Midsummer Hills on the trackway between Theocsbury and Ledbury. These arrangements settled, Rosamond and her brother departed, an early day being fixed for our hunt of the wild boat.

Chapter Two

IN THE days of the Norman kings the forest laws were far more oppressive than they are now, and the Chase of Malvern stretched away for miles with here and there a village and a church rising in the clearings. Even in the time of Edward the First and his son-in-law, Gilbert de Clare, the Red Earl of Gloucester, land which now the farmer's axe has cleared and converted into pastures, was covered with wood, dense thickets and the yellow gorse; the haunts of the wild boar and the wild deer, while the bittern was a common bird in the meres, and the beaver still haunted the Severn at Beverley. But now both boars and bitterns are become rare, and the stag is not nearly so abundant as it was in the days of my grandfather.

Still the chase of boar or deer was far more accessible to the dwellers in the forest than it ever was in the days of the Red Earl, when a man hardly dare venture out of the line of the trackways or cut a new path through the thickets lest he should disturb the wild beasts in their lairs. The owners of the principal keeps and castles – such as Hanley and Branshill Castles, or Castlemereton and Birtsmereton Keeps – now claimed a right of chase in portions of the forest near them, as having been granted to their forefathers for services rendered in years gone by.

The largest range in our neighbourhood was that of the Earl of Warwick in the right of his Countess, Ann Beauchamp, who was the owner of Hanley Castle and other vast possessions. Our forester, Hasting, was a ranger of Lord Warwick's, and so had built a woodman's lodge, which he called the Robin Hood, at Castle Mereton, as being near to the haunts of some of the stags in the Gullet Pass and about the Swineyard Hill, and where, after a deer had been killed, it could be flayed and dressed.

This lodge was a mere log house, but was filled with various implements of the woodman's craft, such as long-bows and cross-bows, bags of quarrels[1], sheaves of arrows, boar-spears, falcon tressels and fishing gear. Against the beams of timber there hung knives and bills, axes for falling timber, large boots made of buck's hides, and leathern jackets which would defy the most thorny thicket.

It was at the Robin Hood that Hasting and I formed most of our hunting plans, and more than once after a long chase and we had been overtaken by nightfall, have we been glad of the rude shelter, and passed the night there with fern for our bedding and deer skins for our coverlids. On the day before the boar hunt, we passed most of our time at the lodge making the necessary arrangements and sending messages to the neighbouring gentry, with requests to bring the particular dogs we required, and whose attendance was often, to us at least, of more importance than their masters.

Thus we invited Sir Hugh Calverley of Branshill Castle across the Malverns, and his son, begging of him to bring his famous boarhounds, Hecate and Styx. Sir John Carfax of Castlemereton was the possessor of several fox curs which he used for hunting vermin, but they had remarkable noses and might be useful, as the ground was parched and dry. Kitel of Pendyke managed his dogs right well, and Bessie would surely join us in the forest. John Berew knew more of kine than hounds, but he was sure to keep his tongue quiet, and was a right sterling fellow if a boar was brought to bay.

Then there was the Rector of Broomsbarrow, a great lover of the chase, and who knew the lair of every stag within five miles of his resid- ence, with the Prior of Newent, who would even hunt foxes on the hill of Maia, if he could find no nobler game. Nay, it was even reported by scandalous tongues that he had been seen chasing hares with his fox curs in Lent.

Another point to ascertain from the Robin Hood was the whereabouts of the boar and his lair. This, as far as we could judge from the accounts of foresters, was somewhere in the Gullet dingle among a thicket of hollies above the Dead Oaks, and where tradition says Sir John Oldcastle lay hid during three days when our house at Birtsmereton was searched by the bloodhounds of the Archbishop Arundel, and even our secret room in the panelled chamber was considered to be unsafe.

The Gullet Pass is situated between the great camp of Midsummer Hill and the hill of the Swineyards, which Gilbert de Clare granted to the dwellers around Ledbury whereon to pasture their swine, and all around the camp there have grown up dense thickets, which form excellent shelter for deer or wild boar, although tradition says that a British town once clustered around the base of these hills.

Early on the appointed morning, I mounted my iron grey, Sir Roland, and accompanied by Hasting rode by the trackway from Theocsbury, past the pilgrims' inn known as The Duke of York, to

Chapter Two

Ledbury and Hereford. This village hostel has for many years been a kind of half-way house or resting-place for religious pilgrims travelling to Hereford to worship at the shrines of St Ethelbert or St Cantilupe, and was frequently the rendezvous of the Red Earl and his son who was afterwards killed at the battle of Bannockburn, when they hunted among the dense thickets of the Hawthorns or the Ragged Stone, or sought the lair of the boar in the wilds of the Howling Heath.

The Duke of York is a rambling wooden edifice with the tabard of the Duke Richard hanging from a pole, which stands on the great open common which surrounds the inn, and is the village green in the forest below the hills. Here we found John Berew engaged with a tankard of cider and a toast with borage, and carrying a huge boarspear. He had also brought some hinds as beaters, and they too were draining horn after horn of their favourite beverage. In a short time Kitel of Pendyke rode up, accompanied by his daughter Bessie, looking like a summer rose as she gave us a cheery "Good morrow," and patted her palfrey's neck. With them also rode Rosamond Berew and the Brydges of Eastington, lovers of the chase, and famous for their skill in archery.

As our custom is when hunting near the only village hostel for many a mile in these wild woodlands, we all partook of the host's cheer, the fair damsels touching each cup of hippocrass with their cherry lips before we drank, cap in hand, to their health and luck to our own spears. Rosamond Berew rode a grey jennet, full of mettle, which she managed with grace and spirit. She wore a dark grey riding gown, cape and hood, with her nut brown hair loose down her back. A look of dignity told of her ancient lineage, which her grandfather used to say was that of 'warriors before the Norman had a beginning'. The expression of her face was grave, tending even to melancholy, when not lighted by that smile, which Hasting used to call the 'angel's look'.

It was now arranged that our horses should be sent by the trackway which led towards Broomsbarrow, in case the boar broke away through the forest before he was brought to bay, and we proceeded on foot up the pass to the trysting-place on the summit, only the ladies riding on horseback.

At the Holly Bush Pass we met a numerous party assembled. Sir Huh Calverley rode up to the meet. With him was Lachmere of Severn End, who was on a visit to Branshill, with Bromwich of Broomsbarrow, the Prior of Newent, and the Rector of Broomsbarrow.

They brought a goodly staff of woodmen to drive the thickets, and dogs of various kinds followed their masters. Sir Hugh was not dressed in hunting gear, but rode up in his gown of violet-coloured cloth with purfled sleeves. The velvet which adorned the sleeves showed his rank of knight. He was a handsome man of somewhat proud bearing, and wore a short beard. He wore peaks to his shoes of considerable length, but not so long as those of his son Roger, who was dressed as if for a Court instead of a hunt of the boar.

We other hunters wore the hunting gear of woodcraft, namely, skull caps of deer hide, surmounted by the feathers of the eagle, the heron, or the bittern, while here and there was a cap with the wing of the wild goose across the front. Then we had boots which came up to the thigh, without the long and peaked toes so ill adapted for charging through a thicket. The forester of Uranshill and Hasting were both equipped, after the fashion of the times of Chaucer, in green hood and jerkin, green baldrics, and large horns by their sides; and Hasting wore on his breast a St Gunhilda of silver, while he of Branshill wore an effigy of St Christopher. All had boar-spears and sharp daggers, but the bows and arrow sheafs were left behind. The parsons rode on dainty palfreys with embossed bridles jingling in the wind, and their gown sleeves were lined with fur, with hoods like those for women.

The Prior of Newent gave us a merry nod and an invitation to see his young dogs course a leveret in the summer, while he invited one and all present to a miracle play on the ensuing week.

Sir John Carfax, of Castlemereton, brought his magnificent sleuth-hound Hercules, and boasted that he "was of the blood of the celebrated dog, Hades, which had been laid on the scent of that arch-heretic Sir John Oldcastle, who had obtained shelter in the neighbourhood, and would, no doubt, have pulled him down on the very crest of the Malverns, if it had not been that some churl had spilt his own blood upon the trail and thus baffled the hound by fresh blood".

"This churl," he said, "lived somewhere near Pendyke," and I observed that Rosamond Berew looked pale and angry; when Hasting blew a blast upon his horn, which summoned us all for the start, and Kitel, well versed in woodcraft, gave directions how the woodlands were to be driven. The sleuth-hounds and boar-hounds were held in leash, but the Prior of Newent's fox curs, and various other dogs that were distinguished for their yelping powers, accompanied the woodmen and beaters, who were to drive the thickets and startle the boar from his lair.

The nobler dogs were not to be loosed until the boar was at bay, or until he broke through the beaters and made for some distant part of the forest. In the latter case those who had horses would mount them, the boar-hounds would be put on the track, and we might follow as best we could. The hope was that he would stand at bay somewhere on the line of the hills, so that all might be up at the death.

The drivers were sent to the base of Midsummer Hill in the direction of the ravine called the Gullet Pass, and we had to force our way through thorns, brushwood, and tangled thicket, though here and there the ground was white with the wood wind-flower, and the primrose blossomed under every tree. Great hollies grew on the hill side, and I could hear Kitel to my right shouting to the beaters, and singing the old song:

> *Holly hath berries as red as any rose,*
> *The forester and hunter*
> *Keep them for the does.*

As we neared the ravine called the Gullet, the yelping of half-a-score curs told us that game was afoot, but it was impossible to see half-a-dozen yards in advance, and I only knew where Kitel was by the whining of his hound, which he led himself. While struggling through a mass of brambles, I was hailed by Kitel, begging me to leave the line of beaters to him and ascend the hill, so that I might get a good view, and signal by voice and horn if the boar should go up the dingle or break across the hill. With some difficulty I found my way through thorns and hollies, to the open space which once formed the camp of Britons or Romans on the hill of Midsummer, and which furnished a splendid view of the surrounding country.

The outer vallum of this great camp encircles the two spurs known as the Holly Bush and the Midsummer Hills. The highest point and deepest trenches are on the Midsummer Hill, and Gilbert de Clare, the Red Earl of Gloucester, has struck his dyke right through mound and vallum. Near the summit was a large pile of wood laid on fern, and surmounted with faggots ready for a beacon fire, which would show a light to the whole country round. To my surprise Rosamond Berew was standing by the beacon looking earnestly on the woodlands below. She started as I addressed her, inquiring what had become of her gallant grey. It seems that Sir Hugh Calverley had expressed his opinion that some sharp eyes were wanted on both hills, and Rosamond had volunteered for the Midsummer, while we could now see that Bessie Kitel had climbed to the summit of the Ragged Stone. They had left their horses in the muddy trackway between the hills and were enjoying the glorious scenery and the animated spectacle below.

The hills were studded with figures on foot or horseback, the sunlight flashing here and there upon the steel caps and corselets of some archers who had run up from Branshill, while the broad trackway below echoed with the neighing of steeds as certain ladies from the castle rode up, hoping to be in time for the finding of the boar. Hot and tired I threw myself down on the hill-top for a few moments by the side of Rosamond, and listening to the shouts of the beaters, the cry of the dogs, and the winding of the foresters' horns, we revelled in the view revealed to us beneath that spring-time sun.

I had often been upon these hill-tops with Hasting in our hunting expeditions, but Rosamond knew the scenes around us as well or better than myself. She had, it appeared, frequently accompanied her grandfather, with whom this was a favourite ride, winding up the pass of the Gullet. So she pointed out the Scyrrid Vawr and Black Mountains among the hills of Wales, and the hills above Grosmont, where Harry of Monmouth won his first battle against the followers of Owen Glendower. We saw, too, the distinct smoke of Hereford with a wooded hill beyond, where Mortimer of Wigmore raised his standard, and Prince Edward galloped on his black charger on his escape from the castle, where he and his father Henry III were confined as prisoners; then nearer was the smoke above Ledbury, which she said was once the home of an ancestor of the Berews, who became a Christian and gave it to the Church.[2]

In the valley at our feet, but sheltered beneath the hills of Eastnor, rose the old baronial castle of Branshill, its four flanking towers glistening in the morning sun. It is but a small fortress, but strongly fortified, and in our troublous times it was an important keep. Sir Hugh Calverley was well known to be a follower of the House of Lancaster, and guarded his castle like a royal stronghold. Branshill is as old as the days of the Norman king, William Rufus, who ordered a chain of forts to be erected along the Marches after he was driven out of Wales, and of such are Branshill and Castlemereton. Branshill has been little altered since

Norman times, and the moat, the walls, the towers, and the loop-holes for the archers remain the same to the present day. The hall has been rendered more modern and the armoury on its walls tells of many a knight who has defended it; while its barbican, narrow archway, strong gates, and portcullis bespeak security for its inhabitants. It has often been the home of highborn dames and gallant knights, and Sir Hugh Calverley was of goodly family and of distinction.

After gazing at the scene around us, Rosamond directed my attention to the great Herefordshire camp with its fire beacon of wood and faggots, which rose like a great haystack facing the north, and looking towards the ancient city of Worcester. She pointed to the Hermit's Cave, a dark hollow in the rocks below the fire beacon. Here, she told me, as the tears glistened in her eyes, was the spot were the blood hounds of Castlemereton had nearly pulled down the hunted and persecuted Oldcastle, but he was saved with the faithful Thomas Payne[3], who accompanied him in his flight from Birtsmereton, where they had sheltered for several weeks.

"It was grandfather," she said in a hollow whisper, "who opened a vein in his own arm and let the blood stream out, and so smeared the turf between the Hermit's Cave and the Wind's Point that it threw the sleuth-hounds off the scent, and allowed Sir John and Payne to diverge into the dense copses of the forest at Newer's Wood, and for a while to escape."

"It was to grandfather, Master Hildebrande, that proud knight alluded, as the descendant of a Saxon churl, and it was my grandfather and yours also who sheltered the persecuted for the sake of their religion and their God, and of whom I am more proud than if I were the daughter of a Norman king."

I knew little of this episode, for my mother's family, the Actons, being Catholics, it was seldom mentioned at Birtsmereton, although my own grandfather assisted much in the escape of the persecuted Lollards, not fifty years before we two were standing on the Midsummer Camp waiting for the breaking of the boar.

Just then a horn winding in the trackway made us turn quickly towards the south; Bessie Kitel still held her post on the Ragged Stone and waved her kerchief as a signal that we should join her, by which I judged that her father and the line of beaters were approaching the Ragged Stone slopes. The sun was now sufficiently high to throw his western shadows over the vale of Eastnor; and, giving Rosamond my ungloved hand while using my boar spear as a support, we quickly descended by the Red Earl's dyke to the trackway below.

When halfway down the steep slope Rosamond stopped suddenly, and exclaimed in an excited tone, "Good heavens! see, Master Hildebrande, it is the Shadow of the Ragged Stone," and she pointed to what seemed to be a black, dark column resting on the Castle of Branshill, while all the rest of the vale was flooded in sunshine.

While we were gazing at this strange scene of brilliant sunlight and local darkness, the tra-la-lirala of half-a-dozen horns on our left gave us due notice that the boar was on foot from his night's lair, and we lost no time in running full tilt to meet the horsemen in the trackway below.

"Mount Sir Roland, Master Hildebrande," said Rosamond, "and let us gallop for the valley of the White-leaved Oak; the boar is safe to go to the Howling Heath." But Sir Roland had been sent to the trackway by the great hawthorn thickets on the way to Broomsbarrow, and besides, it was my duty to proceed on foot to the summit of the Ragged Stone and to signal to those below which way the boar was heading.

Mounting Rosamond on her grey, and giving directions that Bessie Kitel's palfrey should be led to the pass of the White-leaved Oak, I ran rapidly up the slopes, when I was accosted by Bessie Kitel:

"Well, Hildebrande the hunter – though you do not deserve the name for staring in the direction of the Beacon of Hereford when the boar was twice showing himself in the open glades on this side the Dead Oak – you will not be entrusted with the signals again by my father, if you are given to moon-gazing so soon after sun-rise. What have you done with my palfrey, and where is your own Sir Roland? Now, there he is again," and truly again the boar showed himself travelling steadily and without haste in the direction of the Chase End – the last hill in our Malvern Chase.

The hunters were nearly a mile behind, so I wound the signal-note on my bugle-horn, and waved a kerchief in the direction the boar had taken, until I heard a reveille sounded from all the horns below, and the beaters were well on the track of the boar. It was time now to assist Bessie down the deep cleft which gives the name to the Ragged Stone until we came to the White-leaved Oak, or the pass between the Chase-End and the Ragged Stone. Here we found her palfrey, and here those who were not engaged in the chase were assembled. Roger Calverley,

Sir Hugh's son, was amongst them, carrying a huge boar-spear and wearing fine feathers in a very fine hood. His dress was little adapted to the chase, as you might have hidden a fawn in his violet-coloured sleeves. An eagle's feather in a woman's headgear was sadly out of place, and so thought Bessie Kitel, who had challenged him to walk up the Ragged Stone, but he dared not for the tips of his shoes.

A ringing note from one of the boar-hounds told us that the Branshill foresters had let them loose upon the trail, while a whoop and wild halloo from the summit of Chase-end let us know that the boar was well forward in that direction, and heading, as Rosamond expected, toward the Howling Heath. Telling Bessie Kitel to ride straight for the 'halloo', I ran at full speed to the trackway below, where I knew Sir Roland awaited me. The gallant roan bounded with joy as he heard the sound of the horn, and I galloped for the south end of the Chase-end, and pulled up below the Howling Heath.

Here I waited till the hunters were seen crossing the crest of the hill, while Bessie Kitel and the Calverleys rode along the western slope. Again rang out the deep notes of the hounds, when the boar came thundering by and dashed down the glen, avoiding the hill of the Howling Heath. I grasped my spear at the thought that here he must come to bay, but waited patiently for the rest to come up. Kitel, too, had mounted, and, with Rosamond Berew, joined me, when we determined to leave our steeds with the horse-boys and proceed on foot to the glen. Laying the hounds on the track, we surrounded the thicket in which the boar had taken refuge, and each hunter became anxious for first blood.

In the densest part of the thicket the boar turned upon his pursuers, and in a second one of the sleuth-hounds lay ripped up by his tusks. I could now see that he was an enormous animal with tusks that gleamed like white scimitars, and that his charge would need a sturdy arm and an unflinching hold. I now determined to show myself and await the charge, when to my utter astonishment, his sleeves torn to rags, and his feather and hood gone, I saw Roger Calverley, with boar-spear at rest, pushing through the brambles to the wild beast at bay. Struck with his courage, I yet determined not to be forestalled, and again pressed forward.

Hecate and Styx had now come up, and Styx pinned the boar by the ear. Turning short he cut her fearfully with his tusks and charged

Calverley, who stood like a man. The spear glanced aside, and in one moment he was on his back, prostrate amidst the briars. He, however, drew blood, although it proved to be a mere skin scratch. The men hallooed, the dogs yelled, the horns sounded, and the foresters swore great oaths as the gallant beast charged through them all and broke clear away in the direction of Broomsbarrow. Turning to Calverley, I found he had escaped the animal's tusks, and was now coolly engaged in cutting off the tips of his shoes with his dagger.

When out of the thickets and mire, all who had horses mounted and rode away. Calverley without hat or hood, and his vestments in a condition wonderful to behold, mounted the palfrey Sir Hugh rode to the meet, leaving his respected father to find his way back to Branshill as he could. Roger Kitel got a heavy fall, but was soon up again, and Bessie and Rosamond Berew followed at the gallop, Rosamond knowing every forest path and trackway and promising to be guide to her fair companion.

I felt annoyed with myself for halting in the bushes, and that Calverley should have drawn first blood, while I could not but admire the gallantry of one I thought a mere dandy and who now rode ahead of us all; so, shaking the boar-spear I held in my hand, I determined that the boar should serve me as he had done Styx before I waited again for the charge.

I soon overtook the palfrey that carried Calverley, and the baying of the hounds told us that the boar was well on his way to the copses of Hazeldine, where Hasting and I had trapped many a badger. Turning at Redmarley, the home of the d'Abitots in the days of the Conquest, he made for the forest thickets of Corse and the gorse groves of Hasfield, and it was not until we reached these that we saw him again. I was engaged with Hasting and Kitel in encouraging the hounds, when he was viewed by Bessie Kitel crossing the open glades leading to the Severn. We were, with Calverley and Rosamond Berew, all that were left of the meet at the Hollybush, and the ladies appeared to have had enough of the chase.

We determined, however, to endeavour once more to bring the animal to bay, and, cheering on the dogs, we were soon galloping over the open flats below the hill when Calverley exclaimed, "By St George, he will cross the river," and by the time we reached the Severn, we could see the boar ascending the hill of Wainlode, on the other side the water. Shouting to the ladies to ride by the river bank to the lode at Ashelworth, where the de Clares had established a horse ferry more than a hundred years ago, I leaped Sir Roland into the river, followed by Calverley. Kitel and Hasting knew that their steeds were too exhausted for the effort, and joined the fair huntresses as they galloped for the ferry.

The stream was strong and we were carried down a considerable distance before we gained the opposite shore. Calverley had thrown himself clear of the palfrey, and with one hand on the saddle was swimming side by side by his steed.

"Wet work this, de Brute," he said, as I assisted him to land, "my poor horse is half drowned."

We now could hear from the baying of the hounds that the boar had turned upon them in the thickets above. Tying our good steeds to some trees, we faced the thickets together, and soon came upon the besiegers and the besieged. The boar was bespattered with blood and bloody foam, and was evidently much exhausted, but no sooner had I emerged from the dense brushwood to the open space where the struggle was taking place, than he at once charged, though Hecate held on like grim death. Throwing myself on one knee and the whole weight of my body forward, I met his charge with the spear at rest, but the treacherous shaft broke short against his tough hide and brisket, when Calverley rushed up, and driving his spear behind the shoulder into the heart, our gallant prey lay dead. We were both still dripping like otter dogs, and Calverley looked a miserable object in the remnants of his dandy garments. Even my stout jerkin was torn, and I had lost my cap with Bessie Kitel's feathers.

We were now across the Severn in the Chase of Gloucester, which was carefully guarded by the foresters of that Chase. A few notes upon the horn would be certain to bring a flayer or a forester upon us, and yet it was necessary to blow the death signal that Kitel and Hasting might assist in securing the head and tusks – trophies we had so hardly earned.

Sounding then two blasts, we set to work with our knives and daggers to cut off the boar's head – no easy task. Before it was accomplished, we heard, as we thought, the gallop of our friends' horses along the Severn bank, and Calverley went to direct them to the open glade, which was completely hidden though so near the Severn stream.

I had allowed the hounds and curs to blood themselves at the carcase, when I heard Calverley calling "De Brute" in a loud voice. On descending to the Severn an unexpected sight awaited me. Instead of our friends I found a party of four horsemen, and one of them was assuming a very hostile attitude.

"Who are you, young Springalls, who dare to trespass on the Chase of Gloucester, and dare to cross the Severn after one of our boars that has chosen to roam?"

"And who are you," said Calverley, "to talk so glibly to your betters?"

"I am the Master Forester of the Royal Chase of Gloucester," was the reply, "and if you cannot give a good account of yourselves I will very soon lodge you both in Gloucester dungeons; such trespass shall not go unpunished."

"Gently, gently, Master Forester," said a young man of about my own age, "It seems to me we have to deal with gentlemen, and this trespass may not be wanton." The young nobleman, for such his dress betokened him, who now spoke, was of very remarkable appearance – his complexion was fair, with large blue eyes, and long yellow hair with lovelocks in a style almost effeminate. He was tall, more than six feet in height, with a great width of chest and shoulder; his address was most courteous, while at the same time he had the air of one accustom- ed to command.

"Who are you, my good friends," he asked, "and why here on the Chase of Gloucester?"

Calverley bowed profoundly, for he had no cap to doff, and explained who we were, and the circumstances of the long hunt which brought us there. He said also that we were both aware that by the Charter of Edward III we had trespassed, but that the custom and usage of woodcraft now allowed of the following of stag or boar across the boundary for a short distance.

A tall and portly gentleman now introduced himself as Sir John de Guyse, and, offering his hand to Calverley and then to me, said he knew our fathers right well, and would be answerable for the honour of their sons. We had thus smoothed matters when the rest of our party came galloping up. They seemed surprised at seeing us thus surrounded, and both Kitel and Hasting looked ready for a fight, when our mediator, transferring the falcon on his wrist to one of his followers, dismounted, and, walking up to Bessie Kitel, begged to be allowed to assist her to descend from the saddle that she might see the boar which he courteously said "had been so gallantly hunted by youth and beauty".

We now observed the manly form of this young nobleman; in his cap of red velvet he wore a heron's plume, and on a jerkin of red velvet braided with gold there was fastened a silver rose. A greater contrast to my dowdy self and the tattered Calverley could hardly be imagined. Turning to Rosamond Berew, he admired her jennet and asked how far she had ridden, and when she pointed to the hills where the Chase began, he replied that truly we seemed all hunters born!

When Hasting had cut a path with his whinger to the green glade where the boar lay dead and we had gathered round the scene, our friend in need turned to the Master Forester and said, "Good boar, staunch hounds, bold hunters, and fair ladies. Master Forester, we must take no notice of this trespass; and from you, fair damsels we may not part without some slight token of this day's chase.

He then took his heron's plume and gave it to Rosamond Berew, and clasped the silver rose upon the kirtle of Bessie. Then turning to his followers, he said, "Sir John de Guyse and gentlemen, time flies." So, taking off his cap to the ladies, and giving us a slight nod of recognition, he withdrew, and in a few minutes we heard the hoofs of their horses as they galloped down the green turf by the Severn side.

We prepared for our return homewards. The boar's head was fastened behind the saddle of Hasting, and, tired with our exertions, we rode slowly towards the Ashleworth ferry, and talked of the various incidents of the chase and the meeting with the party of falconers from Gloucester. Kitel said he believed the young nobleman to be Lord Berkeley, while Calverley thought he might be Lord Tracy.

Having crossed the ferry, and being in need of refreshment, we determined to seek for some at the manor of the Pauncefortes of Hasfield. Calverley declared he would rather starve than present himself in his present condition before the lovely daughters of Julian Paunceforte, till a hint from Kitel of the probability of a pasty of goose, a Berkeley cheese, and a tankard of hippocrass[4], made him prefer to put off starvation, and we all rode up together to the drawbridge of the moat, when Kitel dismounted to beg the hospitality he knew would welcome us.

Hasfield Moat house differed somewhat in its structure from the manor houses which are now arising in many parts of our western counties. The moat was dug only in front of the dwelling house, which was protected on the north and east by a high wall with steps on the inner side to enable archers to shoot through the apertures, while on the top of the wall was a *chevaux de frise* of strong oaken spikes. The house was mostly built of strong timber, and the only entrance was by the drawbridge; though it might not stand a regular siege, it was right well protected against robbers and raiders.

We had not waited long, when Paunceforte appeared to welcome the weary hunters and, entreating us to dismount, led the way to the Moat House, where at the door ready to receive us with all hospitality, was the fair mistress of the house and her two sweet daughters, Dorothy and Miranda, to whose care our damsels were committed.

Dorothy was a fair girl, with a sharp wit, and was so well taught by her parents that she could read Master Wycliffe's Bible, and had written verses which might have passed for Master Lydgate's; while Miranda had a voice like a mavis, and played with wondrous skill upon harp and spinet. The central hall was hung around with skins of wild animals, which Master Paunceforte, who had been a great traveller, had brought from foreign parts, and which excited much admiration among our party, who had never seen such trophies of the chase before.

The table soon was spread with platters of salted beef, and the goose pastie which Kitel said was a dish to dream of, and loaves of wastel bread. Mistress Paunceforte, too, was famous for her green cheeses, and never ceased to recommend the hot collops. Flagons of hippocrass and cider passed around, and nothing was spared which hospitality could provide.

The afternoon was now drawing to a close, so, making a promise to meet our hosts at the miracle plays at Theocsbury, or at the gluttony feast at Redmarley, we again mounted our horses and partook of the stirrup cup which was handed to us by the mistress herself. I now observed that she had lost her right hand and bore the cup in her left. The history I afterwards learnt was as follows:

'In the days of his youth Julian Paunceforte had plighted his troth to the beautiful Dorothy Ashfield, whose home was in Oxfordshire. He was a gallant sailor, and had arrived at some distinction. Their marriage was deferred, for Paunceforte was ordered to take the command of a vessel and sailed to the distant Mediterranean sea. On this voyage he was taken prisoner by pirates and sold as a slave in the East. A lady of rank beholding his degraded and forlorn condition and seeing that he had been gently nurtured and born in better circumstances, took compassion on the broken-down and nearly dying captive, released him from his fetters, and raised him to a situation of a less menial kind.

By and by love succeeded to pity, and she offered to free him altogether, on condition that he should spend the rest of his life with her in the East.

Then Paunceforte told her how an English girl was weeping over his absence by the broad meadows of the Isis, and anxiously hoping for his return home in love and constancy.

The Eastern lady laughed in bitter scorn at the idea of woman's constancy, and Paunceforte, little thinking that his words would be taken literally, declared that his betrothed would give her right hand for the return of her lover.

"Then be it so!" exclaimed the indignant Princess, and she swore a solemn oath that Paunceforte should be her slave unto death unless the hand of the English girl was sent across the seas as a ransom and pledge of her fidelity.

Tradition tells how Dorothy had gone to Hasfield to visit the widowed mother of her lover, and the girl and the grey-haired woman mourned together over the fate of him who seemed lost to them for ever; when one day a ransomed captive, a fellow-prisoner of Julian Paunceforte's, appeared and related to them the history of the strange oath, which would keep him a captive until the day of his death. This news deepened the shadow of sorrow; which was over the old manor, and two days afterwards Dorothy Ashfield left for the port of Bristol. She in time returned, but bearing her arm in anguish in a sling, for the plighted hand had been cut off at the wrist and gone across the seas as a ransom.'[5]

Our horses were too much exhausted for us to ride faster than a walk and, as Calverley seemed anxious to converse with Bessie Kitel, I rode the whole way back with Rosamond Berew.

We had both of us heard much of the religious questions of the times, for the exactions and encroachments of the ecclesiastics were the constant topic of conversation between my father and Master Berew; and we had read Master Wycliffe's *Trialogues*, and his belief that Christ taught faith, hope, and charity, rather than the persecution and burning of heretics. We had also learned to detest the sight of the 'sompnour', described by Master Chaucer, with his 'fire-red cherubim's face, so scalded, whelked, and bepimpled that children fled from its presence', and whose vocation was that of an ecclesiastical officer, who served citations for trial in the Church courts on the most trivial pre- tences.

Nor were we better inclined towards the 'pardoner', for we had learnt from the writings of the great Reformer of Lutterworth that 'God only can forgive sin, and that therefore pardons and dispensations were not to be sold like an ox or an ass', and that 'the Scriptures assure us that Christ is the mediator between God and man'. Yet a month rarely passed away that our villages were not pestered with these miserable pedlars, who travelled from place to place selling dispensations for sin and exhibiting pretended relics, such as a veil of the Virgin Mary, hand- kerchiefs with the blood of Christ, fragments of St Peter's boat, and such like impostures.

Witchcraft, too, was the subject of our conversation, and we agreed that, although there might be cases in which black magic, sorcery, and enchantment deserved to be punished with the strong arm of the law, nevertheless hundreds of innocent persons were tortured and executed for imaginary magic, as in the case of several poor women executed a few years previously.[6] Indeed, to such a height had the fear of necromancy arisen, that it was unsafe to concoct a potation of herbs, or even to gather plants for medicaments; while the presence of a black cat, or an owl, in a household was absolutely so dangerous that we ever destroyed our black kittens.

Nor were these the only topics of our conversation. It was impossible to ignore the fact that we were living in dangerous times. We were both old enough to remember the excitement caused throughout the country by Cade's rebellion; how the Archbishops of York and Canterbury had to take refuge in the Tower, and the talk of the desperate single combat between Squire Iden and Cade, in which the latter was slain. The great battle of St Alban's, too, in 1454, was hailed as a good omen by our parents, who looked upon the Duke of York as the rightful king, and hoped under him for greater liberty of conscience in religious matters.

At the present moment, it was true, a reconciliation had been patched up, and King Henry was acknowledged as monarch of England by the Yorkists and the great Earls of Salisbury and Warwick, but now, in this year 1459, there were rumours of warlike preparations, and great bodies of troops had been massed at Worcester.[7] Who could say how soon our quiet homes might not be invaded by armed men and made desolate by a reckless soldiery?

While conversing on such subjects we had arrived as far as the rounded hill of Berthhill on the horse hackway to Gadbury Camp and the church of Eldersfield, when a tall figure crossed our path and entered the dense glades of the forest. I had hardly time to see whether the dress was that of a man or woman, but Rosamond said, "There is Mary of Eldersfield; I expect she has been on Berthhill after nettles to make a capon sit,[8] or spurges for ointments."

Mary of Eldersfield was celebrated for her knowledge of herbs and medicaments, but led the life of a strict recluse.

Eastington Court

Chapter Three

As I rode homewards, I could not help thinking of Rosamond, and a change of feeling respecting her, which had come over me of late, and which I did not altogether understand. We had been much together as boy and girl, but I had also seen much of Bessie Kitel and Kate Brydges of Eastington. Yet, I was now almost afraid of Rosamond, afraid of doing something she did not like, or saying something of which she did not approve, and her face always haunted me, go where I would. If I mounted Roan Poland or Bold Harry, they always would carry me towards Berew, and I always blushed when I got there and wondered how they could be so stupid, especially when I found only John Berew at home, and Rosamond away searching for wild flowers on the hills. To her I owed all my knowledge of the herbs of the forest glades, so good for medicaments, taught her by Mary of Eldersfield and the Sub-Prior of Pendyke.

Many a time have I walked across the Malverns, or the Gullet Pass, where alone I could gather sufficient whortleberries for a comfiture for Master Berew, and receive for my reward a smile from Rosamond. Then there was the bee flower which grows upon the hill of Berew, but never in the vale, with which Rosamond loved to deck her hair in the pleasant month of June.

I knew where the first blossoms were to be found in an old stone-pit, among stone oyster shells which look as if fresh from the sea. But Rosamond's favourite flower was the 'nodding star of Bethlehem', with its white silvery blossoms, among the yellow broom and gorse of Broomsbarrow. Long distances have I walked for these flowers and others, such as wild mint and sages, with which Rosamond would make medicaments for the poor and sick, for she was never happier than when doing some kind service for others.

But now, and I could not account for it, we seemed somewhat estranged from each other, and she called me 'Master Hildebrande',” whereas she once said 'Hildebrande'. Thoughts of this kind passed through my mind as I neared my own home.

I found my father and mother seated in the panelled chamber, the internal adornment of which my father had superintended. In my grandfather's time, the walls were bare, or only covered here and there with worn tapestry. The noble chimney-piece was my father's own design, and the armorial bearings of the various friends who visited us from time to time were painted above each panel, and were the work of a foreign artist.

Here are the arms of Scudamore of Kentchurch, whose grandmother was a daughter of Owen Glendower, and the Baskervilles of Erdisley who came over with the Conqueror, Blount of Eye, Bromwich of Broomsbarrow, Throcmorton, Rudhall, Vaughan of Hergest, all old friends of my father and mother. My father was clad in the long manteline which he wore in the house, and which was well suited to a scholar. His beloved parchments were on one side and mother on the other, as was her custom when night drew on. A letter, with the silk only lately cut, lay upon her lap, and tears were in her eyes, and both of them seemed impressed by news of great importance.

When I had related the events of the day, my father said, "You are aware, Hildebrande, that the present King's marriage with Margaret of Anjou has been the commencement of a series of troubles from about the time of your birth to the present day. Within two years of that marriage in the year 1445, the good Duke Humphrey was murdered. Before Margaret had been queen seven years, the noble Duke, Richard of York, who many, like myself, believed to be the legitimate King, was ignominiously cast into prison, and probably would have been there now, or in another world, but for us Marchmen, who rallied round his standard at Wigmore, and frightened the Queen and the Council into setting him at liberty.[1]

"The year of grace 1454 saw the noble York lieutenant to the King, when Queen Margaret was delivered of a son, whom few believe to be the son of the imbecile Henry. Through the intrigues of the unscrupulous Margaret, Edmund Beaufort was placed in power until the battle of St Alban's, when Somerset was killed and King Henry taken prisoner. This occurred four years ago and a peace has been patched up, when now I have just received a letter to inform me that the Queen, dragging the King in her train, has marched on Ludlow at the head of sixty thousand men, and that, owing to the treachery of Sir Andrew Trollop, the Duke of York, and his son the Earl of March, with the great Warwick, are all fugitives from her, who spares neither friend nor foe if they interfere with her ambitious projects.

"This letter informs me that the Duke of York has escaped to Ireland, that his son Edward of March has fled to Gloucester, and the Earl of

Warwick is safe at his castle of Hanley, only a few miles from hence. Edward's situation is most precarious, there are only too many who would betray him to the vindictive Queen, and she would rejoice at getting the heir of York into her eagle clutches. Not a moment must be lost in bringing him safe, by unfrequented paths, through the forest to Hanley Castle,[2] where Warwick may make a stand, until we who love the White Rose can rally round him, and save the country and ourselves from ruin.

"Lord Edward of March is now at the Forester's lodge at Wainlode in the Chase of Gloucester, and it is evident that you have fallen in with him to-day in company with the forester, who is true as he is brave, and would defend him to the death; but Trollop's minions are already on the track, and it is madness for March to be flying falcons when he should be flying for his life. I must ride for Hanley Castle before the sun rises tomorrow, to arrange with Warwick the summoning of the adherents of the White Rose again to arms. You, I would have to ride with the grey dawn of morning to Wainlode. Take Hasting with you, and this letter for Edward of March. It is a missive from the Earl of Warwick, and Lord Edward will not hesitate to place himself under your guidance, while you must be guided by circumstances whether you will conduct him straight to Hanley, or bring him here until we can safely deliver him to the care of Warwick."

"The House of York, Hildebrande," he continued, "is the only hope of those reformers whom men call Lollards, who in this country protest against the exactions and encroachments of the Roman pontiffs, and who hold by the tenets and opinions of such as John de Wyckliffe. These noble Lords are now in the greatest danger, and it becomes you and I, if necessary, to die for our faith, and those who would aid us. In the meantime let me show you a secret of this house, the chamber in which Sir John Oldcastle was hidden,[3] a secret which no one knows but myself and your mother, and I now entrust it to you."

He then led me to one of the oaken panels close to the great chimney, and touching a secret spring a door flew open and revealed a recess large enough to hold two men standing. There was no apparent escape from this recess save by the secret door into the chamber, but my father showed me in the thick wall a large stone, which had been pierced and suspended on an iron rod and fastened on the inside like a trap door. This stone, when swung upwards, permitted the passage of a man out to the terrace in front and the moat, from whence in a boat it was easy to cross to the land and out into the forest. My father explained how in my grandfather's time the secret chamber was hidden only by tapestry, and how he had himself invented the panelled door and spring.

"It may happen," said he, "that we may require to use this secret for ourselves, or others, in troublous times like these, for no man can calculate what may happen on the morrow."

I mounted a fresh horse at sunrise on the following morning, and, accompanied by Hasting, rode quickly by the avenue of great elms, which reached from the moat across the park to the trackway to Branshill and Ledbury. The blackbirds were singing and the swallows skimming over the grass, the young leaves were bursting forth in the trees, and the Malverns were clad in their green spring mantle, with the canopy of a blue sky over all.

My thoughts were so occupied with the sudden fall of the Duke of York and Earl of Warwick, and the dispersion of their followers near Ludlow, that I said little to Hasting as we rode on, until we were close under Gadbury Camp, near to the Norman church of Eldersfield.

This camp was an important stronghold in the forest, when the Romans held the line of the Severn, and the British, under their chief Caractacus, defended the barrier of the Malverns inch by inch. Strongly fortified by nature in its steep sides, there is a level platform on its summit, where a large force could be arrayed for battle. It was now deserted and surrounded by dense woodlands, the only access being a narrow pathway on the south. The camp is a large flat area without trees, and nothing grew there save brushwood, gorse, and long grass.

The absence of trees was accounted for by the fact that the noted white witch, called the Witch of Eldersfield, frequented this isolated spot, and was said to summon the Devil to assist her, and to visit the moon.

Hasting told me that only the previous year no less than forty wondrous cures had been ascribed to the White Witch, who lived on the camp. An instance of her evil doings had happened to the head forester of Gloucester Chase in the thickets on the flanks of Gadbury. He had gone forth in search of a stag of great size, which was known to frequent a part of the Chase known as Pudden Crok, and on climbing the Crok he found the deer browsing beneath a large oak. He was enabled to obtain a close shot, and the animal, badly wounded, rushed down the steep bank and took refuge in the woodlands on the slopes of Gadbury.

Arriving at a dense thicket he heard the stag moaning and dying in the bushes; he cut a path through the underwood, but there was no sign of any stag or struggle, not a blade of grass was disturbed, not a leaf moved, but he heard, on the platform above, a peal of laughter, as if the witch had summoned some unearthly companion to her revels. Night was approaching, and the forester returned to his lodge, convinced that foul spirits obeyed the commands of the accursed witch, and that the black stag was a black fiend.

I listened with a smile to this tale, and, telling Hasting that I had heard that the witch was only a herbalist, touched my horse with the spur, and we trotted as fast as the muddy paths would allow towards the horse ferry by which we were to cross the river at Ashleworth. We had almost reached the river when the sound of a horse at full gallop behind us made us pause to discover who was the rider.

It proved to be Rosamond Berew on her grey jennet all alone, hot with her ride, and looking anxious and alarmed. There was little time for greeting, and she said, as she pulled up her jennet,

"Master Hildebrande, for God's sake, do not attempt to cross at the ferry. Not many minutes after you started, a message arrived from Lord Warwick to your father to inform him that more than two hundred archers, led by the traitor Sir Andrew Trollop, are now in our Chase in search of those Yorkists who escaped from before Ludlow, and that a high price is set upon the heads of all the leaders of the House of York. Your father had started for Hanley Castle, and your respected mother herself rode up to our poor house at Berew to beg of my brother to gallop after you, lest you should fall into some ambush. Trollop himself Is with his bloodhounds, and is sure to make for the ferry at Ashleworth. John was out with the kine, so I mounted Grey Bess, and rejoice greatly, Master Hildebrande, that have overtaken you in time."

This was a dilemma. Swimming the river on horseback was not to be thought of, as we must keep our horses fresh; we therefore determined to ride up the right bank to a boat ferry at a place called the Haw, and that Hasting should remain there while I crossed in a boat and proceeded on foot to the Lodge at Wainlode. Time would be lost, but there was no help for it. Entreating Rosamond to seek the most unfrequented paths on her return, I begged the posie she wore in her bosom, of rue and rosemary – the one for grace the other for remembrance – and arriving at the Haw, I soon was on the other side of the water.

I ran rapidly by the green meadows on the Severn side, where the comfrey, so excellent for bruises, was just showing its lilac blossoms, and soon reached the woodlands, which at Wainlode surmounted the steep cliff above the river.

The forester's lodge was erected near to this cliff, close upon the river bank. It was built much after the fashion of the one Hasting frequented in the Malvern Chase, but much larger, and was opposite the spot where the wains or waggons, loaded with corn for Gloucester, came once a year, when their burdens were placed on rafts and sent across the Severn. Thus it was called Wainlode.

The bark of many dogs gave notice of my arrival, and I was some little distance from the lodge when the forester accompanied by a couple of woodmen, armed, met me, as I was running, with the question, "What tidings?"

Taking the forester aside, I told him that the archers of Sir Andrew Trollop, were searching in every direction on the other side of the water for the followers of York and Warwick, who were now fugitives from the wrath of the Lancastrians, and that I was the bearer of a missive from Lord Warwick to Edward, Earl of March, and who, from my description, my father believed to be the young nobleman I had seen the day before.

"It is he, and no other," said the forester, "and right glad should I be if he was safe at Hanley Castle, for King Henry's scouts are all around this country. Theocsbury is ill-affected to the House of York and Gloucester would shield him if it were possible, but Trollop – may he be accursed as a foul traitor – has arrived there, with a host of archers from Hereford. Only this morning men-at-arms were seen upon our hill. I am not suspected, or they would soon be here."

He then conducted me to the lodge, and we found Lord Edward standing within the high palisades which surrounded it. He was caressing a boar-hound, and received me with a courteous bow of recognition. He did not wear the falconer's dress as before, but as clad in a suit of hunter's green, which showed the proportions of his powerful frame to great advantage. Bending on one knee and doffing my cap, I presented Lord Warwick's letter, which he read without evincing the slightest emotion, and merely remarked, "We shall deal with these tyrants yet. Warwick is safe in his castle at Hanley, and my noble father has by this time crossed the seas to Ireland."

The Master Forester now came forward and informed him that his safety was compromised by the appearance of Trollop at Gloucester, and that Malvern Chase had parties of scouts distributed in hopes of his capture, or that of any other fugitive Yorkist. He therefore recommended Lord Edward to accept my offers of guidance by the unfrequented forest rides to Hanley Castle, as on that side of the Severn many espoused the cause of Henry of Lancaster, while on the other side many of the houses would advance the banners of the White Rose.

The young Earl thus addressed me: "Will you be my guide, good Sir? Warwick says in this missive that the de Brutes, of whom I suppose you to be a scion, are men of honour. Serve me in this strait, and if I live, I will serve you in turn. A Plantagenet never forgets a kindness."

I then hastened to assure him that my life was at his service, and proposed my plan of escape. The forester also suggested that Lord Edward should be disguised, and go forth with the dogs in the direction of the Haw, as if for hunting. The Earl consented, and the forester winding his horn for 'the rally', in a short time a dozen woodmen assembled at the well-known call. Lord Edward was arrayed in a rough leather jerkin and long boots and buskins, a cap with long lappets, which fell over the cheeks and covered his long fair hair, and a billhook in his hand. In this dress it was almost impossible to recognize the dashing young nobleman of the previous day, now turned into John Ball.

We had left the hunting lodge less than half an hour when the glittering of steel caps was seen on the banks of the Severn, and soon we heard the tramp of horses and the clatter of arms. The forester begged of Lord Edward to show himself as little as possible and keep well among the thickest of the wood, acting as a driver of the game. He then called to me to accompany him and descended towards the river bank, where he busily engaged himself in looking for the track of an imaginary stag.

Five or six horsemen armed from head to foot rode up to us, and the officer in command inquired if we had tidings of the escape of certain Yorkists in the general flight from Ludlow, as both the Duke of York and his son, Lord Edward of March, were believed to have taken refuge in the Chase of Malvern or to have crossed to that of Gloucester. Sir Andrew Trollop, he said, had arrived at Gloucester, while the Duke of Somerset had despatched bands of scouts from Worcester, and good hopes were entertained of their capture. Tidings had been brought, he said, of the appearance of a strange nobleman, who was seen searching for herons along the river flats.

The forester replied that Sir John de Guyse and Lord Berkeley had indeed been there, but had both departed for Gloucester the day before.

"Well then," replied the officer, "I charge you in the king's name and of Sir Andrew Trollop, knight, commissioned by the right honourable parliament of England, now assembled at Coventry, to summon your followers and assist me, John Salwey, of Ludlow, in apprehending the followers of the Duke of York, who rose in rebellion against our Lord the King, and who are now believed to be hidden in the Chase over which you have the care and keeping. I am sorry to spoil your hunting, but there are stags on foot better worth our capture, for the heads of these traitors are worth a thousand marks apiece. Sound, therefore, your bugle-horn, and let your woodmen join us in the search."

"Have you," he continued, "for I am a stranger in this country, any idea where these rebels may have taken shelter?"

A gleam of intelligence passed across the face of the Master Forester, which, observed by both Master Salwey and myself, was interpreted by us in a very different light "By my halidame," he replied, "I expect the Rector of Down Hatherley is a malcontent who would gladly shelter any one of the House of York or Warwick," though he well knew the Rector was a staunch Lancastrian.

"Also," he said, "there is Master Paunceforte the other side the water at Hasfield Moat House; we must send a couple of trusty men to invite his aid, until we can ourselves cross and conduct a search."

"But we must first to Hatherley," he said to Salwey, "a thousand marks is indeed a goodly sum."

Then he told me to take John Ball, the woodman, and cross the ferry at the Haw to proceed to Hasfield, and warn them of the party of Lancastrian searchers and the quarry they hunted.

I at once took the hint, leaving Salwey and his men in the care of one whom I perceived was quite capable of putting them well on the chase of the wild-goose, while I carried off the stag. I now joined Lord

Edward in the thickets, and beckoning him to follow in silence, led him in the direction of the ferry by a narrow path through the forest from Wainlode to Apperley.

We had not gone far before we heard the forester's horn calling up his woodmen, and I knew that all the party were well off to Down Hatherley in the opposite direction, so slackened speed, when Lord Edward, coming up somewhat breathlessly, said, "I hope this pace will not last long, for I am well nigh winded, and this leather jerkin and these buskins are not meant for such travelling. Whither now, and what tidings?"

I related what had passed, and he laughed heartily at the ruse of the Master Forester.

We soon arrived at the boat at the Haw, and the ferryman said not a soul had been there since I crossed in the morning. Safe on the other side, a blast of my horn soon brought Hasting and our steeds to the trackway which leads from the river to the forest paths. We now learned that several armed men had inquired of Hasting what he was doing there, and whether any one had passed that way?

He replied that his young master had gone to the lodge at Wainlode seeking to borrow a hound, and that he was waiting for his return. He overheard the leader of the troop say that other riders were stationed along the horse trackways which led through the forest.

Under these circumstances I determined to send Hasting ahead with the horses instead of our mounting them, as the fact of Lord Edward being seen on horseback in the woodman's dress would excite suspicion. So, telling Hasting to make for the church green at Eldersfield by the horse trackway, we at once took the footpaths by Chaseley in the same direction. Threading the narrow and intricate forest paths of Chaseley by ways no horse could follow, we emerged near an open space called Eldersfield, so named from the abundance of elder trees,[4] with their flowers so famous for eye ointments, and their berries for 'honey rob' and black pigments. Here in the wilderness the Normans built a church, and in the clearings of the forest had settled a few franklins and their churls, but the trackways are still difficult to find, and the village is most remote and hidden.

As we emerged from the forest to the knoll on which stands the church, we saw a tall, somewhat masculine, middle-aged woman, with large black eyes of a most searching character, sitting upon a large stone, and carrying in her hand a great bunch of wild sages freshly gathered. I at once knew this could be no other than the celebrated Mary of Eldersfield, whom some called a witch and others a herbalist. In former days, she used to come to Berew and our manor house, but latterly she had led the life of a recluse, going nowhere save to the house of sickness, where with her great skill and famous medicaments she was ever welcome.

She arose as we approached, and, with her peculiar long stride, advanced to meet us. Recognizing me at once from my likeness to my father, she said, "Rosamond Berew bid me watch and tell you that wolves are abroad, and your road by the horse trackway already beset. Follow me."

She led the way by a clearing to the borders of the forest, until we arrived at a rounded knoll, the Pudden Krok, of which Hasting had related the tale of the marvellous stag. The Krok is covered with large yew trees, and Mary bid me mount one of these and to conceal myself as much as possible among the dense foliage while I scanned the valley below. On doing so I perceived that the trackway was full of soldiers between us and our destination, and that no horseman could pass without challenge. Our guide then put her fingers to her lips, and motioned to us to follow her.

Descending from the Krok in the direction of the Camp of Gadbury, she conducted us up a short steep slope to the perfectly level platform on the summit of the ancient stronghold. There were no trees, but the entire area was covered with dense scrub of gorse, honesty, ivy, and brambles, which was impenetrable save by the aid of the billhook. No path could we see, until our guide pushed aside a mass of gorse and passed into a narrow cutting, which led through walls of scrub and thorns to the centre of the platform.

Here was a strange structure of wooden logs, interlaced with twigs and bedaubed with mud. It was circular, with four slits looking north, south, east, and west, down narrow paths cut in the scrub, which were straight for a short distance and then winded through the thick underwood. The apertures could be closed at night with wooden doors, and were large enough to allow of escape from any one of them. The place was a remarkable contrivance for safety and retreat.

Inviting us to enter, our guide drew a bench from under a table and motioned us to be seated. Two brown owls, known as 'hooters', blinked

Chapter Three

upon us from a wicker cage, and a large raven hopped upon the floor. With these, in apparent intimacy, was a large black cat, and outside, in a box of wooden strips, a blackbird was singing with all his might. A small wooden bedstead, a bench, a table, and a wooden cupboard was all the furniture the hut contained.

On the table was a parchment covered with groups of stars, and a number of dried plants arranged in bundles; also several adders were dried and hung by their tails from the wooden logs of the walls. Dried newts hung; about in clusters. Such was the furn- iture within the dwelling of the famed Witch of Eldersfield, who was celebrated for her wonderful cures both of man and beast, and the good which ever waited on her pharmacy.

I observed that Lord Edward surveyed this dwelling and its surround- ings with a suspicious look, as if we had entered into a witch's den, which Mary observing said, "Fear not, Sir, these are but nostrums for fevers and rheumatism, and neither Tab or her mistress ever injured man or beast."

We had not, however, been long within the dwelling when the sound of a bugle-horn among the gorse showed that the Lancastrians had ascended the hill and might discover the retreat of the herbalist. On this, Mary led us down one of the paths through dense scrub down the hill, and below we could see the glitter of the steel caps of the soldiery, and hear their shouts to their companions on the platform.

Pointing to a large oak, the trunk of which appeared as firm and sound as that of any tree of the forest, she whispered to Lord Edward that there was a hollow in the middle fork where he might lie hidden, and begged of him to ascend the tree and there wait in shelter until we returned on the removal of the soldiers.

Having seen him safely hidden in the hollow of the oak, Mary re- turned to her retreat upon the platform, while I descended the hill towards the trackway, as I had no fear, clad as I was in the hunter's dress of the Malvern Chase, that I should be mistaken for a fugitive Yorkist. In the meantime it struck me that the hollow oak might be the cause of the sudden disappearance of the Witch of Eldersfield, which certain tales of the surrounding peasantry recounted.

On reaching the trackway I saw our own horses and Hasting sur- rounded by a troop of men-at-arms. They were led by an officer clad in a stout jerkin of green, with yellow buskins, and wearing a steel bonnet projecting far over the face. He was speaking roughly to Hasting when I walked forward, boar-spear in hand.

As I wore the crest of our house, the *talbot*, embroidered upon the sleeve of my jerkin, he saw I was of gentle blood, and said, "Pardon, Sir, I asked your follower a plain question and I cannot get a plain answer. I inquired if he had seen a young man of tall and comely stature, with blue eyes and fair hair, and he tells me 'he knows the spoor of a boar from the stud of a stag' – at least such I understand to be the drift of his unintelligible speech."

I apologized for Hasting, who spoke only the Saxon dialect so prevalent in our forest land, and was ignorant of the French parlance of the more cultivated classes. Observing the velvet with which his jerkin was trimmed, I knew that the Lancastrian was of knightly order, so I made the low bow usual in addressing one of his rank and station.

"I am Sir Andrew Trollop," said the Knight, "and am engaged in searching for rebels and traitors to our Lord the King, and there is little doubt, from all we hear, that Edward of March, the eldest son and heir of that foul traitor the Duke of York, is in these wilds, having escaped from Wigmore."

"And," he continued, "I never saw a better hiding-place than this Gadbury, or more abominable thickets to search for boar, or stag, or traitor. There are fifty men in those woodlands, and another half-score are gone to the summit, yet not a sign can be seen of any one of them. However, here come some of them."

As he spoke, several men-at-arms appeared leading, or rather dragging, Mary of Eldersfield, with the cry too often heard, "The witch! the witch!" One of the soldiers carried an owl with his neck twisted, another had a handful of dried beetles, another displayed some dried herbs and adder skins with as much pride as if they were the honourable trophies of war.

The impeachment of the Duchess of Gloucester for witchcraft; the burning of Margery Jourdayn at Smithfield; and the hanging of Roger Bolingbroke for necromancy, were still topics of general conversation, and were examples of the fate one convicted of witchcraft was likely to meet with at the hands of the highest judges in the land. Courtiers, priests, and bishops went to see the burning of a witch, as they would the baiting of a bull.

Nor was their example lost upon the lower classes. A man who was a student was very apt to be set down as a wizard, and the fact of such animals as owls and cats being seen in the house of an aged woman was enough to satisfy the soldiers of the undoubted witchcraft of our guide. But Mary was not old, nor ugly, nor withered, and, even under the trying circumstances in which she was placed, there was an air of dignity as she raised her tall form, and quietly awaited the judgment of the leader of the boisterous soldiery around.

Having heard the circumstances of her apprehension and looked at the contents of her dwelling displayed by the soldiers, Sir Andrew said, "We can give her the ordeal of the nearest water and see whether she will sink or swim." – a judgment which was willingly acquiesced in by the soldiers, who, more in sport than in cruelty, would have tossed her into one of the large deep marl pits filled with water which are abundant in the neighbourhood.

It was time to interfere, and I said to Sir Andrew, "This is no witch, she is merely a poor herbalist of the forest, who is well known for the cures effected by her nostrums; her witchments, if witchments they are, are for good and not for evil, and every village has some record of her healing."

"I care nothing for her nostrums," said Trollop, with a glitter in his cruel grey eyes. "This is enough for me! I have burnt half-a-dozen hags before now, for having in their possession less cunning means of necromancy and wicked philtering than these," and he held up the adder skins to view. "She sinks or swims in that slough before we part."

"Not while I am present, Sir Andrew Trollop," I said. "I will not stand by and see an innocent woman put to the torture of the ordeal you propose, because a set of ignorant soldiers choose to imagine that she is a witch."

The Lancastrian paled with passion as he shouted: "And pray, Master Springall, what is to prevent me from putting you into that horse pool, or hanging you from that oak? You propose to interfere with my commission, given at Worcester by our royal master, King Henry, which is to take and apprehend all witches and wizards, and malcon- tents such as you, and deal with them according to my best judgment, and that judgment is . . ."

"Gently, gently, Sir Andrew" said the officer in command of a large party of soldiers who had been searching Gadbury, and now joined their comrades, "I may not have you talk of hanging my good and excellent friend, Hildebrande de Brute." Then turning back his steel bonnet, he displayed the handsome face of Roger Calverley, of Branshill, who, at the head of his retainers, had, it seems, assisted the bully in his search for the Yorkists.

"You are not in a country, Sir Andrew," he continued, "where even the king's writ will avail for such tyranny as you propose. It is such conduct as yours," he proceeded in a tone of the highest indignation, "which makes the name of Lancastrian to stink in the land; conduct utterly unworthy of a knight and gentleman."

Trollop was a coward, as all traitors are, and said he merely intended to give me a fright, and the ducking would do the witch no harm. "Ask the crone yourself, Master Calverley," he said, "what necromancy and philtering these portend," as he pointed to a bunch of snake sloughs in the hands of a soldier.

Calverley turned to Mary, and questioned her as to the uses of the various trophies from her dwelling She replied that they were all used in pharmacy, and gave a short description of the different diseases to which they were applied. He then inquired from me what character the supposed witch bore amongst her neighbours in the forest villages, and I informed him that she went by the name of Mary of Eldersfield, and was most notable for her knowledge of herb pharmacy, and the efficacy of her nostrums.

Calverley then called me aside, and advised me to ride homewards and keep quiet for a time, "For you know," he said, "that your father is suspected of being a supporter of the House of York, and the Court is now determined to make examples of any that outwardly manifest their adherence to what now is a ruined cause, as you must know. In a short time the Yorkist leaders must be in the power of the Crown, and Queen Margaret never spares an enemy. This fellow," he said, alluding to Trollop, "is the traitor who betrayed York and Warwick, and I would willingly be rid of his company, for I hate traitors even if they serve our cause. He rode from Gloucester to Branshill early this morning with some half-score troopers, and a letter from Lord Belmore to my father asking for aid to search this side the Severn, as Edward of March is believed to be hiding in this immediate neighbourhood. Now, my good friend and brother of woodcraft, let me beg of you to lose no time in riding to your home at Birtsmereton, and when next we meet, I trust this storm will have passed away."

Chapter Three

"We will ride on, Sir Knight," he said haughtily to Trollop, "it is not impossible that Edward of March may be sheltered in the thickets, though I, for one, would rather meet him on the battle-field, than be seeking for him as I would for a murderer or a thief. Order your sleuth-hounds to stand back, Sir, and follow at a distance" – for Sir Andrew's half-score men-at-arms came round their leader – "they are no company for the retainers of Branshill, who are soldiers, not witch takers, or curs which hunt thieves."

Then sounding three blasts upon the silver horn which hung at his baldrick, Calverley led the way slowly on the road to Hasfield, Trollop following, with a hang-dog look, behind.

I congratulated Mary of Eldersfield upon our escape; then, when the men-at-arms were out of sight, I told Hasting to remain where he was, and, accompanied by the Witch, proceeded to the oak where I expected Lord Edward was chafing at his long confinement. This was the case, and Lord Edward did not improve matters by his excessive hurry to descend from his hiding place No sooner had I assisted him from the hollow Into the branches than he leaped down from the tree to the ground, and, falling heavily, sprained his knee so badly that he was almost incapable of standing, and the pain was very great.

The question now was what we should do. To ascend the hill to Mary's hut was impossible, and it was not easy to reach the horses below. However, Mary was equal to the predicament, and telling me to remain quietly with Lord Edward, she strode up a pathway to her abode and in a short time descended with a small phial of oil and a bunch of the danewort. Begging me to cut away the top of Lord Edward's buskin with my dagger so as to expose the injured limb, she proceeded to rub in the oil.

During the operation, I observed Lord Edward crossing himself from time to time, with a singular expression of fear on his countenance for one who in danger was so collected and unmoved. After the rubbing, he was not only able to stand but, with the aid of my arm, to walk slowly towards the trackway where the horses were waiting, but he refused the aid of Mary's arm, which she offered more than once. I assisted him to mount Roan Roland, and he then thanked Mary for her medicaments, adding, "May God, good woman, preserve you from the wiles of Satan."

Chapter Four

WE REACHED Birtsmereton without further adventure and found my father was still absent, not having returned from Hanley Castle. I resigned Lord Edward, for a time, to the care of my mother and her damsels, and busied myself in superintending the arrangement of our panelled chamber for the comfort of our illustrious guest. I placed a couch near the great chimney, and had a fire of logs lighted. I then looked carefully to the secret chamber, as it was by no means improbable that some Lancastrian men-at-arms, holding a writ from King Henry, now at Coventry, might insist upon the right of search.

Touching the spring, I thoroughly examined the chamber and the swinging stone by which egress could be obtained to the terrace above the moat. I then waited on Lord Edward, and con- ducted him to the couch.

He had taken off the woodman's gear, and was now clad in a loose robe of my father's. Lying at full length upon the couch, he laughed and said, "I wonder what Warwick would say if he saw me now, tended like a sick girl from having a sprained knee. What poor creatures we are, Master Hildebrande, when hurt and wounded. I vow that I should be as useless in a fray, at this present moment, as if I had a broken limb. But I must not complain; I owe you my life, and, what is dearer, my liberty. Have you news of Warwick yet? What men-at-arms has he at this hunting place of Hanley, which I have heard him speak of as part of the dower of his Countess?"

As he thus asked question after question, a damsel entered with the tapers in our noblest silver sconces, and commenced arranging the table for supper. Soon after my mother came with the other maidens, and the repast was quickly served.

I was struck with the grace and courtesy with which he addressed my mother, and he received nought at the hands of the serving maidens without a bow or slight wave of the hand. Supper over, he requested my mother to sit at the foot of his couch, and proceeded to relate to her our adventures of the day – the meeting with Mary of Eldersfield; her hiding him in the hollow oak; the appearance of her dwelling; and his strong suspicion that sorcery intermingled with her pharmacy.

"I have good reason, Mistress de Brute," he said, "to fear and hate sorcery and witchcraft; my young brother Richard, not yet nine years old,[1] was tall and as straight as a young poplar tree, when one day he happened to ride on his palfrey against an old crone. She cursed him by her demons and attendant fiends, and look at him now. The blessing of the Holy Father of Rome, and the prayers of our Archbishop, and all the assoilings of the Church, have been ineffectual in removing some blast which affects him. Richard has crooked shoulders through that hag's sorcery, and I much doubt if he ever lives to be a man."

"Yet," he continued, "I would not find fault with the bridge that carried me safe across the gulf, and I might now have been a prisoner in the hands of the Lancastrians but for your witch of this wild Chase; her nostrums too are good for my injured knee, which is less painful since the application of those herb bracings."

My gentle mother replied that witchcraft was no doubt a device of Satan, but that my father had told her there were wise men, like Master Roger Bacon, and wise women too, who were neither witches nor wizards, and she had always heard Mary of Eldersfield spoken of as famous for her pharmacy.

As the evening passed, Lord Edward made inquiry as to the disposition of various families in the neighbourhood towards the rival claims of York and Lancaster, and he then expressed a wish to retire for the night, finding his knee painful. While assisting him to the great tapestried chamber, he inquired how old I was.

When I replied that I was almost twenty-one years of age, he asked me what age I supposed him to be? I guessed a score of years and five, whereupon he laughed, and said forsooth I was the older of the two. Truly it was difficult to believe such a stalwart form could be yet so youthful.

After I promised to attend him in the early morning, he said: "Good night, my good friend Hildebrande. Edward of March feels as safe under your honest roof tree as he would in his father's halls at Wigmore, or his strong castle at Ludlow; nay, safer, since we may no longer depend upon a Saint's oath[2] nor a Queen's honour."

I could not sleep, however, when I went to my chamber, and stood for a long time at the casement gazing at the reflection of the moon on the moat, and the forms of the dark trees beyond, and listening to the call of the coots as they swam to and fro across the water. I thought of Rosamond Berew, her beautiful smile, her courage, her bright and modest ways, and I wondered if she ever thought of me in that quiet home of hers below the round hill of Berew.

At last I sought my couch and was only awakened by the sunlight streaming in at my casement and the clatter of arms, as my father rode over the drawbridge into the courtyard, attended by the archers who accompanied him to Hanley Castle.

I was soon dressed and waited on him with the news of the safety of our guest, when the expression of his face told me that all was not well at Hanley Castle. I then learnt from him that after the dispersal of the Yorkist camp before Ludlow, the King had summoned a Parliament to meet at Coventry, and had attainted the Duke of York, his Duchess, his sons, the Earl and Countess of Salisbury, their son the Earl of Warwick, Lord Clinton, and many others.

The army of sixty thousand men was broken up into separate corps. King Henry was at Coventry with the Queen, and was expected to besiege Lord Warwick's great stronghold at Warwick, while other corps were massed at Worcester, and two were marching to London.

The Duke of York was believed to have escaped to Ireland from Wales, and Lord Warwick had so few followers with him at Hanley Castle that my father and others had counselled his flight also, as it was impossible to hold Hanley if the Lancastrians should bring up culverins to bear upon it, and which they had at Worcester.

It was therefore necessary, as soon as Lord Edward was able to move, to conduct him to Hanley Castle, where he would be in a safer asylum than in our small moated grange, should his track be followed by those Lancastrians, who would hear of his having been seen in the Chase of Gloucester.

I now proceeded to Lord Edward's bedchamber, and found that a night's rest had greatly relieved him. I was again struck with his courageous bearing as he received the tidings of the complete dispersal of his father's followers, and the apparent crushing out of all his ambitious schemes for power.

"We shall meet that false Queen and her puppet king again," said he; "the White Rose shall yet blossom on the banners of England, while the Red Rose shall perish beneath the rivers of blood of which it is an emblem."

He now accepted my assistance in descending to the panelled chamber, where he received my father with great consideration, and thanked him warmly for the efforts made in his behalf and the shelter afforded him in the hour of need. He expressed himself able to ride on horseback to Hanley Castle as soon as possible, as he did not wish to compromise us with the Lancastrians by being discovered in our Grange.

My father told him of his determination to escort him in person, accompanied by half a score of archers, which he had summoned together with the aid of Roger Kitel of Pendyke. I also begged to be allowed to go forward with Hasting to give notice should any Lancastrian troops appear along the route.

Lord Edward having taken a courteous leave of my mother, our small party started, and, avoiding the road by Castlemereton, we proceeded by the marshes of Longdune and Eastington, the home of John Brydges, a supporter of the House of York, and descended from the champion who was selected by Bishop de Cantilupe of Hereford to defend the rights of chase against the encroachments of the Red Earl of Gloucester in the days of the first Edward.[3]

Riding forward with Hasting, I learnt from Brydges that no Lancastrians had been seen at Upton, a hamlet inhabited by the retainers of the Countess of Warwick; but we found on arriving at Upton[4] that large parties of men-at-arms had been seen on the left bank of the Severn, even as far as the bridge, but they had not ventured to cross the river. We then proceeded at a brisk trot till we found ourselves before the drawbridge of the Castle.

Hanley Castle had been a stronghold of Earl Brithric in the days of the Norman Conquest, and it was here he was seized through the devices of the Conqueror's wife Matilda. It was a Norman keep of great importance before the bridge at Upton was built, as it was near a ford at the quay of Hanley, by which troops might cross the river when the waters were not In flood.

In the days of the first Edward it was a favourite residence of the Red Earl of Gloucester, who married the daughter of that monarch, Joan d'Acre, so called because she was born in Palestine during the siege of Acre. De Clare pulled down the Norman keep and built a strong Edwardian fortress with stone brought down the Severn; large enough to hold a force of a score archers, ten of whom were cross-bow men.

On all sides it is surrounded by water. On the north and east is a double moat, and on the west is a small mere or lake, with a stream issuing from it which turns a mill, and on this side is a postern gate communicating with the moat and lake by a flight of steps. The walls are from eight to ten feet thick and have within them a gallery with œillets, for the discharge of arrows.

The drawbridge over the inner moat is defended by a double portcullis, and at the four corners of the inner area, which is nearly a parallelogram, are four massive towers, one of which, called the Tower of the Princess, was often the forest home of Joan d'Acre when she accompanied her lord, Gilbert de Clare, who was devoted to the pleasures of the chase.

The castle is situated in a little vale by a small stream which rises from the Malvern Hills and, as we rode down a slope towards the drawbridge, we could see the church tower rising from among the houses of a secluded village in a nook of the forest of Malvern Chase. A few archers were pacing to and fro on a kind of terrace within the walls of the fortifications, but the days of Hanley Castle as a stronghold for warlike purposes had passed away.

The Earl of Warwick seldom visited it, except for a few days now and then for the purpose of hunting in Malvern Chase. Since the death of the Duke of Warwick at Hanley there was an air of decay and desertion different from that presented by the great castles of Ludlow and Wigmore, or the strongholds of the powerful Earls of Salisbury and Warwick

My father had given me a pass-word, 'The Black Bull of Middleham' and, on blowing my horn at the drawbridge, a warder appeared at the portcullis and inquired my name and business. I demanded to be conducted to the Earl of Warwick, as I had a message of importance to convey and had ridden some miles to bring it. I then gave the password and was at once admitted across the drawbridge.

The courtyard was nearly filled with archers and men-at-arms, in the centre of whom stood a tall figure armed cap-a-pie, with a huge battle-axe in his right hand, his casque shaded by black plumes, and a face I shall never forget. Gallantry and daring was the expression of those large, bold, and handsome features, and I knew at once that I was in the presence of that celebrated warrior and leader, Richard Neville, Earl of Warwick.

The man-at-arms sent with me by the warder went forward and repeated the pass-word, on which the Earl came forward from among the soldiers he was addressing and inquired who I was and whence I came.

Cap in hand, and making the obeisance due to so renowned a chieftain, I explained that my father had sent me forward to announce the safety of the Earl of March, Lord Edward of York, and that he was close at hand, being conducted by my father himself to the care of Lord Warwick.

The Earl's face lighted up with a sudden outburst of frank and genuine emotion as he said, "Welcome, good sir, you are indeed the bearer of good tidings, and welcome to your worshipful father, whom I little thought, when he parted from us before dawn, would so soon bring back to our safe custody one so dear to the heart of Warwick as the gallant Edward of York. But this is no place for him now, and verily hardly for me. The forces of Henry of Lancaster are all around us, and I know not how I shall make my own way without hindrance to our castle of Warwick."

I then mentioned that my father thought it better to remain in a hamlet near called Upton, where is a bridge across the Severn, until I brought back word that it was safe to approach the castle of Hanley, lest it might be beset by Lancastrians from Worcester, and if so we intended to make for Warwick by Evesham.

"Right!" said the Earl, "Right, and by Pershore and Evesham we must travel, for every other road is closed to us."

Lord Warwick then gave orders that all the troops available should proceed with me to Upton to escort Lord Edward and my father to the castle.

Within an hour we were all safe inside the fortifications, when Lord Warwick embraced Lord Edward, and assisted him to walk to one of the chambers. After a short time a man-at-arms summoned my father and myself to the presence of this great nobleman, and we ascended a stone staircase to a narrow chamber above the massive arch of the gateway, below which hung the grate of the portcullis.

At the door was a richly-dressed page who, in a somewhat supercilious manner, performed the office of usher, and admitted us to the presence of Lord Edward and the Earls of Salisbury and Warwick. The latter with a courteous wave of the hand motioned us to be seated, saying to my father, "We would take you into our counsel, good Master de Brute, and also your son, of whom, though young, Lord Edward of

York speaks in high terms as regards valour and discretion."

He then spoke aside to the Earl of Salisbury, when that nobleman did me the honour of making me a low bow and smiled kindly, as if well pleased.

Lord Salisbury had much of the gallant bearing of his celebrated son, but was somewhat bowed by age and the heavy armour he usually wore, nor was he so large a man as 'the stout' Earl of Warwick. With a frank manly bearing was united a certain majesty of demeanour, which was never absent from either father or son, and told of ancient lineage, power, and high repute.

Lord Warwick then addressed himself to my father, and said that notwithstanding the present apparent success of the adherents of the Crown, he believed it was only temporary, and could not last.

"Everywhere," he said, "he was met with complaints, not only of the common people, but often of gentlemen and even knights, who no longer lived in security and ease, but were liable to attacks from Lancastrian barons and followers of the Court, who did not hesitate to break into the houses of yeomen and even the manors or keeps of gentlemen, and to commit various acts of depredation in contempt of all law and order. There is not a squire or franklin round Worcester and Coventry who has not been despoiled by the followers of King Henry."

He then inquired of my father if he thought the people would still go on enduring this, or whether knight and squire, franklin and yeoman, would not rather rise and follow the leading of the Duke of York, his father, and himself, who ever loved the people of England, and ever pleaded their cause before King and Parliament.

My father rose, and, making a profound salutation, entered boldly on the many grievances and just complaints of the people. He alluded to the insecurity of property and of the general lawlessness of all classes; to the persecution of the Lollards, and the oppressive power of the Church. The principal grievance, he boldly declared, was the persecution of men for conscience sake, and it was only necessary to be known to be a possessor of a copy of the Bible of Wycliffe to bring down the wrath of priests and bishops and the curses and persecutions of the Church.

"You, my Lords," said my father in his most dignified manner, "are believed to be willing to shelter the persecuted for religion's sake from

Chapter Four

the exactions of insolent priests and a licentious and tyrannical Queen; and it is this which has gained for you the hearts of thousands such as myself and my son, who will go whithersoever you lead to danger, and, if God wills it, unto death. The House of York and its gallant supporters are under a shadow for a time, but they reign in the hearts of the people and will eventually reign over the land."

When my father ceased speaking I could perceive that his pleading produced considerable effect upon the Earls of Salisbury and Warwick, and upon Lord Edward also, until the allusion to the persecution of the Lollards by the Church, when I observed that his brow contracted as if in anger.

Lord Salisbury replied that he could answer for himself and his son that neither Lollard nor Catholic should with their consent be persecuted for conscience sake. He believed also that the noble Lord Richard of York would gladly curtail the powers of the ecclesiastics; powers which should belong to the Crown and the Parliament of England, and not to those whose duty it is to teach mercy and not persecution; peace rather than war; and by convincing arguments rather than the gallows.

Prince Edward was about to speak when a loud blast from a trumpet near the castle sounded through the chamber. Lord Warwick sprang from his seat, and begging of Lord Edward, lame as he was, to remain quiet, and his father also, he called upon my father and myself to accompany him to the men-at-arms assembled below.

As we passed down the stone staircase, he looked through one of the œillet holes and said, "I see our own cognizance, the white bear and ragged staff. I expect our Countess has sent our men-at-arms from Warwick Castle," and before we reached the courtyard we could hear the shouts of "A Warwick! A Warwick!" from the stentorian throats of some two hundred troopers, who rode down the slope towards the moat and drawbridge.

Lord Warwick had guessed rightly, his courier had arrived at Warwick Castle, and the Countess immediately despatched a number of riders under the command of Sir Herbert Lovell to increase the force assembled at Hanley.

Sir Herbert Lovell counselled immediate departure from Hanley, as the Lancastrians would without doubt lay siege to the castle if it once got abroad that the Earls of Salisbury and Warwick were within its walls. The Countess of Warwick, too, had received certain tidings that the forces at Worcester had cannon to batter the walls of any place to which they might lay siege.

On hearing this, Lord Warwick determined to abandon his castle of Hanley and make for Warwick before the route was closed by the approach of troops from Worcester. In a short time the armed men were marshalled in the courtyard, and the horses of the two Earls were brought from their stabling.

Lord Edward was mounted on a charger of Lord Warwick's, when he called me by my Christian name of Hildebrande, and beckoning me to his side, said, "I shall not easily forget the words of your worshipful father, with much of which I quite agree, and so I am certain would my father also; yet still more will Edward of March never forget the succour he received when he most needed it from his friend Hildebrande de Brute."

Then taking a plain gold ring which he wore on his right forefinger, he took me by the hand and placed it on mine, saying, "Wear this for the sake of Edward of March, and if ever the time should come when our House of York can repay their friends for their adherence and devotion, and you have aught to ask that an English nobleman may grant, bring or send this ring in token of our adventures in Malvern Chase, and it shall go hard with me but it shall be granted."

Leaving but a few men-at-arms to guard the Castle, the cavalcade rode forth, the Earls, with Lord Edward between them, in the van, and Sir Herbert Lovell bringing up the rear. We accompanied them as far as the hamlet of Upton, where, receiving the salutes of these great leaders, we parted and rode away for our own home under the southern Malverns.

All this happened in the year of grace 1459. The Earl of Warwick did not remain long in his castle of Warwick, but crossed the seas to his sure asylum at Calais, taking with him his own family, his father, and the Earl of March. In the meantime the Court had appointed the Duke of Somerset to the command of Calais, but the mariners of his fleet deserted him and took their ships over to Lord Warwick, the Duke being glad to escape to Guisnes.

News from foreign parts travels slowly into forest districts in the country, and though my father had friends in London, we did not hear of the safety of the Earls for many weeks.

In the meantime the Lancastrians made themselves more unpopular than ever by the lawless violence they displayed wherever their standard appeared. Sir Hugh Calverley and others of their party were disgusted with the despoiling of corn and granaries, and even burning the houses of franklins, who had sided with neither Yorkist nor Lancastrian.

Chapter Five

WE PASSED a pleasant summer in home pursuits and duties, and visiting our neighbours, which is hardly possible in the winter when slough fills all the trackways up to the bellies of the horses. My father, as a magistrate, put in force tbe Act passed in the reign of Richard II, 'to compel all servants to practise with the long-bow on Sundays and holidays'. He also took care that the arrows were well winged with goose feathers, according to the edict of Henry V to the sheriffs of each county, so that our neighbourhood could furnish a good number of bowmen well equipped, while I took some pains to accustom our own serving men to the use of the cross-bow, which was my favourite weapon.

For the purpose of practice, we repaired to the open green on the mere of Longdune, which on a dry summer furnished us with a long range for the flight of the arrows and bolts; and sometimes after our exercises we would repair to the village green for a dance and a merry-making in the evening's sunshine.

The damsels of the neighbourhood, too, took great interest in our progress, and would embroider the archer's glove or bracer as prizes, and those worked by the fingers of Rosamond Berew, Bessie Kitel, or Dorothy Paunceforte were eagerly contended for.

It had been thought necessary to decree that no common man or servant should wear hosen[1] which cost more than fourteen-pence, or kerchiefs that cost more than ten-pence, and that the women should not wear girdles garnished with silver, prizes fairly won being excepted, so any prizes ornamented by the ladies around were esteemed highly.

All the farms in Malvern Chase were held by a tenure of military service to the knights, esquires, or franklins around, for we had no great baron in our parts. The Earl of Warwick indeed married the last of the Beauchamps, but he seldom visited the estates of his Countess in the County of Worcester, and thus the yeomen in the parishes around us were seldom called upon to follow the lead of any but the gentlemen who lived amongst them and had at different times received grants of land from the Chase.

My mother, seeing the interest we took in the progress of our archers and pikemen, proposed that there should be a day fixed for rural sports and competition in archery among the Yeomanry around, and that the meeting should be held on the mere of Longdune. She proposed to prepare a feast for the occasion, and said she would request all the damsels of the neighbourhood to embroider prizes, and grace the gathering by their presence.

My father liked the plan, for he never lost sight of the fact that in those troublous times it would be well for our parishes to be united, in case it might be necessary to band together to resist the demands of some insolent baron, or perhaps to defend some attacked dwelling-house or keep. Hitherto we had been preserved from the effects of the quarrels between the houses of York and Lancaster, but none could tell how soon war might break out again, and we might be involved in the struggle and give offence either to one side or the other.

The whole country round on our side of the Malverns responded to my mother's summons, and great preparations were made for the entertainment of our guests on the great green glade on Longdune mere. Days were passed in preparations for good cheer, consisting of chines of pork, beef and mutton without end, with manchetts of bread, and casks of cider and ale in abundance. Then there were provisions for the high table in the great shed where the gentry were to dine. For this there were brazed peacocks, and herons, and multitudes of capons, with a great boar's head, into which was inserted the tusks of a real wild boar, to add to the ferocity of the garniture. Also dishes of 'blancmangers of pounded capons, with pottels of milke and pottels of creame', and above all, for the centre of the table, was a magnificent 'soteltie', which was to be carried in amidst the sounding of bugle-horns. For the preparation of this soteltie my mother held a long consultation with Dame Brydges, who rode over on her palfrey from Eastington to lend her aid and advice.

It was composed of jellies and blancmangers, preserved fruits and confectionaries, built up to imitate our manor house at Birtsmereton. There were figures of men and animals admirably cut out of the pith of wood by Rosamond Berew, and the water in the moat and fish-pools was represented by cream. Dorothy Paunceforte, too, sent a pleasing riddle in jelly and blancmanger, made with her own fair hands, and which was of the most subtle kind, for no one could interpret it until they came to the illuminated scroll inside.

It was on a bright morning in July that I marshalled our little band of ten archers and cross-bow men of Birtsmereton in our courtyard before conducting them to the mere of Longdune. Hasting wore his forester's dress and a heron's plume in his cap. In honour of the day I had put on my best jerkin of rich green cloth and a crimson baldric with our crest, the *talbot*, worked in silver thread by Bessie Kitel, while my cap was adorned with a silver arrow, and on my forefinger was the massive gold ring presented to me by Lord Edward of York.

My father wore a new doublet of damask cloth trimmed with satin, as only knights were entitled to wear velvet, and my father was ever careful not to presume upon his ancient family as a grandson of Sir Giles de Brute. 'Win your honours before you wear them', was one of his precepts. My mother was robed in her newest gown from Worcester, with long trailing sleeves and a silver girdle. Her head-dress, of the newest fashion, came from London itself. It rose to such a height it was difficult to think that the steeple of the church of Longdune had not come among us. I much preferred her heart-shaped head-dress, but my loved mother looked well in anything.

Arrived on the shooting-ground, we escorted my mother to a great wooden shed, which had been erected for the occasion to afford shelter in case of a passing storm. In the centre was a raised dais for the Queen of the Sports, who was to be selected by the most successful archer of the day to distribute the prizes to the winners.

Roger Calverley had arrived before us, dressed in archer's green, with his jerkin and baldric trimmed with black. Kitel of Pendyke brought half-a-dozen cross-bow men and the fair Bessie, and announced his intention of challenging me to a cross-bow contest at a hundred yards. Pauncefortе of Hasfield brought six archers, Sir John Carfax the same number, and Brydges of Eastington six, while Bromwich of Broomsbarrow headed ten.

Lord Warwick's forester came accompanied by three picked archers from the castle. Old Master Berew, as he was usually called, was accompanied by Rosamond and her silent brother. The inhabitants of most of the villages round, old and young, attended, for it was made as much a holiday as if it were a gluttony mass. All the ladies came clad in their best, and most of them wore some light gossamer stuff adapted to the heat of a July sun. Bessie Kitel had a chaplet of red and white roses round her hat, as if the wearer hoped and trusted the present antagonistic factions would blend together, while Rosamond Berew had a single white rose on the side of her dainty little head.

Chapter Five

My father, who acted as commander for the day, had so arranged that parties of three and six were to act as skirmishers. When arrived at a calculated distance, they were to shoot at figures of men made of straw and gorse. Then all the archers were to stand in a body and shoot at a large target of straw with a black bull's-eye, as if they were discharging their arrows at a clump of spear-men.

Loud shouts arose from the spectators as Hasting, accompanied by two of our picked archers, pretended to creep on hands and knees through imaginary thickets and then, rising suddenly, shot all their arrows into a maukin's head at the distance of two hundred paces. Nor was Kitel far behind, with his Pendyke yeomen, in a performance which required much practice. He and his six men started from one of the maukins, and running at full speed turned round sharply at the distance of a hundred yards, when all seven arrows struck the figure, Kitel's arrow penetrating the head.

These displays and evolutions went on for a couple of hours, when the cross-bow men exhibited their skill, and though, with Kitel's men, we made a fair score, it was by no means equal to the performance with the longbow. Each arrow, in this kind of practice, is privately marked, and each archer claims his own, and hits are scored accordingly. Head-hits in the maukins and bull's-eyes in the targets entitled the archers to contend in the single strifes which succeeded to decide the superiority of single archers. Thus Hasting and three of our Birtsmereton archers with myself were enabled to contend, while Kitel had two, Lord Warwick's forester two, and Paunceforte of Hasfield one. Broomsbarrow had three.

It was not till the winning archers had been told off that I observed a man of middle age, dressed in a suit of sober grey, and wearing a baldric covered with arrows worked in silver thread, the signs of success on many previous contests. He shot with the Broomsbarrow archers, but did not wear the badge of Bromwich, or of any house around us, and it was evident by the great skill he exhibited that the competitors for the principal prize would have a most formidable opponent.

A hearty cheer greeted the rivals for the great prize as they selected their arrow from the sheaf or tested their bowstrings. The mark was a white pigeon fastened by the legs to a pole, the height of a man's head. The distance was two hundred yards, at which the bird looked but a white spot. Roger Calverley wished to be a competitor though he had not shot in the melée, and was admitted on handing in a baldric as a prize for the shorter distances.

We were now shooting, 'each for our own hand', as it was termed, as competitors who had displayed a decided superiority over others, and now endeavoured to establish our superiority over the best. Before we shot at the white dove, we aimed at the great target at a distance of four hundred yards, and only those who were within four inches of the bull's-eye could claim a right to shoot at the pigeon.

This trial at a long range weeded us out considerably. My own arrow was not within a foot of the bull's-eye, and the only archers who struck it were Lord Warwick's forester, Hasting, and the stranger in grey. Lord Warwick's forester hit the post not two inches from the pigeon, and the arrow remained quivering in the wood. Hasting now came forward, and I believe would have transfixed the bird had not Bessie Kitel called out, "Now, Master Hasting, shoot for the honour of Birtsmereton, and I will work you a winter kerchief with my own hand." I saw Hasting grew nervous, and though he ruffled the feathers he missed the mark.

The stranger in grey now advanced amidst breathless silence. He did not appear to take much precaution in drawing the bow, but gave a short, quick pull, and his arrow transfixed the pigeon through and through. The spectators cheered loudly, but not so heartily as they would have done had the successful archer been one of ourselves; they then crowded round the post, the maukins, and the targets, criticizing the shots and the archers.

My father now invited the successful archer to come forward and give his name, and to exercise his privilege, as champion, of naming the Queen of the Sports. The grey marksman, who did not seem the least elated by his success, gave his name as Robin of Elsdune, a name well known on the Welsh Marches of Kington and Wigmore, as that of a bold rider attached to the House of York, and of remarkable skill in archery. He disclaimed the intention of accepting any honour beyond the congratulations of those present, and begged that the honours of this trial of skill might be bestowed upon Hasting, whom, he declared, "Would have struck the mark but for the challenge of the beautiful lady with the golden hair".

The applause of the spectators was now unbounded, for Hasting was a favourite with all, and as the prizes were intended for competitors from the neighbourhood, no demur was made to the request of the archer.

I saw Hasting was much embarrassed and, modest even to shyness, would rather have faced the charge of a wild boar. Blushing like a girl, he came forward, but without awkwardness, and casting a look of half reproach, half admiration at Bessie Kitel, knelt on one knee before Rosamond Berew, and led her to the dais amidst the shouts of all, gentle and simple, who now surrounded the shed.

Bestowing one of her winning smiles upon the champion who selected her, and a curtsey to my mother and those around her in the shed, Rosamond took the throne of the Queen of Sports, and my mother, assisted by Mistress Brydges, placed a wreath of roses on her head. She was not so fair as Bessie Kitel, nor so handsome as Kate Brydges, but there was a calm dignity in her whole bearing, and an indescribable expression of countenance which told of a mind of more than common culture.

The first prize of the day was now handed to the Queen. It was a magnificently worked baldric, and in receiving this, the champion was privileged to kiss her cheek, while the other prize winners only kissed her hand. She received the salutation of Hasting with grace, and handed him the baldric with a few words of congratulation. My mother insisted upon presenting Robin of Elsdune with the silvered girdle she wore round her own dear waist, in token, she said, "of the courtesy shown to a brother archer, and in memory of a day with the archers of the South Malverns".

The Grey Marksman, as the people called him, seemed surprised at this courteous gift, but received it with evident pleasure as he knelt at the feet of Rosamond and kissed her hand. The other prizes were then distributed to Kitel, Lord Warwick's forester, and among others to myself, for the best hits with the long-bow and the crossbow, at shorter distances than the test of the white pigeon.

The ceremony over, my honoured father, holding my mother by the hand, came forward on the dais, and congratulated the archers upon their skill. He said that "such men united would be ever ready to protect the homes in which they lived". "A score of such steady men," he said, "might avail to turn the scale in many a battle when large numbers were engaged. They could not all expect to equal the marksman from the Marches, but all might practise till their aim was well nigh certain." He then invited them to partake of the refreshments, and the bugles sounded for the feast of good things.

The winners of the prizes were placed at seats of honour at the high table. The boar's head was opposite my father at the extreme end, and there was abundance of spiced wine, morat, and hippocrass for the gentry, with ale, cider, and honey wine, or mead, for the people. It was my office to see that all were well supplied with the drinks they preferred, while the waiting maids were handing the simnel and wastel cakes and spiced bread.

I observed that Roger Calverley was particularly attentive to Bessie Kitel, pulling off the wings of a capon with his own hand; while I upset a flagon of hippocrass at seeing Rosamond Berew reading a scrip found in the soteltie to Robin of Elsdune, and I longed for the time when I should be released from the office of cupbearer to my father's guests. I had gone with a flagon of choice morat, a drink as old as the time of the second Henry, and challenged Robin of Elsdune to drink to my mother's toast of the 'Archers of merry England', when he said to me in a quiet tone, "After the feast, Master Hildebrande, do me the favour to grant me a few minutes of your time, to hear a message from one who trusts you."

Feasts like frays have their ending, and when every one had partaken to the full, the fragments were gathered into baskets, and sent to the Church for distribution to the poorer classes. The Sub-Prior of Pendyke gave thanksgiving, and then all prepared for the jig and the dance before the sun went down.

It was a merry sight. On one side of the great green some of the common people engaged in the game of bob-apple, and many got a good ducking at the end of the plank. Another group gathered round a Welsh harper, who sang the achievements of Rollo and of Robin Hood. Sir Hugh Calverley had sent his fool, who was a tumbler and dancer as well as buffoon, and drew numbers around him to witness his agility. The Queen had given her orders for the old Saxon dance of *Thread the Needle*, and begged each archer to select his maiden, when Robin of Elsdune beckoned me on one side:

"You will trust me," said he, pointing to my forefinger ring, "when I tell you that he who gave you that ring sent a message to you."

"From Edward of York," I said, in great surprise, "he is safe in France."

"That is quite true," said Robin; "nevertheless I only parted from him ten days ago, so you may judge I have lost no time in reaching you."

He then informed me that Lord Warwick had command of the whole English Channel, and had taken two fleets sent out by the Lancastrians, that he purposed sailing to Ireland to bring away the Duke of York, and that the Earls of Salisbury and March were safe in Calais. Lord Edward sent to beg of me to try and induce my father and other followers of the House of York to be in readiness to support their cause when once their banner was displayed again in England.

"The days of tyranny and priestcraft are numbered," said Robin of Elsdune, "and before a year has passed, York and Warwick united will summon a new Parliament, and I for one, hope that Richard of York will be King of England, as we Marchers know full well is truly his lawful right."

I then sought my father and told him of this unexpected message. He bade me request Robin of Elsdune to take up his abode with us for some days, in order that measures might be concerted without exciting the suspicions of the Lancastrians who were still in considerable force at Worcester.

On returning to the merry-makers, I found Hasting still dancing with the Queen, so I sought the hand of sweet Dorothy Paunceforte. *Thread the Needle* was now changed for *Hunt the Shoe*, and we were soon engaged in the evolutions of this well-known dance, enjoyed by our grandfathers and grandmothers ages before our time.

Somehow in the scramble I managed to kiss Rosamond the Queen instead of Dorothy, and so I got sentenced to stand 'in durance vile' in the centre, while they all danced round me with good-humoured jeers at my discomfiture, and my partner and place in the dance were taken by John Brydges. So the merriment went on until the sun went down and the horns of the foresters reminded us that we must all wend homewards.

My mother invited the Queen, and her grandfather, with the Kitels, Pauncefortes, and Calverley to our supper at the manor house, and bidding farewell to the numerous villagers, who still lingered round, we strolled homewards, discussing as we went the various adventures of the day.

Robin of Elsdune walked by my side and told me how he had attended Lord Edward of York from his childhood and had taught him to shoot with the bow and wield the battle-axe, and I found that he was far more educated than his appearance indicated from his dress, which was in those times the outward sign of a superior station. He had associated with some Lollards in his youth, and was one of the bodyguards of Duke Richard of York, when he was Protector during the lunacy of King Henry VI.

Robin had been present at the Battle of St Alban's, when the Lancastrians were defeated and Henry their king was found hidden in the tanner's house; and later on he was with the Duke when Sir Andrew Trollop deserted the cause of York and went over to Henry. In the flight which was rendered necessary by this defection, he had accompanied Richard, Duke of York, to Ireland, while Lord Edward escaped to Gloucester; but Duke Richard, being anxious for the safety of his son, despatched Robin to Lord Warwick, hoping that his son would find shelter with that powerful baron till he could cross the Channel.

Robin had just arrived at Hanley Castle when we rode in with Lord Edward, and afterwards accompanied him as his body servant in the train of Lord Warwick to Calais.

The heir of the House of York had not failed to observe, when he was at Gloucester and in the forest of Malvern Chase, that other classes besides the great barons and their retainers would have to give their adherence before the throne of England would be secured either by the Red Rose or the White. He thought much of my father's words, that support would be given to that leader who would conform to the laws of the land, and guarantee greater freedom for conscience sake in religious matters. Lord Edward therefore determined to send Robin to England, with instructions to see first my father and myself, and to beg of us to prepare as quietly but as surely as possible for a time, not long distant, when he, Lord Edward, would raise the standard of York at Gloucester, and call upon the knights and gentlemen of the neighbourhood to join it.

As we neared the moat, Robin remarked that he knew the place from the description of Lord Edward, who was astonished at the comfort and safety of these well-defended manor houses, which were becoming so common in the land, and were all able to send their six or ten well-trained archers to the field of battle. Robin had this day seen how some of us could shoot, so he had respect for the middle classes, though he had been accustomed to the great following of such powerful peers as the Duke of York, and the Earls of Salisbury and Warwick.

The supper was laid in the wainscoted chamber, and when the archer observed the emblazoned shields above the panels, I told him that these were the bearings of knights and gentlemen who were the equals and friends of my father and mother, who would, if called upon, with one or two exceptions, rally round the House of York.

In the conversation after supper, allusions were made to the Miracle Plays which were soon to be enacted at Theocsbury, and my mother gave a general invitation to all present to rendezvous at Birtsmereton and attend these fashionable religious displays. All seemed gladly to accept the invitation save my father, who said he had other business to attend to, old Master Berew, and the Queen of the day, who looked down in silence. Bessie Kitel clapped her hands, and Roger Calverley, presenting her with a red rose, said he should reckon upon escorting her, as Theocsbury had the best Devil in all the country, and the Angels were well spoken of.

The moon had now risen above the tall elms of our great avenue, and our friends rose to depart. Calverley was to remain the night, so I proposed to him and the archer that we should accompany them part of their way home. We walked over the greensward in the direction of Berew, the Kitels coming partly out of their way with us. I took the opportunity of asking Rosamond Berew if she would go to the Miracle Plays of Theocsbury, and she replied, "No, Master Hildebrande, I do not like such amusements; they are innocent to many, but brought up as I have been by my grandfather, I may not behold them without sin."

I asked somewhat angrily if she thought my mother was likely to invite her friends to visit sinful places of amusement. Rosamond replied very quietly, that the case was different. That my mother had always conformed to the customs of the country, although it was believed that my father would gladly abolish miracle plays, and see some things altered in the services of the Church.

"But I am a simple girl, Master Hildebrande, and have no right to talk to you on such subjects; nevertheless, though I love a chase or a merry-go-round, it is against my conscience to go to these plays in God's house, and therefore I may not do it."

I pressed her to tell me why it was against her conscience.

"Not now," said she, "Master Hildebrande; it is too serious a subject, and I am too tired with the exertions of the day. You should ask grandfather why he would sorrow if his Rosamond was in that noble house of God, the Abbey of Theocsbury, looking on at a devil dancing, or an archangel trumpeting."

I told her that I objected to any approach to profanity, but that miracle plays had been considered for a long time a good way of instructing people who were without education in some of the facts upon which the religion of Christ was founded, and that such instruction was better than none at all. Although, no doubt, many of the ecclesiastics of the time were a disgrace to their profession, as in former days was William of Ledbury, who was prior of Malvern. Yet there were good Catholics as well as good Lollards, and I instanced Prior Alcock, who even then was engaged in the rebuilding of Little Malvern Priory, and I thought people should be allowed to worship God in their own fashion without being considered sinful. Rosamond said no more, but I could see the tears glistening in the moonlight as they rolled down her cheek

We had now come to the top of the hill where the road to Berew crosses the trackway to Theocsbury ford, and a good-night was said by all as we parted from our friends.

Many questions passed before my mind ere I slept on that night of our archery on Longdune mere. Were my father and I about to engage definitely in the cause of the House of York against the reigning king of England and his young son? Then I thought on the words and conduct of Rosamond Berew.

My father had given much time to my education, but he had not influenced me in regard to the theological differences between the Lollards and the Church of Rome, leaving me to follow my own bias, while never concealing his own opinion. He thought the teaching of Wycliffe in advance of the age, and that the attempt at propagating the views of such men as Roger Bacon, Bishop Grostete, Wycliffe, Robert Langland and others, was but as the casting of pearls before swine.

Liberty of opinion for Lollard as well as Catholic was his demand, and he was ever ready to defend the persecuted for conscience sake, nay, even the proscribed Jew. I have seen his cheek pale with anger when recounting the martyrdoms of Oldcastle and others in the days of Henry IV and Henry of Monmouth, but he was equally indignant when speaking of the horrible cruelty of Richard Coeur de Lion towards the persecuted Jews.

Chapter Five

Not many days later, our party assembled for the miracle play, and we rode by the ford of Fordington, where the Abbot of Theocsbury has his country residence, crossing the Severn a mile below the town. We rode past the Abbey to a hostelrie on the banks of the Avon having a tabard painted with the arms of the Earl of Warwick.

The landlord of the Black Bear reminded me of Chaucer's landlord in his Prologue to the Canterbury Tales, as fit to be a 'marshall in a hall; a right merrie man, wise and welltaught'. The stables were opposite the hostelrie on the banks of the river. The space in front was crowded with franklins and their wives and daughters, and monks skilled in hunting with greyhounds and hawking; and friars who were favourites with the franklins and ever ready to beg from those who had anything to give. As we rode up, the head forester of the Chase of Gloucester was quaffing a goblet of hippocrass with a monk of Bredon, who was begging a puppy for his kennel and taking his share of the potation for which the forester paid.

Then there were country gentlemen and their dames, some quaffing goblets of ale and others attending to their steeds; with nuns from Gloucester who could sing right sweetly as in Chaucer's time, and pretty country girls with country bumpkins fresh from the plough. All these had come in for the miracle play at the Abbey, and had assembled round the best hostelrie in Theocsbury. The landlord had the 'best victual' and plenty of it, but those who wished to eat had to feast under a wooden shed by the side of the Avon, for all the chambers were occupied by persons of quality.

I was surprised to find Robin of Elsdune entering into conversation with the forester of Gloucester Chase like an old acquaintance, till I remembered that Lord Edward of York had taken shelter at the lodge at Wainlode, and found upon inquiry that the forester came from Ludlow. I joined them and inquired after the dogs and falcons, when our friend of the Chase of Gloucester said, "Ware snakes," and on turning round I saw Sir Andrew Trollop, with his cruel eyes, ride towards the Abbey down the street from Bredon.

He was dressed, like the gay gallants of the time, in a short but gorgeous gown of satin with enormous sleeves of velvet, and his boots had tips as long as those of Calverley. He vociferated a series of astonishing oaths as the crowd somewhat interfered with his progress. He was followed by two men-at-arms, and used his riding whip very freely upon men and women alike as they barred his way. "Damme," he said, in a loud voice, "but I will ride over you country louts if you do not clear a path," and spurring his horse he actually rode down an infirm woman who was trying to get out of his way.

I rushed forward just in time to save the old body from being trampled to death, and if I could have left her would have pulled him off his horse for his pains, but she lay senseless in my arms and the gal- lant knight rode on; not, however, before he had recognized me, as he said, "So, Master de Brute, it is you again with another accursed witch!"

Robin now came up and assisted me in taking the helpless woman to the hostelrie, when she proved to be a person employed on the premises and was attended by the servants of the house.

I lost no time in telling Calverley of the arrival of Trollop, and while we speculated on what could have brought him to Theocsbury, Robin came up and said he should remain at the hostelrie while we went to the Abbey, as Trollop would be certain to send back his attendants and horses to the stables, and he should keep a watch on the men-at-arms and make out, if possible, their master's errand and what mischief he was brewing.

"He is the man," said Robin, "who betrayed us at Ludlow and went over to King Henry. I owe him a debt I may sometime repay him, but it is not one of gratitude." He then addressed himself to the landlord, and ordered a couple of measures of spiced ale to be prepared, mixed with a measure of the strongest wine, as he expected guests, and that soon.

It was now time to wend our way to the Abbey, which is so famous for its early history and the many tombs of worthies of note who lie buried there. Fitz-Hamon, who was a follower of the Conqueror, built the Norman nave and tower of the Abbey of Theocsbury, so grand in their proportions; and the solemn round arches of massive stone were brought, men say, up the Severn from Caen in Normandy. The founder was buried in the chapter house, and the Abbey was finished by Robert Fitz-Roy, the bastard of Henry I, whom he made Earl of Gloucester.

Here, too, in front of the high altar, are the magnificent tombs of several of the illustrious de Clares, the descendants of Strongbow, the conqueror of Ireland. Of the noble family of the Despensers there are several tombs. The body of Hugh Despenser the younger, the favourite .of Edward II, who was hung, drawn, and quartered at Hereford, lies in the lavatory[2], but his limbs and head were sent to different city gates. There is a magnificent monument to Guy de Brian, standard bearer to Edward III. I have stood with my father at this tomb, and fancied I could hear his shout at Crecy, "Advance banners, in the name of God and St George!"

A magnificent tomb of modern date rests over the remains of Isabella Despenser, the mother of the present Countess of Warwick, near to the chapel she erected to the memory of her first husband Richard Beauchamp, who fought at Agincourt and was created Earl of Worcester.

We had examined the tombs and admired the splendid proportions of both Abbey and Monastery, when the sound of trumpets called us to our appointed seats and we joined the multitude who were assembled in the nave, between which and the choir was arranged the stage for the *Mystery* which was to follow.

After a procession of the monastic clergy, headed by the Abbot, a celebrated preacher preached a sermon[3] which impressed the audience much. The subject was summoning the congregation to the services of the three days called Tenebrae, or the three days preceding Easter.

"Worshipful friends," said the preacher, "holy Church useth the three days, Wednesday, Thursday, and Friday; the service to be said in the eventide in darkness. And it is called with diverse men Tenables, but holy Church calleth it Tenebus, as 'Rationale Divinorum' saith, that is to say, Thirus, or darkness, for then is the service said in darkness. But unto the service of Thursday at eve is no bell rung, but a clapper the sound of a Tree, tokening that every man and woman should come to the service without noise making. Also in this service called Tenebras, before the altar is set a hearse with twenty-four candles burning, for twelve apostles and twelve prophets, which candles be quenched one after another in tokening that Christ's disciples went from him every one after

But when all be quenched yet one is kept light, which light is secretly, while the clerks sing the kyries and the versts, and that signifieth the holy woman that made lamentation at Christ's sepulture. Then afterwards that candle is brought again, which betokeneth Christ in his manhood dead and laid in sepulture. But soon after he rose from death to life, and gave light of mercy and of grace to all that were quenched by despair. The strokes that the priest giveth upon the book betoken the thunder-claps when Christ brake hell gates and destroyed the power of the Devil in his resurrection."

The preacher continued at great length, and then came the moral of his discourse, that his hearers "should not be unkind to the merciful Lord that suffered for us; for unkindness is a sin that stinketh in the sight of God". And then he told how "There was some-time a knight came from far countries and would seek adventures. So it fortuned to a forest where he heard a great noise of a beast crying. So this knight drew nigh, and there he saw how an adder had clipped a lion, and venomed him, and bound the lion to a tree while he lay and slept. "

"When the lion waked of his sleep, and perceived himself bound, and might not help himself, he made a horrible cry. Then the knight had compassion on the lion: he drew out his sword and slew the adder, and loosed the lion. And when the lion found himself unbound, he fell down to the knight's feet, and ever after he served the knight, and every night lay at his bed's feet; in tournaments and battles ever helped the knight, insomuch that all men spake of the knight and the lion. And so Christ loosed mankind out of the bond of the Devil with the sword of his precious passion, and made him free. Wherefore must every man and woman show kindness to that good Lord as the lion did to the knight, to be obedient to him and thank him of his goodness, and of his unbinding of the bonds of the Devil."

The miracle play, which followed the sermon, was written in the time of Edward III. The subject was the descent of Christ into hell for the liberation of Adam and Eve, the Prophets, and John the Baptist.[4] The play was conducted with music, and John the Baptist was arrayed in real goat-skins, the prophets in long gowns, and Adam and Eve as lightly dressed as decency would allow.

Then came a Morality Play, in which the Devil and Vice were the principal characters. The Devil appeared first as a handsome gallant of the time, dressed in the extreme of Court fashion. His shirt was of fine holland, with a stomacher of clear reynes. His gown was three yards in length, and his hosen of the most costly cloth of crimson with two dozen points of cheverelle, and the aglets of fine silver. He had a goodly pair of peaked shoes, a dagger for devotion, and a small high bonnet.[5]

Vice was a wicked buffoon, but merry withal; he assisted Satan in all his wicked seductions, until at last they quarrelled, when Satan appeared in his proper character, with horns and hoofs, and shaggy hide and tail. Vice attacked him with a great wooden sword, but the

Devil mastered him with fire and smoke, and carried him off to hell on his back.

All this was sufficiently well played, but I could not see in what the morality consisted, and how it could add to feelings of devotion. I was glad when it was over, and thankful that it did not last as some did for eight days; beginning at the creation of the world, and going through the whole of the gospel history.[6]

I left the church convinced that Rosamond Berew was right – that the services in God's house should ever be adapted to devotion, and not 'to make sport' and to 'glad the hearers'.

Chapter Six

WE LEFT the Abbey and were wandering among the cloisters of the Monastery, when the Abbot passed us, clad in a magni- ficent dress of scarlet and gold, and attended by a large group of ecclesiastics. I saw also Sir Andrew Trollop glide by, and follow the Abbot among the clustered columns.

The Abbey was now emptied of the crowd and we re-entered it, as Bessie Kitel wished to see the tomb of the Skeleton Monk.[1] This monument is in the north aisle, not far from the tomb of the Standard-bearer at Crecy, and is the representation of a skeleton on which are the creeping things which prey upon the dead – a good rebuke to human pride.

We were regarding this stone effigy with somewhat solemn feelings, when Robin of Elsdune appeared, coming up the north aisle, beckoning as if he wished to speak to me alone. I passed on, when he said in a low tone, "It is time for us to leave this place, and you should leave at once. Get to the Black Bear of Warwick as soon as you can."

I now learnt that he had discovered from Sir Andrew's followers that Trollop had obtained a writ to arrest one Master Hildebrande de Brute of Birtsmereton, for conniving with a cunning necromancer known as Mary of Eldersfield, and had taken it to the Abbot and demanded his aid to arrest my person for examination before the Archbishop of Canterbury.

This was indeed a serious affair in the hands of one as unscrupulous as Trollop. It would be of little avail to show that Mary of Eldersfield employed her knowledge of herbs and nostrums for the benefit of her fellow-creatures. Adder skins and beetles, owls, and a black cat had been found in her possession; she was therefore a sorceress, and as such was liable to be brought to the stake.

Joan of Arc saved France, but Joan of Arc was burnt; Cardinal Beaufort and several bishops being present. Roger Bolingbroke was a learned astronomer, but learning did not save him. Margery Jourdain was a poor woman, but poverty and obscurity, especially in aged women, was a signal for their ill treatment.

If the Abbot of Theocsbury aided Trollop there was nothing to prevent my being seized at any moment and tried for the terrible offence of consorting with a witch, and perhaps assisting at her sorceries. 'Thou shalt not allow a witch to live', was a text quoted by the Church against the white witch as well as against the black hag, and a yeoman archer had been accused of obtaining the aid of a white witch because he hit the mark at which he aimed with unerring dexterity.

I lost no time in acquainting Calverley with Trollop's abominable accusation for, if he should attempt to arrest me on my road home, we were none of us armed beyond our daggers, and were incapable of resistance. He saw the danger of the situation, and undertook to escort my mother and our friends home with his men-at arms, begging of me to absent myself from home for a time until means could be taken to disprove the charge.

"I never knew," said Calverley, "how it was that you fell in with that Mary of Eldersfield when I saved you from the clutches of that false knight, who, I regret to say, has too much influence in high places since his treachery at Ludlow."

We then consulted with Robin of Elsdune, when he proposed to accompany me and that we should take boat to Gloucester, where some friends of the Yorkists would gladly give us shelter. Having arranged matters with our friends, who seemed somewhat surprised at our sudden departure, we entered a boat on the Avon, which impelled by two stout oarsmen soon brought us to the waters of the broader Severn.

I had borrowed the cloak of Kitel, and Robin that of Calverley, so that our persons were well concealed as we lay back against the flat bottom of the boat. As we passed the Lower Lode, or ferry and ford of Fordington, we saw on the left bank Trollop and his men-at-arms, accompanied by others who wore the badges of the Abbot of Theocsbury, and the knight was evidently waiting there to intercept our party. But he was disappointed, for Calverley returned by the Bushley lode, which crossed the Severn by the ancient Roman ferry leading to the Roman causeway at Sarnhill.

As we passed Wainlode, the scene of my meeting with Lord Edward of York, Robin inquired if I was acquainted with Gloucester or any of its inhabitants, and I replied that I had twice ridden there with my father, who knew Master Nicholas Walred, a clerk who lived near the church of St Mary-de-Lode, and that I had no doubt he would show us hospitality for a few days.

He then explained that he had been sent several years before on a mission with a large troop of men-at arms to bring up the body of

Richard Boulers, a former abbot of Gloucester, and to take him to Duke Richard of York,[2] and during this expedition he had become well acquainted with the city and some of its inhabitants. I therefore determined to resign myself into his hands, for the more I saw of this unobtrusive man, the more I became convinced of the sterling qualities of his character.

The moon had now risen on the waters, when, landing near the western gate of the city, Robin led the way to a woolmonger's near the castle, who lived in a fine timbered house, containing a large store for woolpacks besides many chambers well adapted for concealment. Robin led his friend to suppose that we were Yorkists who had compromised our safety and, being a Border man, he had no hesitation in allowing us to make an asylum of his dwelling, especially when he found there was little chance of our being recognized in Gloucester. He conducted us to a chamber we were to share together, showing us at the same time a door behind some woolpacks, by which, if necessary, we might escape into a narrow street which led to the city walls and the castle bridge.

I lay long awake thinking over the stirring events of the last few months, which had so changed my hitherto quiet and unruffled life and, when I fell into an uneasy sleep, I was wandering with Rosamond Berew in the ancient Abbey of Theocsbury among the monuments of the dead, while the miracle plays were going on in the nave, and the 'He, he', of Satan resounded through the aisles. Then a thousand fantastic shapes flitted up and down, and we heard whisperings and murmurings and suppressed voices close to us, and we saw rise from the surface of the tomb the figure of the Skeleton Monk.

Rosamond clung in terror to my side when all the effigies on the different monuments began to move. The marble draperies lost their rigidity; the features relaxed into living expression, while each figure rose slowly and solemnly from its recumbent posture and stood erect. The Abbots in their robes, the Crusaders in bright armour, the warrior knights and their dames came slowly towards the Lady Chapel, until a crowd was assembled there of the illustrious dead. Suddenly the door of the chapter house opened, from whence issued a flood of light, and numbers of choristers and acolytes in white surplices appeared bearing lighted torches reversed, and pointing to the nave where the Devil and Vice were fighting; and shouting.

Led by the Skeleton Monk, that strange procession marched in solemn order towards the nave as if to expostulate with the performers at the profanity offered to the Abbey and their graves. I heard the skeleton feet rattling on the pavement in strange and unearthly tread; it was the rattle of dry bones. A lurid light glared from sockets which once eyes did inhabit. The Skeleton Monk approached nearer and nearer, leading the risen dead towards the nave, which nave ceased,was crowded with playgoers. The noise in the nave ceased, the organ wailed, Rosamond screamed with terror, and I awoke, in broad daylight, among the woolsacks.

Rising from this disturbed dream, I proposed to Robin to take a plunge in the Severn, and passing through the western gate we went out to the rich meadows beyond. A swim across the river and back drove off the feverish feeling a bad night's rest had produced, and we returned in time for our host's early meal with appetites sharpened by the morning's dip.

We now learnt that Gloucester was more Yorkist than Lancastrian, and Robin was careful to indicate that Richard of York was far more likely to befriend the trader and the merchant than was Henry of Lancaster or the advisers of his Queen. Still, the Lancastrians were triumphant and Master Ferley opined that prudent men should not let their tongues wag. "If," he said, "the Duke of York or the stout Earl Warwick were in Gloucester with a goodly following, hundreds of Gloucester men would rise to their call, but the one was in Ireland, and the other at Calais, and King Henry and his Queen at Windsor. It would be therefore wise not to flaunt the white rose when the red was the fashion in the ladies' hoods."

The day was passed in visiting some old acquaintances of Robin, and in the evening we were admiring the statue of King Edward II and his queen on the splendid high cross[3],when to my utter astonishment I saw Rosamond Berew ride up with Mary of Eldersfield seated behind her, while her brother rode by her side. Robin of Elsdune seemed transfixed with astonishment at the sight of Mary of Eldersfield. "Who is she? Who is she?" he repeated, looking almost aghast, and seeming not to comprehend when I tried to explain. I walked up to them and inquired of Rosamond what could bring them to Gloucester. She told me that she had gone down the evening before from Underhills to Birtsmereton, with a message from Master Berew, when Calverley had arrived at full gallop, in advance of the rest of the party, and informed my father of the cause of my flight, and the wicked accusations of Trollop. He therefore counselled that I should remain in hiding until it could be shown that my acquaintance with Mary was of the most innocent kind.

He declared his own belief that it was impossible that Mary, who went about doing good with her herbs and nostrums, could receive her powers from the wicked one. Sorcerers and black hags he would have exterminated, whenever wicked necromancy was proven against them ; but Mary had never done aught but good to any living thing.

"But I knew," said Rosamond, "how little mercy she might expect at the hands of such men as Sir Andrew Trollop and his myrmidons, so I begged of grandfather to let me go to Eldersfield, and rescue Mary from the fate I knew would await her if that cruel knight and his bloodthirsty men-at-arms should find her in her cottage on Gadbury, so full of the medicaments which they would consider proofs of necromancy. Thus I brought her here, and we know an honest clerk, Master Nicholas Walred, who can discern between white witches and hags, and the good deeds of Mary from the evil of the Devil, who will give her refuge and hospitality until better times come. Eldersfield is no place for Mary now, or Birtsmereton for you, until our forest Chase is rid of such wolves as, no doubt, at this moment are prowling in search of you both."

I admired Rosamond's courage, though I expostulated with her at the danger she incurred if taken in the very fact of assisting a supposed witch to escape. It was far greater than mine, for the utmost of which Trollop could accuse me would be interference with his cruel order of the test of the water ordeal at Gadbury, while here was Rosamond riding in the streets of Gloucester with the noted Mary of Eldersfield behind her. Rosamond would hardly be recognized; she was so little known, but Mary had often visited Gloucester for the purpose of healing some sick- ness, or anointing some sore, while some of the monks had used her pots of herbage, and salves of the danewort and rue. Reports of her presence there might reach the Abbot of Theocsbury, when her arrest and trial would be certain to follow.

I determined to accompany them, and we proceeded to the New Inn in Northgate Street. This is a fine hostelrie, only just constructed of goodly timber, and the chambers are built round a courtyard. Here

Chapter Six

John Berew led the horses, and after assisting Rosamond and Mary to dismount, I asked Robin to inquire the way to Master Nicholas Walred's. He stared, as if frightened, at the tall gaunt form of Mary, who was clad in a homely peasant's gown, with a hood that nearly concealed her face, but could not hide the brilliant eyes which flashed somewhat wildly.

Having ascertained the direction of the clerk's house, Robin, still in a maze, led the way through some narrow streets by the Abbey, I following with Rosamond and Mary, who had now learned the position I was placed in, and the charge against us both. She begged of me to leave them and not expose myself to further danger, but I would not consent, and Rosamond's smile thanked me more than words, when Robin stopped at the door of an ancient timbered house, with an entrance under a great archway of stone.

Over the archway was the cognizance of the de Clare – three chevronels *gules* in a field *or* – known as Strongbow, the conqueror of Ireland, whose remains lie buried in the chapter house of the Abbey. Master Nicholas Walred opened the door and appeared astonished at the arrival of so large a party. His form was somewhat bowed with age, and what little hair escaped from under his skull cap of black silk was as white as snow. He held forth both his hands to Rosamond, who kissed first one and then the other, and he then extended them to Mary, with an expression of gladness at their arrival, but he looked with an inquiring eye at Robin and myself, as if to say, 'What brings you here?'.

Rosamond begged for his assistance and advice, and entreated that we might be allowed to enter his dwelling to tell him the business we had on hand. Robin excused himself, saying he wished to go to the Castle, but, advising me to wait for the night before I traced my steps back to our host's at the wool-shop, departed with a frightened glance at Mary.

The residence of Master Walred must formerly have been that of a person of distinction, as, being built entirely and substantially of wood, it was ornamented in many places with rich carving, though the beams of the roof of the chamber into which he conducted us were so low I could hardly stand upright. It was scantily furnished with a few wooden benches, but the rushes were clean, and in the middle of the chamber stood a massive carved table covered with parchments and scrip, copies in Master Walred's own hand of rare manuscripts from the library of the Abbey, which had just been enriched by the donation of Richard Boulers[4], who, after he was imprisoned at Ludlow Castle by Duke Richard of York, became Bishop of Hereford, and, dying, left his librarium to the Abbey of Gloucester.

Master Walred now begged us to be seated, and he placed refreshments on the table, apologizing for the poverty of his larder. He gave us a flask of good wine, which he said was made at the vineyards at Tortworth, a Berkeley cheese, and some manchetts of bread of fine wheaten flour. He listened to our story as he attended to our comfort, but when he learnt that Trollop had applied to the Abbot of Theocsbury to take up the matter, he sat down suddenly and his benevolent face was shaded with apprehension.

Abbot Strensham, he said, was a noble-hearted and humane man, and could draw a distinction between a sorceress and a herbalist; but if the writ was issued by the officers of the Crown, he would be compelled to employ the Witchfinder in pursuit of Mary, if Trollop should find at her dwelling suspected spells or charms. He then in- quired what they might find, and looked very grave when Mary said she had left adder skins[5] in her cottage, and when I reminded her of the star scrip on a parchment, and the broomstick without a broom, lying there also.

"There is no doubt," said Master Walred, "from Holy Scripture, that witches were permitted to work their sorceries, and that through all time the Devil had been able to impart to his agents on earth supernatural powers of injuring and tormenting others, of necromancing, of bewitching cattle, and taking various shapes of animals, such as cars or hares; but," he added, "I will never believe that the Almighty would allow Satan to usurp his own gracious goodness and work for the good of God's creatures! God and the Devil never work in the same fashion, and Mary has cured diseases by her medicaments, as I know from my own experience."

Still, this was not the belief of uneducated people, and the white witch was liable to be prosecuted and brought to the stake; therefore Mary must be sheltered from the Witchfinder, and Master Walred said he would do so to the best of his power.

Master Walred then advised me to remain in hiding or go to a distance until Trollop had left the neighbourhood. Rosamond he begged to return to Berew as soon as possible and to say nothing of what had occurred. It was then arranged that Mary was to be arrayed in a

Chapter Six

serving-man's clothes and to attend upon the clerk, while he advised me to dress after the fashion of a woolstapler, when, as I was a stranger, I should be safe enough in Gloucester. He then went into another chamber, and, bringing thence a sharp dagger, proceeded to cut off my love-locks, much to my annoyance, and I should have hardly allowed it but for the entreaties of Rosamond and Mary. Then putting on my head a vile woollen bonnet, he completed the disfigurement of my head and face to such a degree that Rosamond laughed aloud.

The good clerk could not give the damsels a sleeping apartment for that night, but said he would obtain a room close by, at a friend's he could trust; and taking Rosamond on one side, he spoke to her for some moments. She then came to me, and, blushing to her temples, asked if I would join them at the Lollards' meeting for prayer and praise, as she would wish to ask God's help in our present troubles. I at once acquiesced, glad to take the opportunity of seeing and hearing the religious service of a number of men and women known for their goodness to others, and yet obliged to worship in secret for fear of persecution. Master Walred now led the way towards the Abbey Church.

The masons engaged on the new tower of the Abbey had left their work and night had set in, but we met Master Robert Tully, to whom the Abbot Sebroke[6], had left the completion of this noble structure. He saluted Master Walred and told him of the fine tomb just erected to the memory of Abbot Sebroke, in the chapel west of the choir. With the usual curiosity of his order, he inquired who we were, and Master Walred replied that we were young people from the country. Mary had remained behind, and was strictly enjoined not to appear in the streets until disguised as a serving-man.

We then entered at the western door of the nave, and looked down the whole length of this noble Abbey to the far east end, where the Chapel of Our Lady was then rebuilding. The abbey was flooded with the light of the moon, not a person was within the church, and the only other light was the small lamp burning in front of the high altar.

We passed through the great columns of the nave in silence, and on by pillars and buttresses to a small doorway, when, descending a narrow stone staircase, we found ourselves in the gloomy crypt, which was filled with a labyrinth of short stone pillars of massive solidity, and lighted by a single lamp. Among the arches moved here and there a human figure hardly discernible in the darkness, but when we came to the eastern extremity we found a small altar on which was burning a taper before a tall crucifix of wood. This was the simple church in which the Lollards of Gloucester, some two score in number, assembled to worship in silence and in gloom.

In the days of Henry IV and Henry V, such worship, if detected, would have led to the gallows and the stake; but in these days, when Richard, Duke of York, had not hesitated to imprison an Abbot of Gloucester[7] at his Castle of Ludlow for tampering with Rome, and the 'stout' Earl of Warwick was known to be inclined to favour the Lollards, the ecclesiastics thought it wiser not to interfere, and more expedient to allow them to assemble in this dismal crypt than in some more public place within the precincts of the city. Since the late success of the Lancastrians, the monks of the Abbey had begun again to talk of the desecration of the crypt, but Master Tully was a monk of known liberality and superior education, and hinted that 'if Richard of York returned to power again, he had small respect for ecclesiastical prejudices and opinions'. So the Lollards met in prayer and Master Walred was their clerk and conducted their services.

I could now discover in the gloom that we were in the presence of a number of men and women kneeling on the stones, engaged in prayer near the altar. Rosamond knelt and I remained standing by her side, when Master Walred appeared, clad in a pure white robe which reached to his feet. He carried two tapers, which he lighted at the taper on the altar and placed them on either side. He then knelt down in silent prayer, and when he had arisen he stretched his arms as it were over us, and besought a blessing for us all in the name of Christ, not in Latin, but in plain Saxon English, and as he offered up in deep and solemn tones the prayer for God's aid and blessing, I thought of the contrast between this old man's devotion and the 'ho! ha! ho!' of 'the best Devil in England' in the nave of Theocsbury Abbey.

Then there arose in those dismal arcades a choir of voices, clear and distinct as evening bells, and those who knelt now stood upon their feet. All present joined in the chaunt until the dark arches themselves seemed filled with song and sound. Again the assembled people knelt, and again rung the deep tones of the clerk offering humble and solemn prayer for mercy for sins committed, and grace to forgive the trespasses of others. Then once more arose the voices of the hidden choir in a song of praise, and the hallelujah seemed to shake the roof as if it would

Chapter Six

ascend to heaven. The effect in that dark and sepulchral place was startling; it seemed as if some spirit was leading us to praise God and give honour to him from whom all good proceeds, even amidst the gloom of sorrow and the terrors of death.

Master Walred then addressed a short sermon to those assembled, and reminded them that our Master Christ taught His disciples to worship His Father and our Father, who was long-suffering in mercy and plenteous in goodness. He spoke of the simplicity of the teaching of Christ, and of the devotion and morality inculcated by Jesus, and that we should endeavour by God's grace to obtain pure hearts and gentle loving tempers. He inculcated the spirit of a Christian life instead of a religion full of ceremonials and outward observances. He said that the popular Christianity of the times was not the religion of Jesus, and that personal righteousness with its roots going into the inner soul was more needful than ceremonial rites of feasts and fasts.

He condemned the indecent familiarity of the Miracle Plays, and the gross sensuality of the Gluttony Masses, and repudiated the notion of pardons and pardoners with purchase-money for indulgences and future salvation; and he hoped the time would come when the abominations which now shrouded the simplicity of the teaching of our Master should be cleared away from our public worship, and that our churches should become the resorts for devotion, rather than that of playgoers and mystery seekers.

Another simple but devout prayer concluded the service, and I arose from my knees by the side of Rosamond thinking that this simple faith of the persecuted Lollards should be mine through life and unto death.

The service over, we dispersed in the same silent manner in which we had assembled. My heart was too full to say much even to Rosamond, and we reached the door of Master Walred's dwelling in silence.

Telling me the road, by a narrow street, to the house of the woolstapler, and bidding me come on the morrow when I had put on the woolmonger's garb, we parted, and I gave Rosamond's hand a gentle pressure, which I fancied was slightly returned. I found Robin fast asleep on his couch, and muttering, "He's come back again"; and, with a mental prayer for right guidance and purity of thought, I was soon once more at the old home under the Malverns, dreaming of my father, and mother, and Hasting, among the dear old woodlands and the meres, with the bitterns and the herns.

We both arose at early dawn, and Robin was surprised at the transformation of my head, but he approved of the clerk's plan of the woolmonger's dress and declared that in such a garb and without my lovelocks my mother would pass me in the street. He even indulged in a quiet laugh at the appearance he expected I should put on. Ever active and fertile in expedient, he insisted on going for a proper garb which, when I had donned it, affected his risible faculties more than ever. He then told me that he had ascertained that the Governor of the Castle and the garrison were well disposed towards the cause of Richard, Duke of York. We started, after breaking our night fast, to find out John Berew at the New Inn, as it was advisable to send Rosamond safe back again to her home, and we found him standing as silent as the statues at the High Cross.

I begged of him to get the horses in readiness while I would escort his sister to the mounting block. Returning through the Abbey Close, we saw Master Walred with Rosamond engaged in conversation with the monk Master Robert Tully, who was pointing out to them the works of the new tower commenced by abbot Sebroke, and underneath the western arch of which Tully afterwards inscribed the words:

HOC QUOD DIGESTUM SPECULARIS OPUSQUE POLITUM
TULLI, HAEC EX ONERE, SEBROKE ABBATE JUBENTE

He then took us over the works of the Chapel of Our Lady, just commenced by the Abbot Richard Hanley. Finding we were interested in the grand old Abbey, he conducted us through the Norman nave, the choir, the transepts, and the chapels or oratories, but no allusion was made to the crypt where three of us had been the night before. He led us also to the famous whispering gallery, and showed us on the way the little altar by which the abbot and other high ecclesiastics stood to witness the elevation of the host or the performance of miracle plays, of which Master Tully expressed a hope that no more would be performed in the Abbey of Gloucester.

In the whispering gallery the sounds of the gentlest whispers are carried as if by magic, but are conveyed to no other ears save the single one applied to the wall. Master Walred talked by it to the monk, and I tried it several times with them and at last with Rosamond. What I said to her the dead wall conveyed and she made no reply, but when I joined her the blush upon her cheeks revealed the secret which had been carried to her. We then visited the tomb of the murdered Edward

Chapter Six

II, and the monk told us the recumbent figure was supposed to be the work of Peter Cavalini, who came to England in the latter days of Edward I. We also saw the oaken figure of Robert, Duke of Normandy, who was tortured in Cardiff Castle by his own brother, Henry I, by the searing out of his eyes with hot irons, and buried in the Abbey. We also visited the great cloisters built by Abbot Froucestre and only finished some fifty years before.

As we proceeded through the cloisters we heard steps behind us and, on turning, perceived an elderly ecclesiastic approaching. He was dressed in the fashion of the time, with little to tell that he was a Churchman with the exception of his hair, which had no love-locks. He wore a red tunic and surcoat of purple, trimmed with amber-coloured velvet; the buckles were of gold, and his shoes had spikes so long that they were fastened with cordons to the knee.

He spoke to Master Tully, who made a profound salute and passed on, when the monk informed us it was the Abbot Winchcomb, who had ridden over to consult the Abbots of Gloucester and Theocsbury on a matter of witchcraft and sorcery. I exchanged glances with Master Walred, and Rosamond's rosy cheeks grew pale.

Having declined an invitation to inspect the Monastery and taste the celebrated ale at the buttery, we bid our courteous guide farewell and once more sought the chamber of Master Walred's house. Here we found Mary of Eldersfield so absolutely disguised in the suit of a serving-man that I failed to recognize her, her tall and somewhat gaunt form being well adapted for disguise in men's attire. Her long black hair was now rounded into a black poll, and little remained to identify her, save her sparkling dark eyes and intellectual expression.

We held a consultation, in which it was determined that Rosamond should leave as soon as possible with her brother, and that Robin should accompany them and go on to Birtsmereton with tidings for my father, and bring me back news of what had transpired at home. Master Walred undertook to find out through Master Tully what the Abbot of Theocsbury proposed to do, while I was to await the result of his investigations. Rosamond insisted upon my keeping her grey jennet and on riding on a pillion behind her brother, while Master Walred borrowed the horse of a burgess for Robin.

We now proceeded to the New Inn and, in front of the arch which led to the courtyard, stood Sir Andrew Trollop, talking to a peculiar-looking man with long white hair, a pasty face, and eyes as red as a ferret's, with a shifting restless expression. He was dressed in a long black cloak which fastened with a buckle round his waist, and he carried a black rod. His eyes moved restlessly as he listened to the knight, and he looked first at one and then at the others of our little party, as a snake watches for his prey.

I trusted to my disguise and walked steadily on with Rosamond. The knight did not seem inclined to make way, when an unfortunate kitten, escaping from a dog, rushed between his legs as if for protection, and the brute seizing her in his great hand, strode out into the street, and dashed her against the stones. This made way for us, and we walked into the courtyard, past the red-eyed man in the cloak, to the stables, where we found John Berew, and the horses saddled.

Honest John Berew made no difficulty about the alteration in the horse arrangements, or the loan of his sister's jennet, and I therefore settled to ride with them part of the way as a sober woolstapler on his road to make a bargain with a farmer or franklin. We rode through the Westgate and over the bridge across the Severn, up the hill by Maisemore towards the forest at Hartpury. Here we halted to admire the beauties of the view.

The sun was shining on the city walls of Gloucester as they encircled the houses and various church spires, while the scaffolding of the new tower rose like a great skeleton towards the skies. A large banner was flying from the castle keep, and the waters of the Severn glistened below the stout defences, which had defied the forces of Prince Edward in the contest between Henry III and his insurgent and rebellious Barons. The smoke arising from the old city spoke of the busy haunts and occupations of men, while the view in the opposite direction was a great contrast.

The Malverns rose like a wall from what apparently was one great forest, and only here and there a village spire peeped through the trees, indicating the abodes of men which from their very obscurity had been allowed to rest in peace. Yet within the last few months there had been mutterings as of a distant storm, the hiding of Lord Edward, the presence of such men as Trollop in our Chase and the accusations against Mary and myself seemed to belong to a dream, as I looked across the scenes hitherto so peaceful and well beloved.

I now alighted to tighten the saddle girths and bid farewell to my friends, when John Berew observed that their horse had loosened a shoe, and, before entering the deep trackways of the forest, proposed to have a nail driven at the smith's furnace, which fortunately was situated close by. He therefore drew a nail from his holster and proceeded with Robin to the smith's dwelling.

Throwing the bridle rein over my arm, Rosamond and I took shelter from the rays of the sun beneath a large oak, and awaited their return. I now asked Rosamond if she heard what I said to her at the whispering gallery. She blushed but said nothing; when I reminded her that we were about to part under circumstances that might separate us a long time; that evil times and evil tongues were around us, and that I would willingly take with me in my troubles and trials the assurance that she was not offended with my whisper, and would believe in the truth and fidelity of my affection.

She looked almost frightened, but at last said, between smiles and tears, "Oh! Master Hildebrande, I am not a fitting wife for such as you, I am but a simple girl, whose lot should be among those who have no ambition beyond that of a village life and village duties. But you, Master Hildebrande, are destined for a very different career. Lord Edward and Lord Warwick must ere long be back again, and you will live among arms, and knights, and lords, and ladies, and you will be persuaded to join these dreadful wars. Oh no! Better seek some nobler mate than poor Rosamond Berew, and one more fitted to admire the deeds of emprize such as warriors win."

While she was speaking I took her hand and kissed it, when, in the struggle to get it free, there fell from her bosom one of the love-locks Master Walred had so ruthlessly deprived me of the day before. Old as I am, I do not now forget the thrill of happiness that ran through my heart as I saw what she had so secretly treasured. But Rosamond was deeply affected, couching like a hare, with her face hidden in her hands. At last the flood-gates of her heart were loosed, I knelt beside her, and soon the tears that flowed from her eyes wetted my own cheeks.

Presently we heard the whistle of John Berew returning, and we endeavoured to regain our usual demeanour, but Silent John changed his whistle to the sweet tune, 'My love is like the red rose' which made us still more confounded.

The New Inn, Gloucester

Chapter Seven

ON MY RETURN to Gloucester, I took Rosamond's jennet to the New Inn and, remembering my character of woolstapler and trader, made myself acquainted with the method of conducting business and the prices of fleeces. Master Ferley made no remark upon the transformation of my dress and appearance, and allowed me to go in and out without question. He appeared to hold Robin in high estimation, and to think that I must be some person of importance in disguise. I was so much struck by the simple character of Master Walred and his unostentatious kindness to all around him, that I passed much of my time at his house, listening to his learned conversation, while anxiously expecting the return of Robin of Elsdune.

Two days elapsed before Robin again appeared and brought me the welcome news that all was well at Birtsmereton. Trollop had lost no time in seeking to arrest me at home when he found I did not cross at the Fordington ferry, but he seems to have had a dread of Calverley, so behaved better than I expected, expressing his great regret to my father that duty compelled him to search the premises, under the warrant of the Crown Commissioners and the Abbot of Theocsbury.

They next went to Gadbury, and it would seem that Rosamond and Mary had hardly left an hour when the knight gave orders that her dwelling should be set on fire. This was done, and the fire spreading to the surrounding gorse and bushes, a conflagration took place on the summit of the old camp which was seen for miles around.

Robin said that Trollop was said to be accompanied by an extraordinary-looking man, with long white hair and red eyes, who carried a black wand, and that the men-at-arms declared that he was John Hum, the Witchfinder, or Snakes as he was generally called, who had been sent to examine the house of Mary of Eldersfield, and give his opinion upon the sorceries therein. From this description we had no difficulty in recognizing the man in the company of Trollop at the New Inn.

Robin now announced his intention of again visiting the New Inn, as he declared he was particularly interested in witchfinders and their ways. He thought also that the character of Trollop required study, as it was somewhat remarkable to find a belted knight turned witchhunter, as well as Lancastrian.

I then adjourned to Master Walred's, and, as he was absent, I took the opportunity of acquainting his serving man, John Tandy, as Mary was now called, with the fate that had befallen her dwelling, and inquired what it contained that would compromise her as a mistress of the black art of sorcery. She now told me that she was the daughter of the unhappy Roger Bolingbroke, the friend of my grandfather, who, about the time I was born, was executed at Tyburn for necromancy against the young king, Henry VI.

"I was once," she said, "a prosperous woman, for my father collected around him all the learned spirits of his time, and he was the friend of the great Duke of Gloucester, who did all in his power to promote his skill and encourage his studies. I was attached to the person of the Duchess, whom I dearly loved, when there came about those horrible accusations of cunning necromancy of which you must have heard so often. My father was the most learned man of his time, and had written books on mathematics and optics, chemistry and magic, and had made a star chart of the heavens.

He also made a large round glass which would set fire to any dry wood or straw by means of the rays of the sun, and through it you could see the spots on the wings of the smallest insect. But all the power of the Duke of Gloucester could not save him; for when his own young serving- man John Hum, whom he had brought up from childhood, swore that he had seen him melting the waxen figure of the king in the hot sun with his burning-glass, it sealed his fate."

"The Duke of Gloucester did all he could to save him, but the Archbishop of Canterbury condemned even his Duchess to do public penance for sorcery, and my father to the gallows and the fire-brand. John Hum by his falsehoods obtained the King's grace, and turned Witchfinder, and is now known as John Snakes.

I went upon my knees before the young king entreating for the life of my beloved father, which he would have granted me but for the Lords around him, who persuaded him that his sacred person was in danger."

"I was carried senseless from his presence, and when I recovered I was ignominiously turned adrift into the streets of London as the daughter of a wizard. I hardly remember now those days of misery, so horror-stricken was I, but I was rescued by good Master Berew. He loved my father and was present at his death, and he received his last words and prayers respecting myself. He brought me down to Berew, and for a time I was mad, Master Hildebrande, stark mad with sorrow, and I could not rest, but roamed a wild woman through the forest and the Chase. Then I begged Master Berew to let me be alone, and for well-nigh twenty years I have lived as you saw me in my little but loved home."

"When my father was executed at Tyburn," she continued, "the commissioners took all his wise treatises and burnt them, and they broke his wonderful glass into a hundred pieces, for they said that it must have been annealed by the Devil. All that was rescued of his many wonderments was the star parchment you saw, and which Master Berew saved, with some receipts for nostrums for fevers, and rheumatism, and catarrhs, with specifics for salves for wounds and bruises."

"It used to calm my melancholy to search in the wild woods and on the Malvern Hills for herbs and plants for the salves, and the beetles and the adders for the nostrums; and I have walked miles and miles to heal a poor man's wound or to give my mashments to a sick child. I never harmed a living creature save the beetles and the newts and the snakes, and I ever spared those when I did not need them for pharmacies. I never saw the Devil, unless he had entered into the body of the Archbishop of Canterbury, when he persuaded the king to turn a deaf ear to my solicitations for my father; and he never entered into my cat, for she was loving and gentle, or into my owls, as I am surely certain."

"The Devil," she said with energy, "is in the hearts of men; he is among kings, and princes, and lords, and persuades them that the things he loves are God's, and those God loves are his own. So they killed my father and burned poor Margery Jourdain, and they call me a witch, although they say I am a white witch, and they fill the churches with mock devils and persecute God-serving men and women, and call this the religion of Christ!"

"I sometimes think, Master Hildebrande, that it is now, as was said in the days of King Stephen, and as William of Malmesbury hath written, that 'Christ and his saints have fallen asleep', or horrors such as these could not stalk throughout our land. Yes, I believe in the Devil, but he is in the souls of the rich and mighty and not in poor maligned men and women, and I do wonder sometimes that God allows him such marvellous power!"

We were interrupted by the entrance of Master Walred, who had seen the monk Tully and learned from him that a meeting had been held in the chapter house respecting the orders of the council brought by Trollop, 'to search into the witchcrafts, sorcery, and dealings with the Devil in the neighbourhood of Gloucester and Theocsbury, and hitherto permitted to go unpunished'.

Trollop and Master Snakes appeared before the meeting, when Snakes declared that 'evidence had been found in Gadbury sufficient to convict a score of witches, for that the place was full of devilish and unholy charms. There were adder skins, the powder of which would give the palsy, and infernal beetles, which would make the cows' udders discharge the milk of their own accord; and there was a broomstick, which enabled the sorceress to go to the moon and to milk the lunar cow, thus obtaining 'lunar butter', which would heal incurable wounds, and consequently persuade those who knew no better, that the wicked sorceress was no witch but a wise woman, and so lead them on to their own destruction'. It was then agreed that Sir Andrew Trollop deserved the thanks of all the clergy and laity of the neighbourhood, and the meeting entreated Master Snakes to do all in his power to apprehend and bring before them 'the foul, pestilent, and devilish sorceress the Witch of Eldersfield'.

Trollop now stated his indictment against myself, and how, when he was in search of the traitors, the Duke of York and his son, he had come suddenly upon me in the forest in company with the witch herself; and how I had interfered with his just and praiseworthy attempt to submit her to the ordeal of water.

Here the Abbot of Theocsbury expressed his opinion that I had not been guilty of a major but only a minor connivance, and that it was possible I knew nothing of the witch's sorceries, and supposed her to be only a wise woman and herbalist. One of the holiest of the monks observed that a nostrum of the wise woman of Eldersfield had been given him by the Sub-Prior of Pendyke, who was himself a learned herbalist, and that he always carried it about with him as a cure for cuts and sores. Upon this the Abbot requested to be allowed to see the nostrum and, on passing a box of brown salve to Master Snakes, he pronounced it to be lunar butter[1], at which all assembled were intensely horrified, while the box was ordered to be committed to the flames.

It was then determined that I should be arrested and brought before the council at Gloucester, in order that it might be seen if one so young had really connived at the sin of witchcraft, or, it may be, have already sold myself to the Devil. Snakes shook his head, and said, "he had known younger men with the tokens of the Devil, and that there were young imps of Satan as well as old warlocks."

The Abbot of Gloucester, like the Bishop of Beauvais and Cardinal Beaufort in the time of Joan of Arc, was a great foe to witchcraft, while the Abbot of Theocsbury was believed to be somewhat sceptical; but scepticism about witchcraft in those days was worse than heresy, and those who were unbelievers had to keep it to themselves. To have expressed a doubt was to cause suspicion that one had tampered with the Evil One, or as my father would say, 'the pearls if strewed will be trampled on, and it is a waste of breath to argue with bigots'. He used to declare that such men as Master Walred and Master Berew had been born centuries before their time, but that the days would come when all educated men would think as they did.

After the council was over, Master Walred strongly urged our departure from Gloucester, as there was no knowing what devices Snakes might pursue. Our persons at present were unknown and our presence unsuspected, but if Snakes found us out, Mary's fate would be certain, and even the respectability and position of my father might not protect me from the questionings of the Witchfinder if I was handed over to his discipline.

These detestable impostors frequently used the torture of sleeplessness, or hot pincers, or running needles into the flesh of their victims, in order to make them declare their own guilt. In this dilemma I thought the best plan would be to consult with Robin, whom I felt assured would be ready with some expedient; I therefore determined to seek him at the New Inn.

I found the quadrangle filled with merchants and traders, for it was market day, and there were also many yeomen and franklins from the country. Among these was our friend Kitel, and I tested the disguise I wore by passing close to him without recognition. Robin was not in the crowd, but standing at a projecting window was Snakes, and behind him I could see the well-known face of the Archer. He perceived me and came out from the chamber. I then told him the result of the meeting at the chapter house, when, without being disconcerted, he said that without doubt it would be expedient for Mary and myself to get farther from the presence of the Witchfinder and the knight, whom, he informed me, employed his time in tampering with those men-at-arms at the Castle who were supposed to be still faithful to the cause of York and Warwick.

He then proposed that before we relieved Master Snakes of our presence in Gloucester, we should pass an hour or so in his interesting society, by which no doubt much profit might arise, and we might possibly learn how to distinguish a witch or warlock at a glance. He then ordered another goblet of dainty morat, and led the way to the chamber where the Witchfinder had seated himself, and was now engaged in draining the last contents of a former tankard.

It was difficult for me, after hearing Mary Bolingbroke's sad tale, to restrain some expression of the scorn and horror I felt when I first entered into the presence of this scoundrel. Here was the man, the trusted servant of Bolingbroke, who had grossly perjured himself to obtain money by falsely accusing the master who trusted in him, and who had since lived on the plunder accumulated by false accusations.[2] Seated in a large wooden chair, his lithe form wriggling and twisting, I could now understand why he was known by the very appropriate name of Snakes. He was nearly fifty years of age, but notwithstanding his white hair he looked younger than he really was, and his red eyes bleared and I blinked as he surveyed me from head to foot. Robin presented me as an honest woolstapler who 'well knew the haunts of the Witch of Eldersfield and detested all sorceries and necromancy'.

I felt so disgusted at the presence of the Witchfinder that I maintained a rigid silence, pretending to listen to the accounts he was giving to Robin of his peculiar art in discovering witches, warlocks, and wizards, and how within the last few years he had given evidence on no less than two hundred trials before committees of inquiry, and had succeeded in obtaining sentences of capital execution against most of them. I listened to some of the details until he gave an animated account in his shrill, squeaking voice – for the morat had mounted to his brain – of the way in which he drove an aged woman stark mad by keeping her from sleep, when I was obliged to obtain relief by going out into the quadrangle.

I noticed before I left the peculiar manner of Robin throughout all these revelations. He never moved from his seat, but sat watching the Witchfinder like a cat does a mouse. Not a feature moved, not a movement of the muscles changed the expression of his countenance. But this was a forced and unnatural calm, for, when he joined me outside, every feature of his face was convulsed with anger and indignation. "Infernal scoundrel," he said, "accursed Witchfinder, justice shall find you yet!"

He then spoke of our immediate departure from Gloucester, but when I confided to him the fact that Mary was the daughter of Roger Bolingbroke, he started as if shot with an arrow. "Then, now it is account- ed for," he said ; and he then related to me how, as a youth, he had known Bolingbroke well, and had been so struck by the marvellous likeness of Mary to Bolingbroke, that he had almost believed that for some purpose Bolingbroke had been allowed to appear on earth again, perhaps to confront the Witchfinder, who had been the principal cause of his torture and death.

Then, as if some plan struck him on the instant, he begged of me to return to Master Walred's, where he would join me in the course of an hour and we would arrange plans for our departure. "But one night more in Gloucester," he said, "we must pass one more night in Gloucester."

In the course of two hours Robin appeared at Master Walred's, when, seating himself before the large table, he inquired for John Tandy. When Mary appeared he was deeply affected, and silently gazed at her by the light of the lamp, which was now burning on the table. At last he told us in a hollow voice that he had undertaken for a bribe to show the Witch of Eldersfield to Master Snakes that night, in order that he might recognize her when he saw her again, and might proceed to her arrest. He said that he should require my aid, and that all Mary would have to do would be to accompany us, and prepare to meet her father's murderer for a few seconds.

He then informed her that Snakes was John Hum, and he hoped that night, with our assistance, to submit him to some of that 'discipline' which he had found so efficacious with others. "You are now," he said, "about the age of your dear father when he suffered, and you look as if his wraith had returned to earth to rebuke the wickedness of men." He then observed the ring she wore on her fore-finger, and kissed it, saying that he had often seen it on his right hand, and he wondered how it had been rescued from the flames which burnt alike his corpse and the gallows. He declared that her hair, now cut short, was exactly as Bolingbroke wore his, as he disdained long hair and love-locks.

Requesting Mary to array herself in the long black gown she wore before she assumed the dress of John Tandy, he told us that he had undertaken to guide the Witchfinder to the crypt of the Abbey of Llanthony that night at twelve o'clock, to see the Witch of Eldersfield searching for creeping things among the bones of the dead; and that Snakes, notwithstanding his boasting and vaunted courage in detecting the emissaries of Satan, had strongly objected to the idea of visiting graves at night, but had given way on the representations of Robin that nothing was to be attempted beyond his becoming acquainted with the witch's person, when the consideration of the emoluments to be derived from her future arrest in some safe place quite decided him.

The first Abbey of Llanthony stands in a wild and secluded valley among the hills of the Black Mountains of Wales, and Giraldus Cambrensis, the great scholar and tutor to King John, describes its situation 'as truly calculated for religion, and more adapted to canonical discipline than all the monasteries of the British Isle.

Notwithstanding this, the monks of Llanthony were continually ill-treated and pillaged by the Welsh, so that in the year of grace 1136 a second Monastery was erected at Gloucester, and now Master Dene[3] is Prior'. Llanthony is famous for its crypt, where many noble corpses lie buried, but is even more dismal than that of the Abbey of Gloucester, for there is a perfect labyrinth of stone pillars and dismal arches, with corners filled with grinning skulls, while a fearful echo reverberates at every sound, making night hideous.

Robin had made arrangements to conduct the Witchfinder to search for the Witch of Eldersfield among the bones of the dead in this weird crypt of Llanthony. Here, he said, he knew she was coming after some of those unholy beetles necessary for her charms, and which are found only in human charnel houses.

Robin then revealed his plan, which was for me to proceed with Mary to the crypt a little before midnight, taking with us a lanthorn. I was then to fasten a cord to one of the centre pillars, and carry it on to the narrow doorway of the only entrance, so that we might guide ourselves, after Snakes had seen Mary and the lights would be put out, to the only means of escape from that dark and sombre dungeon. At a signal from him we were to put out the lights, and find our way out by means of the cord, leaving the Witchfinder to pass the night amongst the columns and the darkness of the crypt.

Having entered into the plan for 'administering discipline', as Robin called it, to Master Snakes, he left us, and we made preparations to fulfil our part of the undertaking. The night was wild and stormy, and the moon only now and then appeared from behind the clouds. The inhabitants of Gloucester had retired to rest, when, lanthorn in hand, accompanied by Mary, we wended our way to Llanthony. Not a sound was heard, save the bark of the watch-dogs, the wind howling, and the patter of rain against the casements.

It was so dark within the crypt that, notwithstanding the aid of the lanthorn, I had to take Mary by the hand, and I felt her trembling as we groped our way to the centre of the gloomy labyrinth of archways. I now laid down the cord, and fastened it to the entrance doorway, when we heard in the distance the shrill tones of Master Snakes, and the deep-chested solemn voice of Robin.

It was arranged that Mary was to be found searching with the lanthorn, among a heap of skulls and bones, for the supposed potent charm. We reached the heap of bones, and I had hidden myself behind a column, when the Witchfinder entered bearing a large lanthorn, while Robin carried a taper, which he lighted on entering the Abbey. Snakes did not seem happy, as he continually urged Robin on no account to leave him.

"What can you be fearful of, Master Snakes?" said Robin, "you have traced scores of witches, and warlocks too."

"But this is a most dismal place, and dark, so dark," replied Snakes, "and the devices of the Evil One are innumerable."

"Do you believe that the spirits of the dead are allowed to walk this earth again, and to come back in their mortal bodies" asked Robin. "Even now I think I behold a dead man's face glimmering through that slit," and he pointed to one of the narrow openings through which the light of the moon waved and flickered.

"Saint Ethelbert defend us!" ejaculated Snakes, in a tremulous squeak; "Master Robin, it would be far better to retire and leave the accursed witch, if she is here, to search for her unhallowed nostrums by herself!"

"Not so, Master Snakes," replied Robin, in a stern voice; "you promised me half the reward if I assisted you to see and know the Witch of Eldersfield, and I am determined to carry this venture out."

The Witchfinder was now silent, and as they approached the column behind which I was hidden, I changed my position and moved stealthily to another, when Snakes again spoke in a tremulous voice: "Good Master Robin, there is a shape before us, let us be gone."

But Robin had a firm grip on his long gown, and dragged him onwards, saying, "No, no, Master Snakes, we must go through this venture if all the shapes from hell were to hit around us."

They had now come in sight of Mary peering with her lanthorn over the dry bones, when Robin said "Hist! hist! There she is! Now, Snakes, go up and speak to her, and speak her fairly, so shall you see her face and form, and then the reward! the reward! Oh, speak her softly, noble Snakes!"

"Yes, good Robin, kind friend," replied the coward, "I will speak to her, and speak her fairly; but come with me, bold Robin, and do thou hold the light and speak her fairly too, we must not anger her here, lest . . ." Here a rat ran across the bones, making a great rattle in the dead silence of the crypt, and Snakes again became so frightened that Robin had almost to drag him up to Mary, who now drew up her tall form to its utmost height.

"How are you, good Mistress Eldersfield? How are you, kind lady?" I could hear Snakes muttering, as if in deadly fright.

Mary slowly raised her lanthorn, and, throwing its full light upon her countenance, turned slowly to meet the Witchfinder face to face.

My blood creeps now, though long years have passed away, as I recall the fearful shriek of the Witchfinder as he once again looked upon the face of Roger Bolingbroke, his kind and indulgent master, and the victim of his perfidy and perjury. It seemed to penetrate through the dismal solitudes of the crypt, and to resound through the vast arches of the Abbey; a cry of such mental agony, and a wail so fearful, that it sounded out into the streets and alleys, and was followed by the howling of a hundred watch-dogs.

The Witchfinder had thrown himself flat on his face, and there he lay, shriek after shriek ringing through the crypt. Even Robin felt some compassion for the miserable wretch as he led Mary away, and, beckoning me to follow, we passed quickly through the crypt door.

All was now silent as the tomb, and Robin said, "I meant to lock that fiend in for the night, but he may find his way out if he can, or hang himself with the cord we have left behind us"

But Snakes never moved from the spot where he fell. The workmen, going to their work at the new Lady Chapel next morning, found the door of the crypt wide open, and seeing the cord, they followed it to the western angle, where, facing the heap of skulls and bones, they found the corpse of John Hum, his glazed eyes starting from their sockets, and his teeth fast clenched in death. He had died of fright, the 'discipline' he had administered to others.

Leaving Mary at Master Walred's we proceeded to our room at the woolmonger's, where it was long before sleep closed the eyes of either of us. Robin now told me that his own mother died through fright at the machinations of this scoundrel Hum, who had endeavoured to convict her of sorcery.

We were awakened in the early morning by a loud fanfare of trumpets, announcing the arrival in the city of some person of consequence. I jumped up, and looking out of the casement I was just in time to see the commanding form and handsome countenance of the Earl of March as he rode past at the head of a troop of horsemen, whose steel casques and spear points were flashing in the morning sun. All the troopers wore the liveries of the House of York, and were clad in buff leather coats and jack boots, while several of the leaders rode in complete armour. On describing what I beheld to Robin, he bounded from his couch, saying, "Then the standards of York and Warwick are again raised in England."

Telling me to leave my woolmonger's dress for woolmongers to array themselves in, and once more to don my own, he proceeded to resume his prize baldric and his archer's cap, while around his neck he hung a gold chain, which I had not seen before; it was evidently a guerdon of good service and a badge of distinction.

"We must follow Lord Edward to the Castle," said he "as soon as may be, for there will be stirring work to do in these stirring times. Is he not a gallant youth? A noble son of a noble father! I doubt not Hildebrande, but Lord Edward will retain you as a squire of his own body-guard, and then we must see you fully equipped and armed. A rush for that traitor Trollop now; I will warrant he is out of Gloucester already!"

Robin then led the way up the Westgate Street to the Castle. The warder knew him, and with a hearty greeting admitted him without further question. Lord Edward had dismounted, and was standing in the midst of two hundred men-at-arms, whose horses seemed somewhat jaded. He held his velvet bonnet in his hand, for he was not in armour, and, as the sun shone upon his golden hair and noble features, he received the homage of the Governor of the Castle, as if he was the monarch of the realm himself.

Waiting till the bustle of reception was somewhat over, Robin, bending on one knee, saluted his young master, who welcomed him with the words, "Honest Robin, ever faithful, ever true, right glad are we to see thee!" Then taking him on one side, they entered into earnest conversation. Robin evidently drew his attention to myself, for, looking towards me, he beckoned me to come forward. His greeting was courteous and kind as he alluded to our forest rides, and bade me attend him later on in company with 'honest Robin'.

"We must have your gallant father, too," he said, "for we shall need all the aid we can gather round us, to rid my noble father of the meshes thrown around him by the Lords' party and the Lancastrian Queen." He then retired with the Governor of the Castle, it being understood that we were to be admitted to his presence soon after mid-day.

In the meantime I went to see how Mary fared, and found her not a little exhausted from the meeting with her father's murderer. I told her of the arrival of Lord Edward, and to prepare for immediate departure. Her name and former residence had been so prominently brought forward before the ecclesiastics and their tribunal that we thought it necessary to arrange for her to leave the country for some time. With Lord Edward's arrival, there would be no longer any fear for me, as he well knew that it was on his behalf I sought the home of the Witch of Eldersfield; but it was not so with Mary.

Lord Edward had shown himself somewhat suspicious of her, and, brave as he was, this noble youth was easily persuaded to lend an ear to any tale or information respecting sorcery and magic. Robin therefore undertook to find Mary an asylum at his own home of Elsdune on the Marches of Wales, where he had a sister who would give her shelter until the storm had passed away.

On our return to Lord Edward, we learned how the Earl of Warwick had landed in Kent and marched on London at the head of thirty thousand men, and that the City of London welcomed him as a friend and a deliverer. Edward himself had ridden through the City, accompanied by the Earls of Warwick and Salisbury, and five bishops had followed in their train[4].

They had sent to Ireland to beg of Duke Richard of York to return forthwith, and Lord Warwick had marched with a large force on Northampton. It was Lord Edward's intention to occupy the Castle of Gloucester, and raise troops to reinforce the army of the north, until he

Chapter Seven

received an intimation to join his father and the Earls of Salisbury and Warwick.

When we were admitted to the chamber where he held conference with Lord Berkeley, Sir John de Guyse, the Abbot of Gloucester, the Prior of Llanthony, and Sir Nicholas Alney, the Governor of the Castle, we found him inquiring into the state of the military lines and entrenchments, and the resources of the city, with all the gravity of an experienced general.

Giving us a look of recognition, we waited till the conference broke up, when the young Earl came forward, and, with a winning smile, said he hoped I would accept the post of esquire to his own person. "It is not" he said, "a post of purses, but there may be some hard knocks before long." Bowing low, I accepted the appointment with gratitude, and he then addressed Robin with all the familiarity of an old friend.

"I trust, bold Robin, that you have taught Hildebrande to use the battle-axe and the brand as you taught me, and that he has attained to that goodly swing which those of less stalwart build have acquired under your tuition. Let those who like it charge with the lance or sword, but give me the battle-axe for men of sinews and stature!"

"Now, Hildebrande," he said, "you must to your new duties, and first I would send you to that right courteous and learned gentleman your own father, and beg of him to come hither and assist Edward of York with his counsel and advice. This done, you shall be my messenger and esquire to various knights and gallant gentlemen, who will, I doubt not, rally round our standard, now they may see it flying from the summit of the Keep. My noble father will soon arrive in London from Ireland, and we must hold this city, so close upon the Marches, against all comers, for a powerful party is in arms for Margaret of Anjou and her son, whom the Lords' party pretend to believe is the son of Henry of Lancaster. Away then with you, Hildebrande! Take a week to prepare your horses and your arms, and raise the neighbourhood round, should these Lancastrians dare to march upon our borderland. You, Robin, will remain with me, I shall need your wise head and cool tongue, and, it may be, your ready arm."

On retiring I arranged with Robin that Mary should be sent with the first plump of spears that departed for Ludlow or Wigmore. I then mounted Rosamond's jennet at the New Inn, and rode off by the western gate for Malvern Chase and Birtsmereton. As I crossed the ridge above Maisemore and Hartpury, I turned to look back at the ancient abbey and the castle keep, where now the standard of York floated proudly in the breeze, and pondered on the sudden change in my fortunes since I was rowed down the Severn in a boat with Robin to escape from the abominable accusations of the traitor Trollop. And now I was the chosen esquire of the heir of the House of York, and the bearer of important tidings!

Then the troubled thought arose that civil war may now rage amongst our once peaceful homes, and the bloody scenes of St Alban's be enacted by the Severn stream and in our woodlands of the west, when the rays of the sun lit up the grey church tower of Berew by those green groves where Rosamond gathered her early primroses and first sweet violets. That tower seemed like a beacon in the forest, bidding me to be a *man*, and bear myself as became the lover of Rosamond, and the esquire of the heir of York. The jennet, too, arched her neck, and bore herself more proudly as I pressed her to the gallop, and she soon carried me right gallantly to the home of Rosamond Berew.

Rosamond was walking on the greensward when she heard the sound of the jennet's feet, and, turning round, saw her own mare and the rider. She dropped a basket of flowers in her surprise, and stood with pale cheeks, looking somewhat frightened, until I had alighted and pressed her to my heart.

I then explained the reason for my sudden appearance, and she said, "Am I not the witch now, dear Hildebrande, and did I not say that Lord Edward and Lord Warwick would come back again and summon you among arms and knights, and lords and ladies, and is it not all come true? Well, I say again, that I am but a simple country girl, and you will find a fitter wife for a gallant soldier, and, it may be, a gallant knight."

I replied that no girl was poor who possessed the love of an honest man, and that no man was rich who had not the love of a chaste woman. I told her that, young as I was, her love had made me a man, and I expected from her a true woman's constancy. If good times came we would meet them with gratitude; if bad, we should look forward to facing them together. 'Faithful and true' was the rue plant and motto of the Berews, and faithful and true we would be to each other.

Rosamond did not reply, but her expressive face told me that all I had said was responded to in her heart. Promising to see her soon, I rode off with the setting sun to Birtsmereton.

The Market House, Ledbury

Chapter Eight

IT WAS gladsome to see my mother's face when she met me as I rode across the drawbridge, and she listened with wonder to the story I had to relate. My father, however, was not surprised, for he knew well how the Church, the State, and the people called for inquisition into the damnable sins of witchcraft and heresy. I then opened my heart to them both, and mentioned the plighting of my troth to Rosamond Berew. Their reply was what I expected, as they assured me that my affianced wife should be to them as their own daughter; but my father reminded me that Master Berew was an undoubted Lollard, and that probably Rosamond was also.

I then mentioned how my faith had been shaken in the Popish religion and their 'wallets of pardons hot from Rome', and above all by their anti-Christian spirit of persecution ever since the time when the Pope of Rome censured King Edward II for not making use of torture[1] against the Templars, and for persuading the English clergy to introduce instruments of torture into the land. Machines for horrible cruelty had now become common, and for this we had to thank the Roman pontiff. I then related how, with Rosamond, I had attended the religious service of the Lollards in the crypt of Gloucester Abbey, and was well pleased with the devotional simplicity of the service.

My father in return informed me how he had received intimation from Hanley Castle that the Earl of Warwick had returned from Calais and was received with great joy by the people of London, but until my arrival he was not aware of the presence of Lord Edward, Earl of March, at Gloucester, and had indeed little thought I was his chosen esquire. He declared that no time should be lost in summoning the gentlemen and franklins in Malvern Chase and on the borders to be in readiness to support the cause of York, and freedom from religious persecution.

Having determined to lose no time in rallying our neighbours and friends to prepare to resist any incursions of the Lancastrians and to be ready to join the standard of Lord Edward, he despatched Hasting with messages to the Prior of Newent, who openly declared for the House of York. The Pyndars of Kempley also were to be visited, and the Wynniatts of the Old Grange at Dymock; while my mother sent a message to Mistress Pyndar, saying that she would soon ride over behind my father to see the wonderful paintings of the twelve Apostles which so embellish the roof of their Norman apse. Master Wynniatt's father was said to have once sheltered Owen Glendower from the bloodhounds of Henry IV, so we felt sure we might depend on him.

My father arranged to ride to Worcester and take counsel with the Governor of the Castle and others who were supporters of the White Rose, while I undertook to see Master Stone of the Glynch near Ledbury, and Bromwich of Broomsbarrow, with Master Kitel and others of the neighbourhood. I then mounted the roan Roland and rode off in the direction of Underhills, intending to persuade Rosa- mond to accompany me on her jennet.

On arriving there I found that she had confided to her grandfather the relation in which we stood to each other, and the fine old man seemed well pleased. He advised me to lose no time in seeing Master Kitel of Pendyke, who had much influence with many of the landowners and franklins in the neighbourhood of Bredon Hill, but to beware of the pretty Bessie, who loved the red rose and abjured the white; why, no one could tell or think! Passing across the little drawbridge to the avenue of elms where our steeds were pacing to and fro, we were soon on the trackway from the portway of Pendyke to the little church and monastery.

This little monastery of Pendyke owes its establishment to lands in Pendyke having been presented in Saxon times to the Church of Worcester. It is therefore not in Malvern Chase, and is now a sub-priory of Little Malvern. The monastic buildings face the grange and barns of Prior's Court, where the Prior of Little Malvern occasionally takes up his abode for a few weeks among his brethren at the monastery. The Sub-Prior and his four monks pass their time, when not engaged in ecclesiastical duties, in the cultivation of the land, assisted by a few hinds or vassals, who occupy their cots of wood and mud in the adjoining hamlet. They seldom venture beyond their monastery and their farm, save when sent for to some bed of sickness in the wild regions about Cromer's pit, or to the portway of Pendyke, once a Roman road but now only a forest pathway.[2]

At the monastery we found the monks engaged in netting the piscatorium, which the Norman builders of the church had dug right in the middle of the old dyke. The Sub-Prior was selecting the luce and perch for the next fast-day, while the others were restored to the pond. The tramp of our horses' feet arrested his attention, and he greeted us with a hearty "What cheer, what cheer, my children!"

The Sub-Prior was ever a great friend of my father's, one report said that, for one of his calling and position, he had seen a good deal of the world and the people in it. He had travelled in foreign lands, but was now growing old and led the life of a recluse. On telling him I wished to speak with him in private, he led the way to his cell in the long, rambling buildings of the monastery. The walls of his chamber were covered with wooden shelves, and these again were filled with all kinds of wonderments which he had brought from foreign parts. There were snake stones from the sea coast of Dorset, and pilgrim scallops from the mountains of the Alps, with stone butterflies and grubs of most curious texture. Then there were bunches of dried herbs famous in pharmacy, with whole piles of parchments written out in his own hand.

I told him the position of affairs as regarded the Red Rose and the White, and how my father trusted he would say a good word for the cause of York to his friends Masters Kitel and Jackman, who could both furnish good archers and pikemen if they would. The Sub-Prior's reply was that as regarded political questions he thought the less the clergy had to do with them the better, but for his own part he should ever be on that side and party which would protect the people from wrong and persecution. Religious persecution was the curse of the times, and would surely end eventually in bitter retaliation.

He was, he declared, a firm supporter of the House of Lancaster until they had become the persecutors of the Lollards and had sent them to the gallows and the stake. If the House of York and the stout Earl of Warwick would insist upon religious freedom and equality and sternly forbid the persecutions of Lollards by Catholics, or Catholics by Lollards, they should have his good word amongst his own people.

"A most horrible thing has come into our land, Master Hildebrande," said he, "when men think they are rendering God service by burning God's creatures in His Son's name, and forsooth, for the sake of Christianity!"

I could not refrain from reminding him that a former Archbishop of Canterbury, Arundel, and other Bishops of the Church, were mainly responsible for burning Master Sawtre and Sir John Oldcastle, and that the statute 'De heretico comburendo' flourished particularly under the Lancastrian kings. I also asked him what he thought the Master, Christ, would say to the 'successors of the Apostles', if he could behold them presiding over such horrible persecutions. The old monk sighed, and made no reply beyond giving me his blessing, and I fancied that he would not trust himself to speak of actions which emanated from the Church of which he was a member, but against which he felt a just indignation.

We now joined Rosamond and the party at the fish pool, when the Sub-Prior showed us a fine patch of the Danewort growing near the monastery, which he told us indicated that Pendyke was once a Danish settlement, and that Danes had been massacred there in the time of the Saxon king Ethelred, and hence sprang up this bloodwort now so famed for sprains and bruises.[3]

He also pointed out a young and rare tree planted among these herbs, called a Wall-nut, which he had brought from Italy, and with nuts four times larger than our hazel nuts. He told us, too, about the little Saxon church of timbers, which was raised where now stands the monastery, and how the font for holy baptism – the stone of which was brought all the way from Caen in Normandy – was all the stone in the church until the Normans came and occupied the forest clearing where Saxons and Danes had been before them.

The old Norman apse at the east end of the church had fallen into disrepair, and the monks were engaged in building a new chancel; but they were careful to preserve the rood-loft[4] and the great crucifix before which for centuries Saxons and Normans had worshiped in these forest wilds. The tower, too, built in the time of Edward III after the staying of the plague of the Black Death, was also under repair, as indeed at this period seemed to be all the churches of the land.[5]

Rosamond told me that she gathered from the conversations between her grandfather and the Sub-Prior that the latter had very strange opinions, inasmuch as he believed that much knowledge respecting the Deity might be gathered from studying the stars in the heavens, the rocks of the mountains, the flowers of the woods, and all animals, birds, and insects. Also that he held some heretical notions about the infallibility of the Pope, believing that there is an infinite universe presided over by an infinite Deity, of whom popes and priests had as yet conceived a very finite and limited notion. Still the Sub-Prior thought that such ideas were little suited to the vulgar and ignorant, and so said little about them.

We did not dismount at Kitel Keep and had to bear a good deal of banter at thus riding side by side, with a malicious proposal from Master Kitel that he should bear us company. I had no difficulty in obtaining his promise to join the Yorkist forces if necessary, and bring with him the gallant young Brydges, who lived at Eastington across the mere. But Bessie chose to make herself disagreeable as soon as she heard of my proposition.

She wore a red rose as large as a wild peony in her bodice and, when the goblet of cider was brought in the stirrup-cup, she allowed her father to hand it to both Rosamond and myself. On her wrist she bore a falcon which I knew came from Branshill Castle, and allowed the bird to take morsels of food from her cherry lips; while her eyes flashed fire as she inquired if I had heard of the burning of the habitation of the Witch of Eldersfield, with all her 'sirrups and juleps, and the strange parchment, which was believed to contain Hell's black grammar'.

I laughed at the idea of the Devil assisting Mary in the concoction of juleps; but Bessie crossed herself and said that "Wise women were but skeely neighbours we could all well spare." She also commented on the pursuits of their near neighbour the Sub-Prior, declaring that "It would be better for him to pay more attention to his breviary instead of star-gazing all the night, and, may be, getting moonstruck and wander-some."

She then reminded me of the good old times, when, in my archer's jerkin, bonnet and feather, I loved to hawk at a boomer or a hern, or shoot a bolt into a plump of young flappers on the mere, instead of riding over the country inciting honest and peaceful people to arms. "For be assured," she said, with a high colour and a flashing eye, "all this will end in a stricken field, and you and my father may become the prey of foul corbies in a quarrel which concerns ye not. And ye will leave Rosamond and me lone lassies through your folly. Out upon all civil wars, and may a just judgment await those who begin them!"

I could not avoid asking her, in return, for whom she worked the last red rose, knowing well that it was for Roger Calverley, and why she always wore the red rose herself when her father and best friends wore the white? She only pouted, and declared that King Henry was a right royal King and a foe to all sorceries, a far better man than Richard of York, who consorted with Lollards and wise men, and even had imprisoned a Bishop of the Church.

Chapter Eight

Wishing her a good-morrow and a better mind towards old friends and true, we cantered away with a wave of the hand from her father, and a smile, through tears, from herself. We now turned our horses' heads for a long gallop through the forest glades to the Hook Grange, the home of Master Bromwich, of Broomsbarrow, which lies just under the Chase-end hill, or the end of our Malvern Chase. It is a beautiful spot, surrounded by goodly trees, with fine open glades, and not far from a sure stag's lair at the Howling Heath.

Master Bromwich was a well-furnished gentleman, well beloved by all his neighbours and his kindred, and a great lover of the chase. He was likewise a good bowman, and could swing a battle-axe with most men. He met us at the doorway of the Grange, as we rode up, attended by his noble boar-hound, Black Hector, and accompanied by his fair daughters, the Lily of Broomsbarrow, and the Snowdrop of the Chase, as we loved to call them, when we toasted their healths at an archers' gathering or a village feast.

But the stately Lily wore a red rose on her bodice, a sure sign of her Lancastrian inclinations, while Mab, her sweet sister, wore the white; so constantly in these days did members of the same family differ respecting the hostile claimants for England's crown. Master Bromwich was true to the House of York, as was his relation, Pyndar of Kempley.

The fair damsels made Rosamond dismount, and while the Snowdrop presented me with a stagshorn beetle for hunter's luck, the Lily gave Rosamond the Nodding Star of Bethlehem, which grows hard by, and is good for potions when any one is sick for love.

Having partaken of their hospitality, and looked at the dogs, the horses, the bows, and the battle-axes, we rode on to Master Stone's of the Glynch. Giles Stone was a franklin, whose ancestors had lived at the little moated grange, which he now occupies, for well nigh two hundred years. The grange stands hard by to a brawling brook which runs from the mere of Eastnor, a stream famous for the brilliant plumaged kingfisher and the shy dipper, and all around are rounded hills, one famous for its coneys, and so called Coneygre.

We found Master Stone busy among his kine, clad in his frieze gown, and little inclined to do battle for either Yorkist or Lancastrian. His wife, good Mistress Martha, received us with kindness, and insisted on our tasting her metheglin while she dilated upon the antiquity of her husband's lineage, and the days when the Red Earl slept in their best chamber when he had the great dyke reared as a boundary for his Chase. Here, too, was the pot and pan which Mistress Dorothy Stone bequeathed to her daughter in the days of King Edward I, while the kerchief she gave to the Blessed Virgin of Broomsbarrow[6] is still preserved in the church.

Mistress Martha at once forbade her husband donning his buff jerkin and steel morion; but their son was a gallant youth, and had no idea of skulking at home, so he insisted on looking up an ancient sword which an ancestor had worn at Crecy, but which was somewhat rusty. His mother, however, interfered, and declared that the mill was of more consequence than any cause of York or Lancaster, and that on no account could the heifers be left while John went fooling to the wars. Altogether we did not seem likely to gain any recruits at the Glynch, so remounted our horses and said farewell.

We next rode for the broad green trackway which runs from Gloucester below the old British camp at Haffield to Ledbury, when as we were passing the camp we saw the tall form of Master Edwins, the Worcester herbalist, with his long white hair flowing from beneath a black skull-cap, and clad in black buskins and a stout frieze jerkin.

Rosamond knew him at once, for he was a friend of her grandfather's. He had been to the summit of the camp, and searched the vallum and ditch for Good King Henry[7] and Herb Christopher, both famous for mashments for bruises; also for the seed of a fern which grows on the Pudding-stone rock, and which is said, if caught when falling, to render the bearer invisible. Rosamond begged for some of this fern seed. He gave her also a large bunch of the bright green King Henry, so called after that monarch of whom Master Robert of Gloucester wrote, 'The goodness that King Henry and the good Queen Mold did to this land, no never may be told', and told her where she could find frog stools and paddock butts, which were sure specifics for stopping blood, with toothworts, which dried are marvellous for toothaches.

As the herbalist sat upon an old stowl of a decayed oak, with bundles of herbs, and two or three staghorned beetles stuck with thorns to his bonnet, I thought it was lucky Master Snakes never came across him, or he would have seized him as a veritable old warlock He was himself going to Ledbury, to consult about pharmacies with the leech, Master Straggles, who was said to be a learned man.

Indeed there have been leeches at Ledbury from the earliest Norman times. They were introduced by the Bishops of Hereford with the vineyards, the wine of which was apt to affect the stomach, and produce the gripes in some, and in others podagra. Leaving Master Edwins we rode by the Bishop's vineyard, which in the time of King Edward I is said to have yielded 'seven casks of white wine and nearly one of verjuice'[8]. This wine was not in favour with the Bishop, who preferred that of Burgundy, but he praised it mightily when he entertained the poorer clergy; and the monks still mingle it with the juices of the slee, or wild plum, which grows abundantly among the thickets of the old Roman camp on Wall hills near to Ledbury town, as it makes excellent good beverage for the poor.

The Bishops of Hereford have ever been great lovers of the chase, and it was Bishop Cantilupe, now Saint Cantilupe, who quarrelled with the Red Earl of Gloucester about the Chase of Eastnor, and who appointed a champion to fight the Red Earl, if the King would allow his appeal to judicial combat. This champion was Thomas de Bruges, *pugili episcopi Herefordensis*, and an ancestor of the Brydges of Herefordshire, and our friends at Eastington by Longdune.

We did not find the Bishop at Ledbury, he was at Bosbury; but many of his attendants and the neighbouring gentry and clergy had assembled for bullbaiting in the market-place. The town, indeed, was full of men and dogs from the whole country round, Master Baskerville, of Eardesly Castle, having given a couple of bulls of the wildest breed from the Cummy Moors, a wild forest district near Kington, where the cattle run at large and become unusually fierce and savage.

The hostelries of the Saxon Oak, and the Prince's Plume, were crowded as we rode up, and great was the consumption of wine, and greater still that of ales, mead, and cider, while big-headed bull-dogs with deep jowls were led in thongs by their masters and backers.

If there was one of our English sports that Rosamond detested it was bull-baiting, although a pastime much frequented by the wives and daughters of the gentry and yeomen, some of whom had their petted dogs with names by no means appropriate to such animals. Thus one terrific-looking animal belonging to Mistress Straggles was named Rose, and another, the property of the wife of the Bishop's seneschal, was dubbed Beauty. When we were stabling our horses at the Prince's Plume, Roger Calverley rode up accompanied by Silent John and

Master Paunceforte, John having brought with him the dog he so kindly offered to present to me. The bulls were to be baited on the great square near King Stephen's market-house, and Rosamond at once rushed away from the baiting and looked at the church, while we indulged our curiosity and watched this national pastime. We joined the committee appointed to see fair play for the bull, as far as fair play could be obtained for a tethered animal.

It was determined that only one dog should be loosed at a time, and not three or four, as would sometimes be done if the mob had their own way, and the bull proved too good for the dogs. Also we insisted on a fair length of rope and gearing, which the dog owners were apt to make over short, and thus hardly allow a bull room to turn and meet his savage antagonists. We would not sanction any worrying of bulls by a number of dogs let loose at the close of a baiting, as had been done several times of late to the disgrace of the managers, and was altogether contrary to the rules of the sport.

When we arrived at the ring we found the bull already tethered and fastened by a good rope and leathern girdles across the shoulders and round the neck; but Calverley having measured the rope, we called upon the judges to increase the length by two yards.

The first bull was the largest, and though wild and savage was somewhat unwieldy, so some of the younger dogs were matched against him, and very short work he made with most of them, goring some, trampling others, while two he actually tossed into the middle of the excited crowd. At last a Redmarley dog, well known for his courage and power, was let loose at the now infuriated animal, who rushed round the ring, mad with pain and fury. This dog at once pinned the beast by the nose, and notwithstanding his struggles held on until the bull fell exhausted and was declared defeated by the umpires.

The second bull was a much smaller animal, but as active as a cat, and a dark red beast with sharp straight horns. The Red Marley dog was let loose at him, and, being somewhat bow-legged and slow, was caught by his horns and killed on the spot. Silent John now came forward with Saxon, a tawny dog with great width of chest and an enormous head. Saxon, however, fared no better, being met by the bull in full charge and tossed nearly across the street. So powerful, however, was the animal's charge, that the rope snapped close at his neck and set him free in the midst of an affrighted crowd.

Chapter Eight

We all ran away, some rushing into St Catherine's hospital, others into houses, and some up the narrow streets which lead to the church. Just opposite the Prince's Plume the enraged beast overset at least half-a-dozen of the runaways, but fortunately did not gore them with his horns, when at the cross trackways in the centre of the town there stood a little child which had run into the centre of the trackways, and, having on a red cloak, attracted the bull's attention. To my horror, I saw Rosamond come down the trackway from Branshill and Malvern, and, seeing the danger of the child, rush forward and drag it to the corner of the street.

In a moment the bull was upon them, but the gallant girl held on firmly to the child, and, fortunately for their lives, both fell together, and thus missed the fatal toss he gave with his horns at the little red cloak beneath his feet. He then rushed on madly up the Gloucester Street followed by men with ropes and dogs. Rosamond was merely shaken by the fall; but the little girl was badly hurt by the trampling of the bull, and moaned with pain as I lifted her from the ground.

Fortunately Master Straggles, the leech, saw the accident, and came to our assistance. His house was close by, indeed Rosamond and the little sufferer fell underneath its overhanging gables, so I bore the child in my arms, as it cried bitterly for its mother, into his dwelling.

It was the first time I had ever been in the house of a mediciner, or seen a scalpel or an iron for burning a naked stump, so I shuddered at seeing these implements laid out on a table, while we were all thankful when Master Straggles declared he believed he could save the arm. Mrs Straggles was a kindly nurse, and quietly prepared bandages and lotions, her bull-dog Rose, looking on as if she were a mediciner herself and accustomed to such sights.

The chirurgeon having fastened on his ligatures and used the emollients of his craft, the child was carried to another room to await the arrival of its mother, and we had time to look round the laboratory. Besides phials, and pots, and herbs, there were drawings on the wall of the limbs of defunct persons, cleverly executed by the simple means of a burnt stick. But these were not the only evidences of the leech's profession. There was a skull said to be that of Hugh Despenser the Younger, which once ornamented the market-place at Hereford, when that unhappy favourite of Edward II was executed by the orders of Mortimer and Queen Isabella.

Then there was a grinning skull brought from Wigmore and believed to be that of the great earl, Simon de Montford, who was slain at the battle of Evesham, when his head was sent by his nephew, Prince Edward, as a present to the wife of Roger Mortimer. It was concerning this skull that certain other mediciners from Hereford and Theocsbury were somewhat sceptical, thinking it was too small for such a brain as that of good Earl Simon.

Having done all in our power for this unlucky accident, Rosamond mounted her jennet and we rode homewards, being soon overtaken by Roger Calverley. As we passed by Branshill Castle he insisted on our riding up to see a cast of falcons from Norway and another of tercels from the Stanner rocks near Kington.

Branshill had stood many a siege in the times of the Norman kings, situated as it is on the borders, and ever liable to incursions from the Welsh, and now men-at-arms guarded the flanking towers and grim walls. But I could not help thinking that the Eastnor hills rose ominously above the castle, and that such culverins as Henry V used in his sieges in France would render it indefensible. Calverley evidently observed my investigations of the situation, for he remarked that the introduction of filthy gunpowder into honest warfare was the death knell of the age of chivalry, and that the time was at hand when the best tempered mail would be a useless incumbrance before the fire of linstocks and arquebuses from behind every tree and wall.

Branshill Castle is small compared to many of the Norman strongholds, but yields to none in the beauty of its situation, as it nestles below the Malverns and the hills of Eastnor. On the north side, as we entered by the drawbridge and portcullis, all is old and ancient, but a new hall had been added to the interior by Sir Hugh, and this was furnished after the fashion of modern times with fine chairs and tables, and cupboards of the newest oak. The walls of this new hall were hung around with ancient armour worn by the Calverleys at Hastings, Crecy, and Agincourt, while there was also displayed on a figure of wood the cumbrous panoply which Sir Hugh himself had worn at the late battle of St Alban's, when he fought for the House of Lancaster.

We were received heartily by the gallant knight and his portly dame, who did the honours of their ancient keep with grace and hospitality; but no allusion was made to the fears entertained by both parties that we might ere long meet each other in strife on some battlefield in these dreadful civil wars between rival claimants to the Crown. Sir Hugh inquired after my father, but it was with an awkward manner, and I felt myself that the very errand I was engaged on, in recruiting for Lord Edward of March, would excite the anger of our hosts did they but suspect it. We therefore took our leave not without grievous apprehensions on my part, that the friendship with those I was attached to from my childhood and truly respected, might be alienated for ever by the coming calamity of civil war.

We had ridden to the summit of the pass across the Malverns known as the Holly Bush and, it being now nearly Midsummer, the sun was setting behind the Black Mountains where they rise into the peak of the Van-sirgaer as it rises above the Welsh town of Llangorse and the lake of Llynsavaddan. It was indeed a glorious sight.

On the western side the sun was yet throwing a golden light over hill and mountain, glen and valley, save where long shadows stood out to mark the approach of the darkness of night; while on the eastern side the long line of the Cotswolds were glowing in its last rays, but the great vale of Worcester was deepening into evening shades.

We pulled up our horses on the pass and gazed first on one side, then on the other, with feelings none can understand save those who love scenery and can appreciate such views as among the blessings God sends us to behold.

I now pressed Rosamond to ride on, as our time was precious, when she suddenly exclaimed, "Good heavens! There is the Shadow of the Ragged Stone resting upon the church and manor house of Birtsmereton!" and truly, as we looked, there was my beloved home almost hidden by a dense black pillar, which seemed to stretch athwart us right across the forest, while all around was still lighted by the rays of the setting sun.

We gazed and gazed and then looked at each other, and I saw Rosamond's cheek was pale and her eyes suffused with tears. And no wonder, for we both well knew the presage that shadow conveyed. It was the certain omen of the shadow of death, and a warning to some member of our household that their last hour was rapidly drawing nigh. It might be; possibly was; my own summons.

From the earliest date to which records of our Hills go back, the Ragged Stone and Midsummer Hills have been famous for their traditions.[10] There was a time, men say, when Druids and Bards assembled in crowds and dressed in strange and savage garb to worship the Pen Awyr, or sacred mistletoe, where it grew upon an oak in the glades of Eastnor. When the Fires of God were kindled upon the peaks of the Ragged Stone and Midsummer Hills and, as they flashed forth into flame, two snow-white bulls were sacrificed. Great frames of wickerwork filled with human beings were fired also, and the air was rank with the stench of the sacrifice thought to be acceptable to the Lord of Heaven.

These sacrifices went on at different times for centuries, but on one occasion, as Priests, Druids, and Bards were marching through the forest in the vale in long procession for the summit of the Ragged Stone – where the night was to be passed in religious ceremonies previous to the holocaust at the Mistletoe Oak – the dark pillar of the Ragged Stone overshadowed them and not one ever reached the hill alive.

Another tradition belongs to those times, when Archbishop Odo was the persecutor with Saint Dunstan – and a pleasant saint was he – of the beauteous but unhappy Queen Elgiva. It is a tale of love and sorrow and of ecclesiastical persecution, but again fires burst forth and the Ragged Stone was rent.[11] Again the Shadow of the Ragged Stone is said to have fallen upon the spot where Sir John Oldcastle was hidden in our forest wilds, the night he fled from the secret chamber in our panelled room, and where he was afterwards taken prisoner, and was haled to his martyrdom in Smithfield.[12]

It is not, therefore, to be wondered at, that we beheld with dismay my beloved home swathed in its black pillar of darkness, standing out across the forest in a flood of sunshine. Even as we gazed I heard the sound of a distant trumpet wafted on the east winds as they sighed through the trees. It appeared to come from our courtyard, and we urged our steeds at the gallop by the Foxholes down the glen.

It was no imaginary trumpet-call the winds had borne to us upon the pass for, as we rode up to the manor house, we found the trackway filled with armed men, the retainers of the Earl of Warwick from Hanley Castle and Upton-on-Severn, and, when we rode into our courtyard, we found my father mounted and armed from head to foot, preparing for immediate departure with the assembled riders.

He dismounted on our arrival and led us into the house, which was itself filled with our own archers and adherents preparing for a sudden march, and told me the news he had received of the slaughter and horrors of the battle of Wakefield.

The Lords in Council had acknowledged that the hereditary laws sanctioned the claim of Duke Richard of York to the crown of England, and it had been settled that King Henry was to retain the crown during his life, but at his death it was to devolve to the Duke of York, to the exclusion of Prince Edward, the son of Margaret of Anjou. On this decision Queen Margaret was wild with rage, and called upon every Lancastrian to take up arms for her son.

Two great armies had met at Wakefield[13] in Yorkshire, and Queen Margaret had herself led the attack on the forces of the Duke of York, which were very inferior in number. The end was that the Duke himself was slain and two thousand of his men lay dead upon the field. But this was not all. The vindictive Queen, mad for blood, had ordered that no quarter should be given either on the field of battle or after it, so those who escaped the slaughter and surrendered as prisoners were executed at once.

The head of the Duke of York was stuck over a gate of the city of York with a paper crown around the brows, and that of the Earl of Salisbury, whom I had lately seen at Hanley Castle, was spiked above the gate of Pontefract Castle. The worst butchery was that of the Earl of Rutland, second son of the Duke of York, a boy of thirteen years of age, who was murdered in cold blood by Lord Clifford as he was fleeing across Wakefield bridge with his father's chaplain.

My father also told me that I must start at once for Gloucester, and see whether Lord Edward had learned the dreadful tidings of the massacre of his father and brother and the defeat of the Yorkist forces.[14] For himself, he declared, that attended by Hasting and our own armed archers and adherents, he would set forth for the Marches at Ludlow and Wigmore, summoning all he passed to join the standard of York and avenge the disaster and foul butchery at Wakefield. At one of these places I could send a rider to convey to him the orders of Duke Edward as to where the levies he could raise should assemble, and meet him with the troops from Gloucester.

"It is no easy task, dear Hildebrande," he said, "to read the signs of the times, but to me our own duty seems plain. The Church of Rome, with its exalted position and vast power, seems determined to crush by the weight of Church authority, every aspiration to freedom of thought or freedom of worship. Rome would be accepted as the final and sole authority on religious matters, and it will spare no rebel against that authority. And if Henry of Lancaster and Margaret of Anjou, with the high Catholic party, are to rule this land, all hope of religious freedom must perish absolutely, and we must prepare for a renewal of such scenes as the deaths and torture of such as Sawtre, Oldcastle, and others."

"This, then, is a cause, my son, in which you and I may well shed our blood. Not, indeed, whether the Red Rose or the White Rose shall reign in England, but whether a man and a man's household may worship God and serve his Master after his own belief, without being persecuted by the priests and tortured by the government."

My father then begged of me to lose no time in preparing for my departure for Gloucester. He gave me his own battle-axe, which he had carried at St Alban's, and a splendid hauberk of the finest mail. I was to take Roan Roland as my charger, and a sturdy serving-man, known as Tom of Gulley's End, who was an excellent horse-keeper, firm as an oak with the pike and short sword, and nearly as good as Hasting with the long-bow. He had another good quality, he could hold his tongue, which horse-keepers rarely did, being accustomed as a rule to much talking, not only about the points and paces of their horses, but also about the sayings and doings of their masters, whereas Thomas was seldom heard to say much more than that "He would give a boy a hiding if he 'coused the cat' or 'mullocked the sow". Tom was to ride a big bay horse known as the Badger, a beast well calculated from his size to carry his rider and our double baggage.

These arrangements made, my father embraced my mother, and then folded me in his arms, for we were both setting forth on expeditions of adventure and danger, and we knew not when or where, or under what circumstances we might meet again. Hasting and half-a-score men-at-arms were now mounted and awaiting him just across the drawbridge. His own charger stood in the inner court, and right noble looked my gallant father as he rode forth that evening on his mottled grey. He crossed the drawbridge, and passing down the great avenue of elms, turned to give us his last look, and wave his last adieu.

Chapter Nine

OUR HORSES were ready in the court-yard for our ride through the forest to Gloucester, and Roan Roland looked well with his war saddle, frontlet of proof, and trappings on which was worked in fine colours the *talbot* of the de Brutes. The battle-axe my father had wielded at St Alban's hung at the saddle-bow, and I rode clad in steel morion, a steel hauberk under a buff jerkin, and greaves of steel and leather. On the sumpter horse was other gear in the baggage valise. The sturdy Tom earned a spear as tough as himself, and wore a well-wadded leathern jerkin and steel bonnet dinted with marks, showing the service it had been in saving the wearer's head more than once.

My mother gave me several gold Richards from her own hoard and a jewelled clasp for the vest which covered the shirt of mail. A soldier's wife and a soldier's mother, she did not make a great lamentation at parting, but the tears glistened in her eyes as I knelt for her blessing and received her parting kiss.

We reached Gloucester without adventure, and giving the password at the western gate, of 'The White Rose of York', rode through the streets to the castle. In one of the principal houses we could hear the click, clack of the castanets, with the tinkle of a harp, and the shrill notes of a rebeck, telling of the dance within. In the great courtyard of the castle were groups of soldiers, listening to the songs of minstrels before retiring for the rest of night. Over the Keep floated the rich banner of the House of York, covered with armorial bearings and quarterings.

Sending a message by the sentinel on duty that I brought important tidings, I was shortly summoned to Lord Edward's presence, as he sat in council with Sir John de Guyse, Lord Berkeley, Master Cooke of Highnam, and with others of gentle blood, who were discussing the precarious state of the country from the refusal of Queen Margaret and the Lancastrian barons to allow the claims of the Duke of York, in preference to those of the Prince of Wales, in the succession of the Crown after the death of King Henry.

It was evident from the light-hearted manner of Lord Edward, and the joyous way in which he inquired for the tidings I brought, that no news had arrived of the catastrophe at Wakefield. Bowing low, I said I thought he would wish to receive the intelligence I brought alone, and that I came with a message from my father, received through a messenger of Lord Warwick's from his Castle of Hanley.

Seeing that my face was clouded, he requested the cavaliers to withdraw for awhile, and said as they retired, "In God's name what is the matter, Hildebrande, your face is dark and sombre as a funeral hearse?"

I have charged on the battle-field amidst the startling surroundings of war, and have lain stricken myself and thought I was a dying man; I have stood by the bedside of those I loved, when the last flicker of the lamp of life was dying out, but never has memory impressed a sight deeper on my soul than that look of Lord Edward, as I recounted the sad fate of his beloved father and brother after the battle of Wakefield.

He neither stormed nor swore, nor was he, as I almost hoped he would be, relieved by tears, nor did he, as I expected, start in a frenzy from his seat. He raised himself to his full height, and stood like a magnificent marble statue, and as motionless, but his face assumed a terrible expression for one so young, so handsome, and so noble.

A vow of vengeance was written in those glaring eyes, which just before were beaming with a kindly welcome. Now he looked like a tiger ready for its leap, or a bull-dog, half strangled in the leash, when maddened by the sight of the bull. I have since seen him assume the same stern and pitiless expression when captives of war were brought before him; whom he seldom spared in retaliation of that butchery by Queen Margaret and Lord Clifford at Wakefield.

I stood motionless in his presence for some moments, when at last he said, "Leave me, sir, and tell de Guyse and the others of this accursed woman and her deeds; but let no one enter this chamber or my presence until dawn to-morrow, when you yourself attend us."

I passed out and joined the knights and gentlemen in the great courtyard, and in a few words acquainted them with the sad tidings and the commands of him who was now the head of the House of York. I had no heart for a long gossip, so left them and retired to the chamber I was to occupy as the body esquire of the Duke. I listened to the wind as it howled through the crenelles until I fell asleep, when I was awoke at the grey dawn by the sound of trumpets and the clash of arms. I went first to the chamber where I had left Lord Edward of York, but he was gone, and I found him in the courtyard addressing the troops.

Chapter Nine

During the early part of the day Lord Edward seemed stunned by the severity of the blow he had received but, when he aroused, a total change appeared to have settled over him; the merry-hearted youth was now a stern man, and he evinced a coolness of judgment and sagacity in the conduct of military affairs remarkable in one so young.

He never alluded in private to the death of his father and brother, but busied himself in the preparations for war, and was indefatigable in sending messengers in every direction to summon adherents to his standard and inflame the minds of the gentry and the people against the tyranny of the House of Lancaster. For days and often nights I was seldom out of the saddle, and before a week had passed a force of seven thousand men was ready to march on any point selected by the leader.

In the meantime, a camp was formed in the fields below the Abbey on the banks of the Severn, to which flocked not the great barons with their banners and their pennons, but the gentry of the country, each with their half-dozen or perhaps half-score of archers and pikemen, who, shocked at the cruelties and butchery at Wakefield, rallied round the son and brother of the noblest of the victims. The new Duke of York moved his quarters from the Castle to a small pavilion in the centre of this camp, and he visited every separate corps, appointing the officers, and making himself personally acquainted with them. If his manner was somewhat austere it was always courteous, and on horseback or on foot he carried himself like a prince.

On one occasion, I was sent to the manor-house of Sir John de Guyse, with certain directions respecting the Elmore archers. A noble avenue of oaks leads up to the manor, which, like so many others in England, occupies the site of a Saxon grange. Sir John de Guyse was a man somewhat proud of his ancestors, for they had been knights and gentlemen from the days of the Conqueror, and that is much to say in these times, when some whose ancestors were earls and knights are now hinds, while others, whose fathers half-a-century ago were hinds, are now knights or earls.

He holds his manor on the presentation of a clove of gilliflower at the court of Gloucester, and it was granted to his ancestors by John de Burgh, son of Hubert, the first Earl of Kent, and Justiciary of England. The manor-house is situated between the woodlands of Hockley Hill and the River Severn, where it traverses noble meadows famous for their pasturage, and whose waters furnish the silver salmon and the royal lamprey. A noble hall, of great timbers, with the walls hung with trophies of the chase, was filled with guests, among whom were beautiful damsels and men.at-arms wearing the cognizance of the Swan.

I found a score of archers engaged in practising with the long-bow, while I gave some satisfaction to the knight by so handling the bow of his ancestor, Sir Anselm, that I killed a corbie, sitting on the top of one of the highest oaks, at a distance of over one hundred paces. Sir John himself is one of those learned gentlemen who, like Sir Richard Widville, or his son Anthony, or the Earl of Worcester, follow after learning, and are gallant knights besides. Dame Alice de Guyse was a courteous lady, and banded the guests the wassail cup with her own hand.[1]

Messengers now came in almost daily with tidings from my father that the vassals of the Mortimers, and the gentry round Ludlow and Leominster, were arming and assembling at Wigmore, the castle and town of the Mortimers. He advised the occupation of such villages as Kington and Presteine, that there might be some check upon forces then being raised in Wales on the part of the House of Lancaster, by Owen Tudor, the husband of Queen Katherine, the Widow of Henry V, and their son Jasper Tudor, now Earl of Pembroke. He recommended a movement of the camp at Gloucester in the direction of Wigmore, as soon as possible.

Lord Edward had no sooner read my father's missive than he commanded me to accompany Robin of Elsdune with a select corps of fifty men-at-arms, and proceed to the small town of Kington on the borders of Wales, close to the birthplace of Robin, from whence we were to raise levies in all directions, and await the messengers and orders from head-quarters. He told me that news had been received that Lord Warwick had held Queen Margaret in check on the northern road from York to London, but as she had large forces with her, no help could be expected from Warwick at the present crisis, so he should himself endeavour with his whole army to prevent the union of the army of the Tudors with the forces of the Queen and the Duke of Somerset.

He then bid me keep up constant communication with my father at Wigmore, to trust to Robin of Elsdune in the summoning of the gentry and vassals of the Mortimers on the borders to arms, and to send him word by trusty messengers as to our success in raising levies, till we had orders to join the main army, whether at Hereford or Ludlow.

Chapter Nine

Our preparations made, we rode with a clump of fifty spears for Ross, crossing the silver Wye at Wilton Castle. Some distance beyond the town, we passed the old grange of Sir Howell Powell of Pengethly, where it rose above a green and sylvan vale, and the ancient church of Henlan. Sir Howell was a Welsh chieftain, who claimed descent from Howell Dha, whose pedigree commenced with Adam, and he had ridden forward with my father; his design of the *dolphin* displayed side by side with our *talbot*.

We entered Hereford, which I had never before seen, by the noble stone bridge which spans the Wye. Immediately on the left of the bridge, after crossing, is the monastery of the White Friars, so soon to hold the body of Owen Tudor and other knights and gentlemen, who were beheaded after the field of Kingsland, or, as some call it, of Mortimer's Cross. On the right hand we saw the noble Cathedral and the ancient Castle, a mighty stronghold.

The streets of this city are wider than those of Gloucester, and the houses larger and finer, built of wood and slabber, with great overhanging gables with casements in which are panes of glass as large as a man's hand. There is also a spacious market-place in the centre of the town; the great timbers of which it is constructed are said to have been granted by King Stephen, when he sat crowned in the Cathedral, in the chair which may be seen to this day.

We obtained quarters for our men-at-arms near the Market, and I was the bearer of the epistle from Duke Edward to the Commandant of the Castle, and another to Bishop Stanbury, who was now at Hereford engaged in superintending the building of a chantry.[2]

The Castle of Hereford is remarkable for its situation above the river Wye, which is a complete barrier on the west, while on all other sides it is protected by a wide deep moat. The walls are high and strong, and its central keep rises like a giant in the midst. The drawbridge and barbican are on the north side, and communicate with the town, which is itself defended by dykes and walls, so that Hereford is a city strong both by nature and the art of man.[3]

As I crossed the drawbridge of the Castle, my father's lessons on our country's history recurred to my mind, and I reflected on the many Kings of England and the illustrious dead, who from time to time had trodden the same path and occupied this feudal stronghold. Here had come King Stephen in all the pomp of war; and Henry II when he marched against the Welsh. Hither fled King John when England was invaded by Louis of France.

Here Henry III, with his son Prince Edward, was imprisoned, by his own brother-in-law, Simon de Montfort; and here came Isabella, the traitorous Queen of Edward II, with her paramour, Roger Mortimer; when they hung in chains Hugh Despenser, because he was faithful and true to her husband. Again, that great warrior, Edward III, was here, after the battle of Crecy, and was present at the opening of the monastery of Black Friars.

The Governor, having read Duke Edward's missive, declared that Hereford had many men who swore by the House of Mortimer, and that great indignation was felt throughout the whole city at the ignominious treatment of his father's dead body, and the cold-blooded murder of his brother. He told me of an encampment of some five hundred men-at-arms on the great common of Widemere, outside the city walls, and that he would meet us there on the morrow and himself declare to the troops the coming of Duke Edward in our presence.

Returning to Robin with an account of my interview, I was astonished to hear from Tom of Gulley's End that he had just met Mistress Rosamond Berew walking by the market, but I treated the statement as an absurd mistake, and I fear used no complimentary language to my friend Thomas.

We found Bishop Stanbury the next morning busied with niches, cinquefoils, and other devices, at the new chapel he was adding to the ancient Cathedral, and waited some time before he cut the thread of Duke Edward's letter, borrowing Robin's dagger for the purpose.

He said nothing whatever respecting the claims of York or Lancaster, but contented himself with directing our attention to the tomb of the saintly Thomas de Cantilupe, the opposer of the Red Earl respecting the rights of Malvern Chase. He told us too that no less than one hundred and sixty three miracles had been performed at his shrine in the space of a few months.[4]

I now remembered that I had heard Master Berew speak of one of their family, who became a high ecclesiastic and was buried in the Cathedral, so I inquired where the tomb was to be found. The Bishop informed us it was at the east end, in front of the Lady Chapel, and conducted us to a spot where we could see the effigies beneath an arch, but the approach on this side was blocked by masses of stone and timber for repairs. We could see, nevertheless, the tomb, and although she did not see us, Rosamond Berew, standing side by side with a tall dark-complexioned elderly gentleman, and looking at the resting-place of her relative, Dean Berew.

It is not easy to describe my sensations of anxiety. We had to make a long divergence and go round by the tower, losing our way among the chapels and arches, so that some time elapsed before we reached the front of the Lady Chapel. When we reached the spot, Rosamond, to my dismay, and the gentleman with her, had disappeared. We saw only the stone effigies, and on the front of the arch the Berews' design of boars passant, with leaves of rue in their mouths.

We walked back to the stabling by the Market, wondering what could have brought our forest damsel to the city of Hereford with an utter stranger.

As the time was drawing near for our meeting the Governor on Widemere, we assembled our spears and rode down a long, narrow, and dirty street, with very poor houses, towards the northern gate. Robin and I in the van, Roan Roland carrying his crest and arching his neck as if he was bestrode by a king, and Tom bringing up the rear. We had almost reached the entrance of the monastery of the Black Friars, when we beheld a crowd of the lowest rabble following Rosamond Berew and the gentleman we had seen in the Cathedral.

The mob was hooting and howling, "Down with the Lords' party!" "Curses on all murderers!" "Hurrah for York and Mortimer!" and some of the more ruffianly threatened to proceed to acts of violence.

I dismounted, and throwing the reins of my horse to Robin, ran to the rescue of the soldier-like stranger as he was with difficulty sheltering Rosamond from the crush. They stopped at the Monastery gate, when the stranger, turning round upon the rabble, shouted, "Back, you howling hinds, or I will send some of you to hell's gate!"

This only produced a greater uproar, when one butcher-like fellow seized Rosamond's gown, but, knocking him down, I caught her by the waist, and carried her perforce through the crowd, now scattered by the riding up of Robin and our troops.

Rosamond seemed dreadfully alarmed at my thus seizing her, as my steel cap covered my face, and it was impossible she could recognize me in my war gear. I had only time to say, "For heaven's sake, what brought you here?" when the gate of the monastery flew open, and her companion rushed forward, and, receiving her from me, drew her inside.

At this moment the Governor of the Castle with a score of men-at-arms rode up amidst the sound of clarions; the mob rushing to the side of the street to escape the horsemen. He inquired into the cause of all this uproar, and was informed that a partisan of the House of Lancaster, wearing the symbol of the Red Rose, which he had flaunted in the streets of Hereford, had just escaped mobbing by taking refuge in the monastery of the Black Friars. The knight sternly bade the mob dismiss, saying that neither Red Rose nor White should be trampled on by such city swine. He then shouted "Forward!" and I remounted immediately, as a soldier was bound to do; riding at the head of our men, but wondering marvellously at what brought Rosamond to Hereford in company with a strange Lancastrian.

Soon after passing the north gate, we came upon the large open common, known as Widemere, famous as the place where the gallant Prince Edward, afterwards Edward I, gave the slip to his keepers from the Castle, and rode away to meet Lord Mortimer of Wigmore, who had displayed his standard as a signal upon a neighbouring hill; an exploit soon to be followed by his great victory at Evesham.

Here we found a crowd assembled, watching the evolution of a large body of men-at-arms, and admiring the sham charges which looked like real war, amidst the trampling and neighing of horses, the flashing of spears, the rustling of plumes, and the jingling of spurs.

As we rode to meet this warlike host, their commander, Sir Richard of Crofts, advanced to greet the Governor of Hereford Castle. We all saluted, when the Governor in a few words, and in soldier-like fashion, informed the assembled men-at-arms of the purpose of Duke Edward to ask for aid from the men of Herefordshire to avenge the death of his father and brother. He told them that Duke Richard of York, with his castles at Wigmore and Ludlow, had been one of themselves, and was ever the protector of the persecuted against the tyrannical court of King Henry and his blood-thirsty Queen. He said, too, that his son's standard was raised at Gloucester, and in a short time, perhaps in a few days, Edward of York would be with them in person to lead them to revenge.

The deepest silence pervaded as the knight was speaking, but when he had concluded, the troopers rent the air with a shout of "A York! A York!" and "Mortimer to the rescue!"

It was a striking scene to a novice like myself in matters of war and soldiery, and I thought that if Duke Edward could rally many such soldiers to his standard, the Lancastrians would not have it all their own way, whatever might be their numbers.

Robin now reminded me that it was time for us to press forward to our destination, the border town of Kington; so, making our salutation to the knights, and receiving their hearty God-speed in return, we rode away for the borders of Radnorshire.

We passed Credenhill Camp, where Mortimer of Wigmore hoisted the signal flag for Prince Edward, and where the Romans had a stronghold above their great town of Kentchester at its base[5]. From thence we rode to Kington, a poor Welsh village, but a good place from whence to rally the border men on the side of the Mortimers.

I observed that great deference was paid here to the Archer by every one whom we met. The bustling landlord of the hostelrie doffed his cap, and the big dog, Vulcan, that prowled about the yard, recognized him and came up to be noticed. Soon the news of our arrival spread abroad, and before our riders had stalled their horses, rough and ragged Welshmen surrounded the door of the inn, some on foot, and others scampering in on small ponies as rough and ragged as themselves.

For two or three days I accompanied Robin to some wild places in the neighbourhood, where we held interviews with these border men. There were the noble rocks and broken crags of Stanner, above which the eagle soared and the ravens croaked, and where in the 'Devil's garden' grow herbs most rare, and famous for medicaments.[6]

Then there was Old Radnor, which Owen Glendower reduced to ruins, among the stones of which a bloodwort was blossoming from the soil watered by the blood of the three-score archers he beheaded in the Castle yard.

But the wildest spot we visited was the romantic waterfall of Waterbreak-its-neck, where the hard rocks are scooped out into a deep ravine; the sides of which are clothed with stunted trees and parsley ferns, and down which rushes a fall of water which may be heard for miles. Here, clustering on a steep hill which rises above, we met a number of Welshmen, armed in a rude fashion, some with short scythes, and some with pikes, but all carrying the long knives, which were formidable weapons at close quarters, and which made such havoc among the horses of the riders on many a battlefield.

Robin addressed them in their own language, and I could see by their countenances that his speech was convincing. A bag of rose nobles seemed also very persuasive, if shouting and grimacing were evidences of their acquiescence.

The next thing was to send forth a number of scouts, in order that we might become acquainted with the numbers and whereabouts of the army of northern Welshmen, whom Jasper Tudor, the Earl of Pembroke, was reported to be leading southwards from the mountains of Snowdonia and the wild hills of Plinlimmon. These were instructed to report on every movement of the enemy, and in a short time more than a score had dashed off on their cat-like steeds. Robin now declared that his principal difficulty was with Master Vaughan, of Hergest, commonly known as Black Vaughan, a gentleman of renown, who lived near Kington, was of very determined character, had large possessions in Radnorshire, and was a decided Lancastrian.

"He must be a friend of your father's, Master Hildebrande," he observed, "for I saw his shield and device among the heraldic panels in the oaken chamber at Birtsmereton. It might be advantageous for you to ride over to Hergest; you will be sure of hospitable treatment, and news travels so slowly in these savage wilds that it is possible Master Vaughan has not yet heard of the massacre of Duke Richard and his son. Vaughan is an honourable man, and may be so disgusted with the conduct of the Lancastrians at Wakefield that he may not move a man-at-arms in such a cause. At all events I would give my best baldric to know what he knows and how he intends to act."

On this I at once volunteered to go to Hergest and renew the acquaintance of the owner, whom I remembered in my early boyhood. Taking a horse-boy as my guide, and having previously sent a messenger to announce my arrival, I started on foot for the Grange at Hergest, followed by the bull-dog, Vulcan, who had attached himself to us without my observing his presence until we had gone too far to send him back again.

My companion spoke little English, but I could see that he was a good deal put out by the presence of the dog, and continually looked backwards as if he feared something dangerous might appear in our rear. At last we reached the high palisades which surround the grange, and could see lights flashing from the narrow windows. The building itself is a large rambling fortified dwelling, and the entrance was guarded by two armed Welshmen who could not speak a syllable of English.

These sentinels looked us both well over, and after communicating with the horse-boy, conducted me up a long flight of steps to a narrow doorway. After a loud knocking, a woman, wearing an extraordinary steeple-shaped hat, appeared, and led me by passages to the large interior hall.

The hall was principally remarkable for the great size of its beams and rafters, while its walls were hung with hunter's gear. Here were the heads and skins of noble stags, and the heads and tusks of wild boars, while in a conspicuous place hung the mouldering skin of the last wolf said to have been killed in Radnor forest.

There were also skins of that very rare animal, the beaver from the Teivi, among the mountains of Wales, and whose curious dens are described by the great Welsh scholar, Gerald de Barri[7]. Numerous, too, were the skins of otters from the Arrow and the Lugg, and those of the wild cat and marten from Kingswood Chase hard by.

Master Vaughan was seated at the head of a wide dais, and with him a number of Welsh gentry – at least, such I supposed them to be from the seats they occupied – while at the table below the dais sat some fifty retainers and serving men of the house of Hergest. When the servant went up to him and spoke of my arrival, he arose and advanced to meet me, when, to my surprise, I recognized the stranger I had seen with Rosamond Berew in the Cathedral at Hereford, and with the mob at the Black Friars. He received me with the welcome of a well-bred gentleman. After placing me by his side on the dais he returned to the duties of hospitality, and I had then time to look around me.

I observed that the gentlemen on the dais were all clad in woollen garments that looked home-spun and home-made and, with the exception of Master Vaughan himself, who wore a dark cloth gown with slashed sleeves, not one was dressed after the fashion of the day. They all wore swords, whereas in England the sword is only worn on the battle-field, and the gentry of both sexes wear dirks and daggers.

Only two of them could speak any English. One was a Welsh gentleman from Clyro, who recommended a 'foumarty budding', and the other was one John of Glascomb, who 'spakked' my Saxon tongue in terms it was impossible to comprehend. I therefore contented myself with supping on the various meats and, after washing my fingers in a bowl of bog oak with a silver rim, quaffed some spiced wine, which I preferred to the favourite drink of 'cwrda' or Welsh ale.

No opportunity was afforded me to broach the claims of the Duke of York upon the Marchmen, and the Welshmen seemed inclined to carouse all night. At last Master Vaughan gave a signal, and there entered the hall one of the most picturesque figures I ever beheld. It was that of a handsome old man dressed in a long gown of grey serge, with white hair falling upon his shoulders, and wearing a wreath of the green holly. He carried the celebrated Welsh harp, and I never listened to such music before; neither the githern or the rebeck are to compare to it, even when accompanied by the reed pipe and the castanets.

Song after song accompanied by the harpist resounded through the hall, and, although I understood not the words, some of the airs were plaintive, and others martial and stirring beyond aught I ever listened to before. They had a great effect upon the Welsh gentlemen, who sometimes rose together, drew their swords, flourished them, and stamped with their feet, but all was done in harmony with the music, so that I sat entranced with the strange sight and marvellous effect.

Finally, the white-haired old bard concluded the entertainment by singing words to a pathetic air, in which, in after years I learned, was conveyed the Welsh ballad written in honour of Margaret of Anjou, 'Farwel iti Peggy bach'.

The time for retiring came at last, and all prepared to occupy their various couches. Master Vaughan was in the act of conducting me to my chamber, when Vulcan, whose presence I had forgotten, made his appearance at the door, as if he wished to pass the night with me. He had hidden himself in some of the passages until he heard my voice. Master Vaughan was apologizing to me for putting me into an out-of-the-way and somewhat forlorn chamber, when he saw the dog following us, and appeared quite alarmed.

Indeed, his fine face assumed a weird, frightened expression I shall not easily forget. Nor did he recover himself until I called the dog by his name and made sundry excuses for his unlucky intrusion, begging that he might be allowed to remain with me for the night. On this he merely bowed, said he hoped I should not be disturbed by the brute's company, and, making rapid excuses of having to attend upon his other guests, bade me good night, without giving me the opportunity of saying one word about Rosamond at Hereford, or the claims of Lord

Chapter Nine 131

Edward of York for the support of all border gentlemen and Welshmen.

I now looked round my chamber. It was a large low room, full of great beams, with but two small crenelles or openings in the timber for windows, and by the light of a single Welsh rushlight it was somewhat dismal. The only furniture besides the great bedstead was a bench, a single large oaken chair, before which was placed a deer-hide trimmed with the fur of the otter, on which Vulcan at once lay down. I examined the couch and found a soft bed well filled with hayriff, and a pillow of goosedown, while curtains of tapestry hung around. Not feeling sleepy, I sat down in the arm-chair in a reverie, with Vulcan at my feet, and with the rushlight glimmering on the bench beside us.

The martial songs of the Welsh harper still lingered in my ears as I thought over the scenes of the evening, and wondered if my darling Rosamond had accompanied the master of the house, and was now actually under the same roof as myself.

While thus pondering, and seated in the great armchair watching the flickering of the rushlight, I was aroused by Vulcan uttering a low growl. No sooner had he done this than he was answered by a low 'whimp, whimp', but whether it came from under the bed or outside the door I could not tell. At all events it aroused Vulcan's Wrath, as he sprang up showing his teeth and bristling with ire as if preparing for instant battle.

Thinking that one of Master Vaughan's dogs was loose and prowling about the passages, and not wishing to have a battle royal in my bedroom, I looked to the fastening of the door, and, persuading Vulcan to lie underneath the chair, I proceeded to undress and retire to my couch. Still the dog remained so restless and excited that I determined for a while to keep the rushlight burning, and in a short time fell asleep.

I could not have been asleep above a quarter of an hour when I was awakened by something moving at the foot of my bed, and, starting up, I saw the figure of an enormous black boar-hound with glaring eyes and a most savage expression, making as if he were about to spring upon the bed. Seizing my dagger, which I had placed beneath my pillow, I immediately jumped out of bed, when the black hound moved slowly towards the door, turning round from time to time uttering the 'whimp, whimp', and showing his fangs and glaring eyes. Vulcan too hearing this, rushed from beneath the chair, and there were the two dogs confronting each other, the black hound standing exactly opposite the doorway, ready for a spring, and with his bristles standing on end and eyes which flamed like torches.

I now gave the signal "Hie! Hie!" the well-known cheer to every bull-dog for a rush at a bull at the stake, and Vulcan sprang towards the door. No sooner had he reached it than he cowered down to the very floor, and creeping slowly backwards on his belly with a distressing cry, as if suffering great bodily torture, he crept close to the chair and there remained soughing.

Not liking to approach such an animal, and wondering how the brute got into the room, and at the cowardice of Vulcan, I was about to shout for aid, when gradually the form of the animal faded away, and I saw nothing but the massive doorway with its great ribs of oak.

Having examined the door, I found it was fast, and lifting the latch, I looked outside, but could see nothing and hear nothing but the sonorous sounds of heavy sleepers. I then returned to the great chair and found the dog had cowered underneath. I spoke to him, and encouraged him again and again, but there was no movement, and on examination I found that he was stone dead.

I was more than startled, and felt that peculiar awe which unnerves the boldest heart, and pales the cheek of the bravest who has to face an apparition.

Sleep was impossible, so, leaving the dead dog by the chair, I threw myself on the bed, dressed as I was, and with my dagger by my side, left the rushlight flickering upon the bench. Long did I lie awake pondering upon this strange manifestation. At last, when wearied out, I fell into a deep sleep, and was aroused in the morning by the sound of a bugle horn close by the windows of my chamber. On looking through the narrow opening, I saw the great square filled with men on horseback, among whom I recognized the gentleman who recommended me the 'foumarty budding'. They filed past one by one, and at their head rode Master Vaughan – and by his side was Rosamond Berew.

When I left my chamber, I was accosted by a Welsh damsel, who presented me with a letter from my host. He apologized for leaving me thus unceremoniously, but, having sent twice to my chamber, heard that I was fast asleep. He had been summoned to join the forces which were marching to the aid of the King against his rebellious subjects of the houses of York and Warwick, and hoped at a future time to show me more hospitality at Hergest than was possible under existing circumstances.

Here was a complication of troubles! Not that I cared so much for the utter failure of my mission, or the departure of Master Vaughan to join the army of the Tudors, but here was Rosamond, my Rosamond, riding forth with these Royalist troops, and I had been in the same house with her for hours! My brain swam and I stood on the steps which led from the courtyard, gazing at the surrounding country, but without seeing it, and heedless of the endeavours of the Welsh maiden to tell me the tidings that she had prepared something for me to eat.

I was aroused by the tramp of horses' feet in the courtyard, and then perceived that Robin had sent Roan Roland by one of our men-at-arms, with a request that I would join him without delay. Hastily partaking of the bountiful refreshment provided for me, I left the dead Vulcan where he lay, and taking an inward oath that it should be the last time I slept at Hergest, I was soon on the road to Kington, where I found Robin in the saddle and the men-at-arms assembled.

He now told me that despatches had arrived both from my father at Wigmore and the Duke of York, who had arrived at Ross on his way to Hereford; while scouts had brought tidings that the Tudor army was already at Knighton-on-Teme. As we rode along, I related to him my adventures, when he exclaimed, "By heavens! then you have seen the black dog of Hergest!"

In reply to my inquiries as to what he referred to, he said that it was a strange tale and appertained to an ancestor of the Vaughans, adding that the house must have been full of guests to overflowing before the host of Hergest would have put a guest to sleep in the chamber of the 'shadow hound'[8]. Indeed, Master Vaughan often declared that he would pull down that portion of the building in which this room is situated. I then pressed him, again, to tell me the history of the Black Dog of Hergest, but he replied, "Not now, Master Hildebrande, we have other things to think of! Jasper Tudor is marching upon Presteine and Wigmore."

Chapter Ten

WE FOUND the Welsh village of Presteine occupied by Yorkist troops sent forward from Wigmore, and a messenger was awaiting us from my father telling us to push on and join him there. We saw on our march Pylleth Hill, where the Earl of March gave battle to Owen Glendower, and after a desperate struggle was defeated and made prisoner. The scene of the personal combat between these renowned chieftains was below this hill, on the banks of the river.

I burned with impatience once again to meet my father, but no sooner had we arrived at Wigmore than we found he had moved southwards to join Duke Edward.

Wigmore Castle is built on the site of a stronghold as old as the time of Edward the Elder; and we admired the grandeur of the castle with its massive keep, situated amidst scenes of picturesque beauty. Long before we reached it, we could hear the din and clangour of armed men, and outside the castle was a large village occupied by retainers; the dwellings situated upon a sloping rock and intersected by ravines. Hundreds of men-at-arms were in troops around the castle, while others were marching southwards towards Hereford, their steel caps and morions sparkling in the setting sun.

"Who goes there!" shouted a hoarse voice as we rode up to the drawbridge of the castle, and the reply, "Robin of Elsdune", seemed to be a sufficient password.

Robin now dismounted and spoke anxiously to the warder, who informed him that the widowed Duchess of York, and her sons, George and Richard – afterwards the Dukes of Clarence and Gloucester – were within the walls for safety; that an attack by the Welsh army under the Tudors was hourly expected, and yet the assembled forces were leaving to meet Duke Edward; trusting to the strength of the place, and the garrison, to keep it against all comers.

We then rode down the slippery paths to the village, where large wooden sheds afforded shelter for man and horse for the night, and arranged that our troops should be well cared for and ready to saddle at a moment's notice. This done, Robin invited me to accompany him to an interview with the widowed Duchess of York, to present her with a token and message from her son, the Duke. We crossed a ravine to the eminence on which the castle is situated and, on Robin again giving the password, we were conducted to the Keep, a massive square palace, in which was lodged the widowed Duchess.

The great square was crowded with men-at-arms, with several domestics clad in mourning, and to one of these Robin addressed himself, showing the gold chain which he occasionally wore. In a few minutes the servant re-appeared and summoned us to the presence of the widowed lady.

Knowing that Duke Edward was nearly twenty years of age, I was surprised to see his mother so young and so beautiful. Clad in the deepest mourning, with golden hair and lovely blue eyes, it was hardly possible to believe her to be the mother of that manly son, and yet the likeness was strong, for Edward had nothing of the 'swarthy Mortimers' about him, and resembled his mother, yet without a shade of effeminacy.

The Duchess received Robin with more than courtesy; it was the welcome of a trusted friend, and as he knelt and pressed her hand to his lips, the tears flowed down her cheeks. On his telling her my name, she extended her hand to me to kiss, saying that she had heard from Lord Edward the good service I had rendered.

In the meantime Lord George had seized upon Robin, and was showing him a new bow and a wooden battleaxe, but the Duchess had explanations to receive from the Archer, so she called him on one side, and left me to entertain the boy and his little brother, Lord Richard.

Lord Richard was dark and swarthy like his father, with an inclination to high shoulders; his face was handsome, but his form was then feeble, and I little thought that I should behold him leading the most terrific charges at the battle of Theocsbury, or that he would become a knight renowned for feats of valour and of arms. Even then, as he sat upon my knee, he insisted on showing me Robin's swing with the battleaxe, much to the danger of my head, and his brother's also. Lord George had flaxen hair, and a weak expression of countenance.

The Duchess now addressed me and, noticing the ring on my finger, the gift of her eldest son, she said the service must be good that won such a token of his regard, as it was her own gift on his natalday. She also alluded to my interview with Lord Warwick at his castle at Hanley, and I fancied a shade crossed her countenance as she spoke of him, for, notwithstanding the predilection of her husband and her son Edward, she never altogether trusted this powerful and somewhat unscrupulous Baron.

It was now time for us to take our departure, when the Duchess inquired if we thought she was safe from the raids of the Welshers within the walls of the castle, or if she should take sanctuary in the Abbey. To this Robin replied that there were Marchmen to meet Welshers, and it would be difficult for all the Welshmen in Wales to penetrate to the stronghold of Wigmore Keep.

We now made our salutations, and took our departure, Lord Richard entreating us to take him with us, and once again practising the Robin swing at my devoted knees.

"Is not that a lady a man may die for?" said Robin, as we reached the bottom of the staircase. He now inquired for the Captain of the Archers within the walls, and, showing his golden chain, gave some brief directions, which that leader appeared to accept without questioning. "We must now," he said, "make for the Abbey."

The Abbey of Wigmore is distant nearly a mile northwards of the castle, and here lie buried the remains of the illustrious Mortimers from the times of Ranulph, who, having vanquished Edric Sylvaticus, Earl of Shrewsbury, received from the Conqueror himself the extensive possessions and immense estates which belong to this royal house. When we reached it, masses were being said for the souls of Duke Richard and his son.

It was from his ancestors, who lie buried within the walls of this Abbey, that Edward of York inherited such decision of character, that no sense of personal danger and no tie of kindred, could ever turn him from the attempted accomplishment of a purpose once determined on. I pondered, as I stood among the graves of this proud family, who never seemed to shrink from any violence to gain their end, if such was to be the character of the youth who, if success attended upon his arms, might one day be King of England.

My cogitations upon the Mortimers past and present were abruptly broken by the sound of a war trumpet outside the Abbey walls, and I found that some two hundred archers from the castle and village were assembled, and prepared to follow Robin of Elsdune, fully confident in his knowledge of the country, and his sagacity as a leader.

In the meantime the Archer had sent a message to Tom of Gulley's End, and our own men-at-arms and horses had arrived at this trysting place. Robin spoke in Welsh to the archers, and I could perceive that he was giving precise directions for their guidance.

We waited for the arrival of some of his scouts, when at last two men appeared breathless with hot haste, and in less than ten minutes every armed man had disappeared in the darkness, and with them our own troops, who were directed to follow the captain of the archers, while Tom remained with us and in charge of our horses.

Robin told me, that in order that Duke Edward might have time for his march from Hereford, we must endeavour to give some check to the advancing Welshmen; with some five hundred men to stop the advance for a time of at least ten thousand men. We should meet some three hundred archers from Kington and the Radnor Forest, and pike men, at dawn, and these, with our own men-at-arms, and the archers from Wigmore Castle, were all we could gather, as so many had marched for Avemestry on the south to meet the Duke.

We rode by narrow paths through the dense forest of Darvold, and, on reaching the summit of the hill, we approached an ancient British encampment with a deep fosse still encircling it.[1] Within the encampment the trees had been felled, and we could see a light glimmering from a fire. Robin dismounted from his horse, and beckoning me to do the same, we gave the bridles to Tom and crept almost on hands and knees into the fosse.

The moon had now risen, and looking over the verge of the trench, we could see the figures of several armed men, some of whom were clad in armour. A short but powerful-looking man stood in the midst, gesticulating and speaking in Welsh.

We anxiously watched the party for some time, until Robin gave me a signal to retire. Retracing our steps, we rode northwards for some distance, when he told me that this was the advanced post of the Welsh army, and with them was Jasper Tudor, their leader, ready for the proposed attack on Wigmore Castle.

"Now," he said, "we will have a look at their rear."

We rode, almost in silence, and in single file at a slow pace, for several miles through woodlands and marshes, impassable without a guide who knew every feature of the country, until we reached the valley of the river Teme and the village of Brampton Brian, close to which rose the Castle of Robert de Harley, who, with his men-at-arms, had marched towards Hereford.

The village was now occupied by our men and the archers of Wigmore. This would not long be the case, as Robin had information that the Welsh army had advanced by two routes, the one by the valley of the Teme to Knighton, the other from Denbigh by the great Offa's dyke. They had joined forces at Knighton, and were to march to Brampton, and thence by Pedwardine on Wigmore.

When the sun rose, it shone upon our little army gathered upon the platform of the camp of Cockswall Knoll, below which flows the river Teme. It was here the noble Briton Caractacus made his last stand against the legions of Rome. Surrounded by strong entrenchments, but with no precipices or crags, we led our horses to the summit and, when there, the horsemen and archers were kept well back upon the platform. I accompanied Robin to a terrace cut along the brow of the hill, and here we lay flat, looking upon the lovely valley below. It was now filled with the dark masses of the Welsh army, the advanced columns of which had just reached the village of Brampton. The front corps consisted of spearmen on foot, while in the rear were some three hundred mounted soldiers, with here and there a knight in full armour, and officers clad in leather jerkins with steel caps on their heads.

Robin now whispered to me his plan, which was to allow them to pass through Brampton, and then to attack the rear in the village by the church. He then took command of the archers, leaving me to lead the mounted men, and no sooner had the last Welsh troops passed by Cockswall Knell, than he led the archers down the slopes of the hill through the thick underwood.

The rear of the Welshmen had passed below the church of Brampton, when a flight of arrows from Robin's archers carried death and destruction into the midst of a troop of horsemen, with whom was a tall knight from whose armour the arrows glanced as if from a stone effigy. He turned, and with his lance at rest looked for some enemy to charge, but the active archers had already sheltered among the trees, and we horsemen had not yet reached the bottom of the hill.

Loud shouts of treachery now rose from the Welshmen; the rearguard turned back to face the onslaught, and again a flight of arrows emptied many a seat, while the horses galloped madly about the narrow lanes, carrying confusion everywhere. Robin now occupied the churchyard with his men, and the whole Welsh force turned back in aid of their attacked rear. In overwhelming numbers they rushed towards the churchyard but only to meet a flight of arrows, and, at a signal from Robin the archers were back again under the protection of the wooded knell.

It was now time for me to act, and calling upon my riders to follow me, we charged down the village lane, in which the knight in armour was gallantly endeavouring to rally his men, but could hardly move in the crush without trampling down some of his own followers. Throwing down his lance, he advanced upon me with his long sword, but the 'Robin swing' unhorsed him and he fell heavily.

In the meantime the Welsh borderers from the forest of Radnor and Kington had attacked the van ahead of us, and again the shouts and oaths of battle rent the air. In the narrow trackways, it was only now and then that our riders could act and charge, but Robin and his archers seemed everywhere, and I could hear his long, keen, bugle blast now in the woods and thickets, and now in some copse, from which his men poured their arrows on the flanks of the Welsh forces. Nor did the Welsh forget their wonted bravery. They rushed upon their unseen foes into the churchyard and up the knoll, but only to meet death from the unerring shafts. With wild and terrible clamour, the whole army had now turned back, and closed in tumultuous throng round the village of Brampton Brian. Again and again we attacked them with our little body of horsemen, but some billmen threw themselves under our horses, and I had soon lost a dozen of our best troopers, while several fought on foot, having had their horses killed under them.

I now saw that it was useless continuing this unequal strife, so, shouting to my dismounted men to ride behind their companions, we fought our way foot by foot out of the throng, and made for the village of Leintwardine, which had been appointed for our rendezvous and retreat. Soon afterwards the Archer joined us there, having lost only ten of his men, while the Radnor troops, who attacked the van had retired towards Wigmore, Jasper Tudor having had a narrow escape of being taken prisoner. Our point had been gained, the whole Welsh army was now in full retreat to Knighton.

We now left the village, which in the morning we found in peace and tranquillity, and in the evening was crowded with the dead and dying. The moon had arisen as we rode into the village of Wigmore, and lit up the standard of York and Mortimer as it floated high above the Keep of the noble castle.

Being well-nigh exhausted, I did not awake until after cock-crowing next morning. Robin had already looked to the horses and their riders, and was conversing with a scout who had arrived from Knighton, full of the rage of Jasper Tudor at the retreat of the whole army, owing to the ambush and attack of a few hundred men. His father, Owen Tudor, was with the horsemen of the rearguard, and had been dismounted, so that it was his charger Robin rode back to Wigmore.

It was now the intention of Jasper Tudor to await fresh forces from Clun, and then march upon Hereford, without attempting to besiege the castle of Wigmore, hoping to crush Duke Edward before he could receive aid from the Earl of Warwick.

We found the gracious Duchess had already heard of our success the day before, and we received her dignified congratulations. She then gave us communications she had received from her son, Duke Edward, who had intended first marching to Ludlow, but, from the tidings he had received from our advanced outposts, was now determined to march to meet the Welsh army.

He had sent word to the troops under my father, Sir John de Guyse, Sir Herbert of Crofts, Sir Howell Powell, and other leaders, to join their forces with his on the line of the trackway between Kington and Leominster; and he left his trusty follower, Robin of Elsdune, to organize as he best could, a force at Wigmore, which might hang upon the rear of the Welsh army as they advanced from Knighton and Clun.

Two whole days we now passed within the Castle, during which we collected a considerable number of veteran dependents of the house of Mortimer, who had seen many a bloody field, but whose bows and spears had been laid against their cottage walls, as if their days of adventure were over. But these hours of leisure soon passed away, and a messenger arrived from Duke Edward's camp on Kingsland Field to inform us that he should await there the onset of the Welsh, while a scout from Knighton brought the tidings that Jasper Tudor had this time led his army by Presteine. His army was calculated at over twelve thousand men, but a large proportion were badly armed, and but few armour-bearing knights in the field. In less than an hour the archers and men-at-arms of Wigmore were assembled in the great courtyard, when the Duchess herself bade us God-speed.

Leaving a sufficient garrison for the Castle, we were soon in full march for Avemestry, the village whither my father and the Lord of

Chapter Ten

Crofts had marched the day we arrived at Wigmore. It was nearly dark when we reached this village, and learnt that all the troops collected there had moved to Kingsland, where Duke Edward had set up his standard, surrounded by his whole army, with the exception of our reserves.

The dawn of the morning of Candlemas Day 1461 aroused us from our rough quarters in the village of Avemestry, and before the sun had risen we had marshalled our troops. I then rode for the camp of Duke Edward, to communicate to him our exact position with three hundred good men and true, and the arrival of the Welsh army on the hills of Shobdon. As I rode forward on a sturdy pony, with Roan Roland led behind me, the fog cleared from the valley, and the gloom was passing into a morning's twilight, indicating the rising of the sun. Suddenly a wailing voice rose among the hills, and a noise came through the air, as of people stamping; my companion said it was the 'creening of the Welsh', and on listening to the mysterious sounds more attentively, I heard distinctly the warlike notes of the Welsh march I had heard on the harp in the great hall of Hergest.

The sun rose as I rode upon the field of Kingsland, when a magnificent sight met my astonished eyes. At the eastern extremity rose the pavilion of Duke Edward, above which waved the Plantagenet banner, and on the right and left were the tents of the knights and gentlemen, who were gathered together in front, while a flourish of trumpets announced that the Duke and his retinue were now sounding 'to horse'. Duke Edward was arrayed in splendid armour, across which hung a rich golden baldric studded with silver roses. Behind him were two heralds, and pursuivants clad in their peculiar livery.

In front of the pavilions were drawn up in battle array srome six thousand foot and archers, all armed with bows or cross-bows, and pikes, or short double-edged swords, while troops of horsemen galloped across the field. Among the various groups I recognized the flags and devices of many esquires and gentlemen who led their vassals and tenants in this quarrel. Here floated the *swan* of de Guyse, and my heart beat when I saw on the far left the red *talbot* of de Brute. On the right was the *dolphin* of Howell, and the devices of Scudamore, Baskerville, Bromwich, and many others.

Sir John de Guyse rode by the side of the Duke, and his dark complexion and deeply marked features were a strong contrast to the fair face of the distinguished youth, who looked as much a king's son as the other a tried warrior. The Duke's quick and stern eye, for no one had a sterner eye in battle, glanced towards me as I rode up on the gallop. He gave me a look of recognition and approbation, while he bid me wait until he had discussed some points in question with the knights around him.

The chivalrous spirit of Duke Edward urged him to challenge Jasper Tudor, the Earl of Pembroke, to the ordeal of personal combat, to be waged first with the lance or battle-axe, and afterwards with swords and daggers, until the death of one or other of the combatants. None of the knights to whom he referred encouraged the idea, as, whoever might gain the victory, battle between the forces, now so near to each other, would be certain to ensue.

The Duke was not to be persuaded, so it was determined that I should carry his challenge, accompanied by one of the heralds. The heads of the Welsh columns were now seen advancing on the western side of the great plain; they displayed a few banners, and as there was little doubt that the Earl of Pembroke led the van, the Duke commanded me to lose not a moment, but to ride with the herald bearing a white flag, and to give his solemn challenge to deadly combat. The herald rode in front, displaying the white banner, and I followed, riding slowly across the plain, passing several corps of men-at-arms, until we reached a knight cased in bright steel armour void of ornament, with the exception of a collar of the order of St David of Wales.

His herald displayed the banner of the Earl of Pembroke. The knight's visor was up, and he had a dark sullen look and a swarthy complexion. On his left hand rode an elderly knight with visor up, whose good-humoured expression contrasted forcibly with the stern bearing of Lord Pembroke; his helmet was bruised and dinted, and behind him rode a pursuivant with the banner of the Tudors. The face was that of one who had been extremely handsome in his youth, and indeed it was that face and form which had attracted Catherine of France, the widowed Queen of Henry V.

I had little time for observing more, as the Earl of Pembroke rode forward to receive the message from Duke Edward of York. On the herald's proclaiming the challenge to mortal combat, first by sounding his trumpet, and then in a loud voice, I rode up and threw a mailed glove of the Duke's in front of the charger of Jasper Tudor.

Chapter Ten

His pursuivant was about to raise it from the ground, when the Earl shouted to him to let it lie, and said in response, "Return, Sir Esquire and Sir Herald, to your master, and say that Jasper Tudor declines to meet a beardless boy with sword and lance. Such questions are not to be settled by the death of babes or infants, but by the valour of bearded men. It were better for him to return to the care of his mother until mayhap we drag him thence to answer for being in arms as a traitor to our Lord the King!"

Enraged at this want of courtesy to my noble master, I said something about the fall of knighthood and of honour, when I was told by a knight near at hand to ride back from whence I came, and bear a civil tongue lest perhaps I might return with cropped ears and a slit tongue to them that sent me. I turned to hurl an angry defiance in the teeth of the speaker, when I saw, underneath a bassinet or steel cap which had no visor, the heavy features and sinister countenance of Sir Andrew Trollop.

Shaking my gloved fist in his face and shouting "Traitor!" I gave the spur to Roan Roland, not a moment too soon, for at a loud signal of this treacherous knight a shower of arrows followed me, and my days would have been numbered but for the good shirt of mail I wore beneath a leather jerkin. Fortunately my horse was uninjured, and the herald was untouched. Duke Edward received the reply from the herald, given in somewhat modified terms, in silent contempt, but he was much exasperated at the traitorous and unknightly attack upon his esquire.

The sun had now risen above a dark bank of clouds, which stretched across the eastern sky, and we witnessed a strange appearance in the heavens. which I have never seen before or since. Some say it was delusion caused by the clouds, others say it was a miracle, but the sun rose as three separate suns, each as large as the other, and so continued for the space of half-an-hour. The appearance was hailed by the shouts of our assembled army, also by the loud cries of the Welsh forces, who were still marching on to the western plain.

How little had I realized the scenes on a field of battle. I had imagined that we should shoot flights of arrows and advance pikes, and charge with knights and mailed men on war-horses, and cut and slash, and wield our battle-axes, and the battle would be won; but the field of Kingsland[2] was obstinately contested from sunrise to sunset, and every yard of ground was fought for, for hours together.

It was a slow, surging struggle for life and death, varied by the occasional charges of horsemen and knights as leaders thought fit. I have ever thought that, had it not been for the clear head and splendid qualities as a general, of the youth the Earl of Pembroke sneered at as an 'infant', the battle would have been lost by us.

Although Duke Edward evinced great personal courage whenever there was a sign of the troops giving way, he remained standing for an hour at a time, giving directions through his esquires, and watching the movement of every corps. At the close of that long and eventful day, he exposed his life again and again in terrific charges into the very thickest of the Welsh forces. Neither did he ride his war-horse during the earlier part of the day, but galloped to and fro on a stout palfrey to various parts of the battle-field, directing attacks or repelling the onset of the ever-advancing Welsh, who at one time nearly surrounded us.

Nor was I, or the other esquires, engaged in the melée for some hours, not until towards the close of this great struggle, as we mere engaged in carrying messages and rallying the weary. Neither did I ride Roan Roland, or he would have expired from sheer exhaustion before the fight was over. He was led, like the Duke's charger, behind the great pavilion, and I rode across the field on a stout Welsh pony again and again, until he was killed under me, and then I ran or walked until I caught another, there being no lack of steeds without riders.

It all seems to me now as a misty dream; of trumpets sounding, of shouts of men raving and dying, of horses and riders charging and being overthrown, of archers shooting and bows clanging, of pikemen thrusting, and falling in heaps of slain, of a hell let loose upon earth, and of being utterly worn out with weariness at the end.

During the whole of this long day, I never once saw my beloved father; he had been sent by Duke Edward to bring up the left wing half-a-mile to the left of the pavilion, whereas my duties kept me continually engaged on the right. I rode twice into the village of Avemestry, and the last time I had to climb the crest of the hill above to take a message to Robin of Elsdune, to keep our reserves hidden until strict orders from the Duke himself, or, if he was killed, from Sir John de Guyse. Indeed, it was the reserve led on by Robin that won the battle for us at last.

It was well-nigh four o'clock on that Candlemas evening that fresh

Welsh troops poured down from the hill from Shobdon along the Kington trackway. The principal struggle was near a small stream, which traverses the Kingsland plain, where hundreds of the forces of both sides had fallen. Here was Sir Hugh Calverley killed, and many a Welsh knight and gentleman on the side of the Lancastrians, and here was taken prisoner Owen Tudor himself.

Here lay Baskerville of Erdisley, Roger Kitel of Pendyke, and Howell of Pengethly, among heaps of slain, and here were still fighting de Guyse, Herbert of Crofts, and others, with the numbers of their men-at-arms sadly diminished, and many utterly exhausted with their long and apparently useless efforts.

Duke Edward bade me now gallop to Avemestry and order Robin to advance with his reserves of fresh and unexhausted men, and to attack the Welsh on their left rear, and this time I rode Roan Roland.

Brave as they were, the Welsh could not withstand this final charge. The advancing archers of Wigmore poured flight after flight of arrows upon men who had not an arrow left. Then came the pikemen with their sturdy thrusts, and the charge of the horsemen with sword and battle-axe.

The scene was now terrific. Duke Edward ordered the whole lines of horse and foot to advance for a last and final struggle and, across the stream over dead and dying, the English forces advanced, amidst the roar of the conflict and the stentorian shouts of Robin's troops. It was now that Duke Edward charged with his band of knights and gentlemen, and I saw him gallop into the midst of the throng, and fight his way towards the standard of Jasper Tudor, shouting his war-cry of "A York! a York!" man after man falling under his battle-axe, and the weight of his barbed steed.

Many of the Welsh, though in dense throngs, were borne to the earth by the barbed horses, others were hewn down by the mailed riders, while some actually clung round the legs of the horses, and stabbed them in their bellies with daggers or knives. The combat was thus raging, when I saw Duke Edward's horse totter and reel, and shouting "De Brute to the rescue!" in a few moments I was in the midst of the fight around the Welsh standard.

Man to man was now the combat; no cry for quarter, and in a short time a frightful carnage ensued.

Of the scenes enacted, and of my own share in them, I remember very little. I only know that, when it was over, I found myself well-nigh exhausted, with my battle-axe broken, and my left hand grasping a mace which turned out to be that of the Earl of Pembroke. I then saw Duke Edward standing close by me, having been dragged from underneath his dying horse. I heard him say, "The day is ours! They fly!" and bidding me kneel there among the heaps of the slain, he laid his sword gently across my shoulders, and said, "Rise up, Sir Hilde- brande de Brute, you have saved my life a second time."

But the combat was not yet over. Duke Edward mounted a fresh horse, and again dashed amongst the retreating Welshmen, shouting to me to follow him; but it was not easy to do so, for noble Roland had seen his last field, and there was no horse near. I therefore joined a band of archers, and followed with them on the track of the retreating Welsh. Again they turned at bay at a place called Kinsham dingle, and fought like bull-dogs of the staunchest breed.

I was thoroughly exhausted when I came upon a stream of water, and having taken off my steel morion and laid aside my battle-axe, I knelt down to drink. Before I could rise, I saw Sir Andrew Trollop, who had hidden in the bushes of the dingle, rush forward from behind an oak. I felt that it was all over with me, and, commending myself to God, threw up my hand with the steel bonnet to protect my head. I remember no more save that my eyes gave forth sparks of fire, as I sank beneath the coward's blow.

The Ruins of Branshill Castle in 1731

Chapter Eleven

WHEN SENSE and memory returned, I found myself lying in a small room, on a couch, on which shone the blessed light of the sun, and directly in front of me was the pale, wan face of Mary Bolingbroke, sitting at the foot of the bed. On my attempting to rise, she pressed her forefinger to her lips to indicate silence, and entreated me to lie quiet, as my life depended on it. She then gave me a draught of some potion, and I sank into a refreshing sleep with the happy consciousness that I was tended by friends.

In due time I was allowed to sit up awhile, and ask questions, when I learned that I was at Elsdune; that I had been rescued in Kinsham Dingle by Robin and Tom of Gulley's End, and that, although apparently dying, the former insisted upon having me borne upon a litter to his own home and, although himself wounded, had never left the litter side until he had seen me safe under the care of Mary and his sister Deborah.

I asked for tidings of my father, who, through all that fierce day on the field of Kingsland, I had never once seen, as he was engaged on the extreme left, and I was continually on the right and in the centre, as esquire to Duke Edward. I had no sooner asked the question than I saw from the expression of Mary's face and the little sob she could not control, that my father was dead.

For some time I relapsed into unconsciousness, and remember little, save a pressure at my heart and a choking in my throat, for my father had ever been to me as a loving elder brother and beloved friend.

Then succeeded a kind of dream, and I was back with him in memory, fishing together in the old moat at home, or rambling over hill and glen among the Malverns, or listening to his wise words under the shade of the elms, or by his side in the panelled chamber among the scrips and parchments. I longed once more to hear his kindly voice, and to say to him, "Bless me, oh, my father!" when there came across my mind the numbing, certain feeling that I should never hear that voice again, and I remembered the Shadow of the Ragged Stone as I beheld it with Rosamond, hanging over our home.

The relation of personal sorrow and a tedious illness have but little interest to others, so I shall merely say that, after a long struggle between life and death, I recovered sufficiently to sit at the window, when I knew by the cawing of the rooks, and the song of the storm-cock and the blackbirds, that spring was about to renew the buds and flowers, and that the long nights of winter were passing away.

Sir Robin of Elsdune – for he, too, had been knighted on the battle-field – still wore his right arm in a sling, and was my constant companion; at least as much as Mary Bolingbroke would allow him, and never tired in showing the many kindnesses the sick and weary-hearted can best appreciate.

My first inquiry, now I had again rallied, was for Rosamond. "What brought her to Hergest; where was she during the battle; what had become of her; and where was Master Vaughan, whose pennon I had seen dying at the great struggle round the standard of the Tudors?"

Mary Bolingbroke then reminded me that Master Vaughan had married the only sister of Mistress Berew, which I had forgotten, if indeed I ever knew it, for old Master Berew being a Lollard and Master Vaughan a strict Catholic, they had not met for years.

The Master of Hergest was a widower and childless, and from time to time inquired after his niece's welfare and the way in which she was brought up. Hearing of the rallying of the Yorkists at Gloucester, he expected raids and plunderings would take place between the contending forces in that neighbourhood, and so judged that Berew would be no safe place for a young and motherless girl. He therefore undertook the journey, and persuaded Master Berew to allow Rosamond to pass some time at Hergest, which, situated as it is in the wilds of Radnorshire, he little expected would be so near the scene of battle.

During the battle of Mortimer's Cross, Rosamond was in safety in Clun Castle, and her uncle had escaped after the defeat, but whither no one knew, for neither he nor Rosamond had returned as yet to Hergest, which had been well searched by riders from Wigmore as the stronghold of a bitter Lancastrian. Indeed, it was through Robin's influence that it was not committed to the flames.

Neither had Master Vaughan's prospects improved. The great battle of Towton[1] had been fought, and Duke Edward had ridden royally into Westminster, followed by an immense train of people shouting 'Long live King Edward I'. The hopes of the Lancastrians seemed shattered for ever. Henry of Lancaster was a fugitive somewhere in the wilds of Yorkshire, and Margaret of Anjou and her son Prince Edward were wanderers, with large sums offered for their apprehension.

After a time I was enabled to stroll about among the woods of Elsdune and Lynhales, to admire the grand scenery of the valley of the Wye, the mountains of Brecon and Hay, and the hills of Kenderchurch, Tibberton, and Foxley, as they rose in the noble panorama in front of Robin's home. On the right rose the vans of Brecon capped with snow, and below the dark headland of the Black Mountains were the castle and village of Hay.

Near to Hay is Clifford Castle, once the home of 'Ye fair Rosamond'. Then nearer to us and in the vale rose the great Keep of Erdisley, the home of the Baskervilles, bordering on the Cummy moors; the haunt of wild cattle and big boars. Just opposite we see the Keep of Almeley, and in the distant vale the ever-winding Wye.

Neither was I uninterested in his fish stores, and devices for keeping the trout and grayling in waters ponded for piscatoria. Tame stags would eat from Deborah's hands, and near were woods, where Mary Bolingbroke could wander without fear or hindrance; the forests of Kingswood and Lynhales.

Elsdune, the old grange where Robin was born, is an unpretending dwelling, but right comfortable withal, and furnished with many modern luxuries, which the master had introduced through his long associations with the Mortimers. If the modest hall was small, it was hung around with valuable trophies of the Arche's skill, and the bed furniture of the dormitories was of the best. Nowhere were there such pillows of goosedown and such mattresses of bog myrtle or bed straw as those of Mistress Deborah. Nowhere were there such salted junk and deer's flesh, or such confections and preserves of honey.

But the days passed by, and I was most anxious to return to Birtsmereton, knowing how my widowed mother was affected by my father's death, and how she had been prevented by dire sickness from attending upon me her only child. But health and strength will not return as we wish it, and my head had been so badly injured that all at Elsdune insisted on my remaining a little longer.

Again I was most anxious to learn something of what had happened to Rosamond, and if possible to find out where she had taken refuge with Master Vaughan; and persuade them both to return home with me to Worcestershire, which was now far safer than the borders of Radnorshire, where hundreds of fugitive soldiery were prowling like hunted wolves in the forests.

As soon, therefore, as I could mount a horse, I determined to ride over to Hergest and try if I could not learn, by the aid of some silver pieces, somewhat about the location of Master Vaughan and his niece. Mary Bolingbroke insisted upon accompanying me, as also did our friend Robin. Indeed, this was necessary, in order that the Welsh domestics might be interrogated in their own language.

On our arrival at the great Grange, we found all deserted with the exception of one old gardener, Evan Evans, or as he called himself, 'Ivvan Ivvans', who was plodding among the herbs in the garden. Wonderful to say, he could speak English, so while Robin and Mary went to some of the tenants' houses hard by to make inquiries respecting the master, I remained with Ivvan, resting on the steps of the sun-dial and enjoying the spring sunshine in the front of the quadrangle.

While talking to him about the fair visitor, who had some time since ridden away with his master, I closely scanned the windows of the apartments which opened into the quadrangle, but nowhere did I recognise the crenelle belonging to the chamber where I had passed that terrible night with the dog Vulcan lying dead under the arm-chair.

I then changed the subject from Hergest apples and Mortimer pippins to the subject of dogs, and inquired if Ivvans ever accompanied his master to the chase, and if they still possessed the breed of the celebrated Hergest boar-hounds.

The word boar-hound was enough! The old man grounded his prong, and, shaking his head, said, "Better not talk, sir, about the Hergest tykes, or you may see one of them suner nor you loikes." I then told him that a well-known bull-dog of the neighbourhood, which had followed me, had died in one of the bed chambers under very peculiar circumstances.

Here the old man gave a low whistle, and raising himself up said, "It would have been odd if he hadn't". Then he looked about him tremulously as if he had said too much. I encouraged him to go on, when, peering into the gorse thickets which came up close to the quadrangle as if he expected some apparition among them, he pointed to a narrow crenelle half hidden by ivy, and said, "Is it there ye slept?"

I replied that was about the position as far as I could tell; when he muttered, "Then it's not much sleep ye had, for that's the Black Dog's room, and the room in which his master died."

I tried with all my powers of elocution, backed by a piece of silver, to extract more of the history from the old gardener, but he only peered nervously into the glades around, and then, resuming his prong and digging, said, in a low tone, "The less said the suner mended."

Robin and Mary Bolingbroke now returned from their investigation among the franklins and tenantry, but they had learned little, save that Master Vaughan, accompanied by his niece, had been seen taking the road from Clun Castle to Abbey Cwm Hir, which had already been the sanctuary of many of the unfortunate refugees among the defeated Lancastrians. So we had to return, without learning more of her in whom my happiness was now more than ever concentrated.

On our arrival at Elsdune, we all rejoiced again to see the face of Hasting, who had ridden over with letters from my mother and brought with him the home tidings. Also we learnt that the Houses of Parliament had declared King Edward's right by descent to the throne of England, and had passed a Bill of Attainder against the expelled King Henry and his queen Margaret, Prince Edward, the Duke of Somerset, the Earls of Pembroke and Exeter, Master Vaughan's great friend and ally the Earl of Oxford, with many other lords, knights, and esquires, amongst whom was Master Vaughan himself. An amnesty was granted to all others who would acknowledge King Edward and remain quietly at their homes, and to these he promised to be 'a very right wise and loving lord'.

The accounts Hasting gave of our own neighbourhood were somewhat alarming. Roger Kitel had been killed at the battle of Mortimer's Cross, and Bessie was now a forlorn damsel at the old Keep at Pendyke. Bromwich of Broomsbarrow was found dead by the side of Sir Hugh Calverley, as if they had struck down each other, and my friend and companion, now Sir Roger, lay in a wounded condition and precarious state at Branshill Castle, whither he had been lately borne in a litter from Hereford. Old Master Berew, too, was very sick.

He reported the country around Ledbury and Malvern as being in a most unsettled condition, for roving bands of marauders had sought shelter in the forests of Wyre and Malvern Chase and, although houses well defended by moats and such like barriers had hitherto been safe, the homes and barns of many franklins had been invaded, and many gross robberies committed. Nor was it only these roving marauders that were to be feared. Certain knights and barons had proved to be as

Chapter Eleven

lawless as the worst outlaws, and report said, that on several occasions, the wives and daughters of yeomen and franklins had been carried off to their keeps and castles and their surrender refused until they were ransomed by corn, cattle, or money.[2]

Even the inhabitants of our own Chase had shown unusual lawlessness. The squatters in the dense woods round the Church and Keep of Castlemereton had long been notorious for their poaching propensities and love of deer's meat, and were nominally under the surveillance of Sir John Carfax of Castlemereton Keep and Castle; but of late there were rumours of depredations of unusual character, and it was these squatters who were believed to be the night attackers of Master Lachmere's grange on the banks of the Severn by the red ford.

I now determined to return home without delay, and Robin declared that he also should leave to attend the King at Windsor, so we were both soon occupied in making the necessary preparations for our departure. I owed a deep debt of gratitude both to Mary Bolingbroke and Deb for their kindly nursing, and did not part without exacting a promise of a visit to our home below the Malverns.

Having partaken of the stirrup-cup from the hands of Deb, we were soon on the road to Hereford, all well armed, and two sumpter horses, right well-burthened with our packs and baggage, followed with their riders. We had ridden as far as the great cross on the Hay and Weobley trackways, some furlongs from Hereford – which was erected in memory of a market held there during the plague of the Black Death – when we saw a tall woman, with her face shrouded in her hood, trying to comfort a youth of nine or ten years of age, who had injured his foot with the sharp stones, and was weeping as his mother bound it with fresh leaves from the road-side.

On accosting them, I at once perceived that they belonged to the gentle classes, and that the lady had a dignified and commanding presence. She said that they were religious recluses journeying from the ecclesiastical house at Sugwas to the sanctuary of the White Friars at Hereford, when they met with this accident.

We surmised, too, that it was most probable they were some unfortunate Lancastrians reduced to destitution by these miserable wars; so, without further questioning, we insisted on their mounting our horses and our seeing them safe to their destination at the White Friars.

The lady thanked us, but evidently did not wish to expose her features, and kept her hood closely veiled; but the boy soon recovered his spirits and chatted gaily as I walked by the side of the horse, although without saying who they were or whence they came.

The sanctuary of the White Friars lay the other side the town of Hereford, close to the bridge across the Wye, and it was here that Owen Tudor and eight other Lancastrians of rank had been buried after they had been beheaded in tht market-place by the orders ot King Edward.

Before we arrived at the gate the lady asked me if I knew Master Vaughan of Hergest, as they were in search of him. On my replying in the affirmative, and telling her he was a proscribed Lancastrian and a price set on his head, she relapsed into silence and said no more until, on giving a letter to the friar at the entrance, she entered the Sanctuary, when she thanked us heartily for our attention and courtesy to those who had been brought low by these troublous times.

We now proceeded to the ancient hostelrie of St George and the Dragon, the resort of many a weary pilgrim to the shrine of St Ethelbert and famous for its good stabling. While our horses were being fed and groomed, I amused myself by looking through the lattice at the market stalls, for it was market day, and the country people filled the streets and were engaged in sale and barter with the inhabitants of the town. Right opposite was a stall with Welsh hosen exposed for sale, and around it were country yokels and men-at-arms, some wearing the liveries of the House of Mortimer and York and others those of the Earl of Warwick.

In the midst of this crowd was the tall form of a pilgrim enveloped in the usual long cloak worn by such travellers, and wearing an enormous slouched hat which dropped over the face, so as to hide it very effectually from the passer-by. In the hat was the scallop shell, and the pilgrim carried a stout staff, which he leaned upon while calmly surveying the manners of the mob. I should not have seen his face but that I suddenly threw open the lattice window through which I was looking, when the man turned and looked sharply behind him.

Our eyes met, and I could not mistake the furtive glance and peculiar expression of my bitter enemy Sir Andrew Trollop. Shouting to Robin, who was engaged arranging his baggage, I made at once for the open street, but some delay occurred before we reached the stall, and Trollop had disappeared down one of the numerous alleys.

Chapter Eleven

At Ledbury I parted with my friend Robin, with promises to meet again as soon as possible, and rode with Hasting by Branshill and the Malverns. The sun was setting as we crossed the pass of the Holly Bush, and I once more beheld the grey tower of our church rising from among the trees of the Chase below; but what changes had occurred since I last looked upon that scene. The Shadow had fallen indeed. We neither of us spoke, and a blinding mist filled my eyes as we rode in silence down the Glen of Berew.

I shall not attempt to describe the meeting with my mother. Suffice it to say that, before the night came on, we two were kneeling together by a little mound of earth, now green with the May grass, in the old churchyard. When I awoke the next morning, it was difficult to realise that I was a belted knight and the master of the house, with all the various duties of life before me, and yet only twenty-one years of age.

My time was now occupied in the different business of country property and a country life, and enclosing from the forest sundry grants of land which Hasting and myself had received from the King for our services at Mortimer's Cross. This land we now call The Rye. I rode frequently to Branshill, and found that Roger Calverley had been obliged to submit to the loss of his right arm, and was in consequence sadly depressed and out of heart. There was still no news of Rosamond Berew, and all that we could learn from Elsdune respecting her uncle was that the soldiers from Wigmore were set to watch for his return. I was most anxious and fretful.

News arrived from Robin, at the Court at Windsor, that King Edward had been crowned at Westminster, and had reversed the attainders of the Duke of Somerset, our friend Calverley, and Sir Andrew Trollop, who had obtained pardon, through some court, on the understanding that he never appeared in the presence of the King; but there was no reversal for Master Vaughan.

In the meantime our near neighbour Sir John Carfax, of Castle-mereton Keep, who had a remarkable aptitude of veering with the wind, had become a staunch Yorkist. In his younger days he had been an equerry of Queen Margaret of Anjou, and was then a pronounced, if not a bold, Lancastrian. Now he had arrived at the opinion that Henry of Lancaster was only fitted to be a monk.

One day, when riding with Bessie Kitel by his keep towards the hills, we saw the gallant knight feeding his pigeons, and gave him good-day.

Sir John had never been known to commit his person to the jeopardy of a field of battle. Having received the grant of the Keep and lands of Castlemereton from King Henry, he was most anxious to keep them, whoever ruled, as well as sundry glades, which he had annexed from the Chase at Welland without any authority or deed of gift.

He was somewhat undersized, with red hair and a pasty complexion, not lovely to look upon and, as an equerry about the court of Queen Margaret, he had contracted the habit of making promises, which, like other court- iers, he never had any intention of fulfilling. So notorious had he become for this habit that 'a Carfax' was understood to mean something you would never obtain. Thus he had not been ten minutes in conversation with Bessie before he had promised her a fox, a brood of chickens, a tame squirrel, with several pots of raspberry comfits. He much admired my principal charger Kingsland, and talked of a bridle with silver trappings he should like to send for my acceptance. But Bessie never saw the comfits nor I the bridle.

With Sir John was a very different man, his friend and neighbour Master Marten, whose father some said was a Jew. At all events he had made money, and left his son the possessor of large money-bags. He was a handsome gentleman with a Jewish cast of countenance, but with large benevolent eyes indicating his character.

Simple-minded himself, he believed all Sir John told him, and had taken a small house up the Castlemereton stream, where he devoted most of his time to his garden, his flowers, his birds, and his bees. He had laid out much money on Sir John's property, and fitted up his little dwelling after the fashion of our manor-houses with a small moat, a drawbridge, and terraces, and with the finest garden in all the Chase.

Sir John gave us a pressing invitation to visit his Keep, which I was about to decline, when an expressive glance from Bessie told me she would enjoy the fun. I had not been inside this Keep since I was a boy, for although so near us, my father never affected Sir John's company, but we now rode up and dismounted. It stands just below the old Norman church, and is rather the *domus defensabilis* of Domesday than a castle. It is defended on the north and east by a moat, and on the west and south by a wall and strong palisades, while the so-called castle is merely a strong Norman keep.

The court-yard within the moat and palisades is of goodly size, and the Keep stands on a mound above it. The interior is quaint, ancient, and somewhat comfortless. Ascending the steps there is no reception hall, but a series of small chambers in flats one above another, which are reached by a narrow spiral stone staircase. It is impossible to go over these old Norman strongholds without perceiving how much more civilized and comfortable are our modern manorhouses, but some say that such buildings were well adapted to the robbers who lived in them, and constantly harried the Saxon granges and villages within their reach.

Sir John Carfax was very attentive to Bessie, now the mistress of Kitel Keep and the owner of certain lands in Pendyke. But Bessie was a loyal lass, and even wore the red rose on her bodice notwithstanding the white rose was now in the ascendant. She was not to be bribed by Sir John's honey pots to change her colours as he had done, and was more interested in the conversation of Master Martin and the gardens of Italy, which he had visited, than in the attentions of the gallant knight.

Like all ladies she was wild upon seeing the dungeon, the most dismal place possible, for it lay beneath the floors of the lower chambers, and Sir John hesitated in complying with the request, but Bessie insisted upon the old warder conducting her down the ladder to the filthy hole.

It was a large square chamber, the walls of which were cut deep with the initials of some unfortunates, who from time to time had been imprisoned, and who must have been well nurtured and well bred from the fact of thus carving these writings. Bessie soon had enough of exploring dungeons, and we were glad to regain the chambers above.

Thanking the knight for his hospitality we rode away, past the church with its Norman porch and apse, while Bessie, who was a good Catholic, crossed herself before the statue of the Virgin, which faces the trackway on the western side of the tower. As she strongly affected churches she now begged of me to take her to see the extensive buildings now being carried on at Little Malvern by Prior Alcock, a very learned and pious man, who afterwards became a bishop and the instructor of King Edward's princely sons.

I now proposed to ride to the Wind's Point, where the trackway to Ledbury crosses the Malverns, and on the left of which rises that great Caer, which tradition says was held by the British chief Caractacus against the Roman general Ostorius. We left our horses at the little hostelrie on the pass, and then ascended the Caer, as the day was bright and sunny, and Bessie loved a noble view as well as I did.

But it was not the Caer of Caractacus, or the hunting grounds of the Conqueror, or Gloucester, once the court of kings, that Bessie and I had in our minds. As yet we had neither of us alluded to the battle-field of Mortimer's Cross, but as the sun lit up the hills of Radnor forest and wooded eminences of Shobdon away beyond the tall spire of Hereford Cathedral, I could point out to my friend and companion where lay the field of Kingsland, where her father and mine died for the house of Mortimer, and from whence Roger Calverley and I were borne two stricken and half-dying men.

We gazed in silence, until, remembering that I had not seen my wounded friend at Bransbill Castle for several days, I proposed that we should ride on to enquire how he bore himself after the loss of his right arm and his other injuries.

From that moment Bessie's secret was no secret, at least to me. I now understood fully why she ever wore red roses, and why Henry of Lancaster was a right royal King. I had suspected, but now I knew it. Bessie's face was mantling with blushes, and her eyes filling with tears as she turned from my gaze. But the distance was too far, she was fatigued, and she must return as the hinds would be awaiting her and she had forgotten to feed her tercel.

And all the while I felt certain that she would have walked to Ledbury, or ridden to Hereford, to get one look at her stricken knight, if she could have done so unawares and unseen, and I knew too that this hungry tercel was his gift in happier days.

She now proposed to ride homeward alone, while I went to see Calverley, and much pressed it, but those times were not nearly so safe as they now are, for damosels to ride untended. We went back to the little hostelrie, where mine host was full of the noble appearance of King Edward as he rode across the pass at the head of his army after the great battle of Mortimer's Cross; how he enquired the direction of Gloucester, Birtsmereton, and Hanley Castle in the vale, and gave our informant a good broad piece of silver for pointing them out.[3]

We then mounted our steeds and rode down tho gullet, skirting the pass of the Swineyard, and by those thickets so well known for the haunts of the stag and the wild boar, above the Hangman's Oak, and then a sharp gallop across the forest glades led us by the glen of Berew to the pilgrim's hostelrie, The Duke of York.

This hostelrie is the only one dedicated to St Julian in all our forest

Chase, and was a pilgrims' inn before the times of Chaucer. It was a forester's lodge in the times of the first and second Edwards, and was frequented by the Red Earl and his son – who afterwards fell at Bannockburn – when hunting among our wild woodlands.

The hostelrie lay on the trackway through the forest from the Severn at Theocsbury to Hereford, and was frequented by the pilgrims who visited the shrines of St Ethelbert and St Cantilupe. The first tabard was put up at the time of the battle of Crecy, with the arms of the Duke of Lancaster. When it became the property of my father, he was careful for the good keeping of his inn, and placed there as landlord one of our archers, a man of goodly aspect, management, and bearing, and he changed the arms on the tabard to those of Richard, Duke of York.

In our time a traveller might be sure of a blazing fire of faggots on a winter's night, cider of the sweetest, ale of the brightest, good fat capons with hog's flesh bruised for gravy. Then the beds in the niches were of the cleanest and the pride of the host's wife, who still showed the chamber where at times have slept the Earls de Clare. Here too is a clock which tells the time of day like Master Chaucer's.

But not only is the hostelrie famous in our Chase. Here is the village green, and trackway cross,[4] and tallest maypole in all the country side; the trysting place of the archers and villagers of many a country parish for trials of quarter-staff or wrestling, and the gentler sports of 'club ball' and 'hoodman's blind'. The most lusty bulls, the biggest badgers, and the most gallant cocks ever appeared on our green, and in the days of Robin Hood our forest Chase was more famous for its bowmen than even in the days of my youth.

Of late years archery had been neglected too much, and games were all the fashion. Hence a prohibition had lately emanated from the Crown against over-indulgence 'in cock-fighting, tennis balls, kayles, closh and half-bowls', and commanding magistrates 'to seize and destroy them, and make the people take to archery trials, and practise the long and the cross-bow'.

As we rode up to this village green, on which were a party of villagers amusing themselves in various ways, Bessie told me how just a year ago her gallant father had been judge of the sports, and how, lest she should be thought too proud, she had joined in a game of hoodman's blind.

King Edward endeavoured to gratify the loyalty of his followers by gifts and grants of estates forfeited by the Lancastrians, and it was only through the influence of Sir Robin of Elsdune that I was enabled to preserve to Roger Calverley the domain and castle of Branshill.

Hundreds of Yorkists were seeking for titles, estates, places, or rich wives, and some of them were so doubtful in their loyalty, that if it was not in the King's power to give what they wanted they would turn Lancastrians at very short notice, especially when rumours arose that the powerful Louis of France was raising a great army to support the deposed King.

Sir John Carfax, who ever sailed with the tide, had in the mean time sent to Court a petition for the grant of some land of the Calverleys' which lay up the Gullet Pass on our side of the Malverns, and the only claim to which was that after the battle of Towton he had all his red roses superseded by white, and now never alluded to the time when he was equerry to Queen Margaret.

Having become a decided supporter of the House of York, he was especially active in denouncing any one in our neighbourhood who was, or had been, an adherent to the House of Lancaster. A charge of disloyalty in those times was no easy matter to set aside; it was so serious that I more than once entreated Bessie Kitel to give up persistently wearing a red rose worked on her bodice in the presence of such men as Sir John. But Sir John had other plans for Bessie. If he thought it would be advantageous to add the lands of Kitel Keep in Pendyke to his own, he also thought it would be pleasant to take to wife the fairest and bonniest damsel in all our forest Chase.

Truly Bessie was not clerkly learned, but she could read Master Chaucer with help from Rosamond, and she had practised enough in writing to trace Elizabeth Kitel on a scrip; but neither was Sir John learned, for he always went to the monks of Little Malvem to indite the humblest missive he wished to send. Thus the letters which sometimes came to Kitel Keep were not indited by Sir John in aught but the concluding signature of 'Geon Carfaks'.

Potels of honey and such small offerings now rained upon Bessie, and a day seldom passed that the gallant knight did not ride through the woodlands to Kitel Keep, to enquire how the lone damosel bore herself, and to inspect the snug barn, the kine and the sheep, the cocks and hens, and the dovecot, all of which would make a considerable addition to the somewhat wild and uncultivated manor of Castlemereton.

Chapter Eleven

But Bessie never gave him any encouragement, although she could not always refuse his white doves and other blandishments. When the visits became over-importunate, she would take refuge with my mother until at last Sir John began visiting mother also, who was far too hospitable to show him an averted face, especially as he came loaded with promises, and frequently bore in his knightly hands conserves of honied raspberries, and baskets of dried pippins.

As I was seldom at home during these pippin visits, I had little opportunity of observing how he sped in his wooing, save that I had heard it whispered that one of our wenches had seen him on his knees before Bessie in the church porch, and he arose brushing his buskins and wiping his eyes.

I was now becoming more and more distressed at the continued absence of Rosamond, not only on my own account, but for the sake of her grandfather, who was rapidly failing, with no one but Silent John to attend him, save the serving women and my good mother, whose own health since my father's death had become delicate. I did what I could to help John, but men even with the best intentions are poor nurses, and a sick bed without the care of a loving woman is a very sorry one.

The dying man's one call was for Rosamond, his Rosie, as he called her, but alas she came not, and death waits for no one. Master Berew was rapidly sinking, and my mother declared that he had but a few days to live. Still no Rosamond came, and at last her grandfather passed quietly away and was laid in the peaceful churchyard beneath the hill of Berew.

Chapter Twelve

THE AUTUMN of this eventful year 1464 had now arrived, and the forest leaves were falling all around us; the ring ouzel had come from the mountains to feed on the red berries of the mountain ash; and the serving wenches had gone to the thickets to gather bramble berries for winter conserves.

Messenger after messenger was sent to Elsdune to enquire whether there were tidings of Rosamond from Hergest, and Mary Bolingbroke had continually questioned Ivvan Ivvans, but nothing transpired to afford us the least information of what had become of her or Master Vaughan.

Night was coming on one gloomy October evening, the Malverns were shrouded in mist, the rain was pattering among the falling leaves, and the whole household was preparing to retire to rest, when we were aroused by the blowing of the born which hung against the gateway, and which, when the drawbridge was up, summoned the warder to the portcullis to see who demanded admittance and their business.

Wondering who had arrived, at this unusual hour, I proceeded to the portcullis and found the warder parleying with a woman whose garments were dripping with rain, and whose hood was so closely drawn over her features that it was impossible to make out who she was. She asked for admission to see my mother upon a matter of life and death, and, obeying my orders, the gatekeeper at once lowered the drawbridge and she entered the court-yard. I enquired what her wishes were, and regretted that my mother was retired to her bedchamber, as she was still an invalid and far from strong. Leading her into the house, she threw back her hood, and to my utter astonishment revealed the features of Rosamond Berew.

My first movement was to enfold her in my embrace, and the second to hold her at arm's length and look upon a face I had yearned to see for many a weary day. My mother hearing the unusual sounds of an arrival at the drawbridge after it had been raised for the night, had returned downstairs, and she, too, fondly embraced our long lost treasure. We had, moreover, Rosamond's tale to listen to, and, as soon proved, a good deal to prepare for.

It appeared that after placing Rosamond for safety at Clun Castle, Master Vaughan led his followers to Knighton, where he joined the

Welsh forces under Jasper Tudor, and fought with them at the battle of Mortimer's Cross. After the defeat, on Candlemass day, he feared for the security of Clun Castle, and so removed with Rosamond for the better refuge of Abbey Cwm Hir, the only monastic establishment in Radnorshire, and so surrounded by wild mountains that escape was easy if the Yorkists sent their armed men in search of fugitives.

Rosamond was placed under the care of a lady, a relative of the Vaughans, who lived among the mountains, while Master Vaughan found shelter within the walls of the monastery itself until the pursuit was over, at least for a time.

Resolute and active as ever, Master Vaughan had led the few men he could rally into Yorkshire, hoping to retrieve the losses the Lancastrians had met with on the Welsh borders. Then came the field of Towton, which, although it was fought at the end of March, began in the midst of a terrible snow storm, and Master Vaughan found himself again a fugitive, and lost among wild moors, with every chance of being eventually taken prisoner.

Among those who saved themselves by flight were King Henry, Queen Margaret, Prince Edward her son, and the Earls of Exeter and Oxford. Even to the present time no one knew what had become of the unfortunate Queen and her boy, but they were supposed to have crossed the borders to Scotland.

In his wanderings Master Vaughan had fallen in with the Countess of Oxford and her young son, who were hidden in a small house in Pontefract, and after many adventures and hairbreadth escapes succeeded in conveying both mother and son safe to the sanctuary of Abbey Cwm Hir. Here, and among the Penmelly mountains at the home of his relation, Mistress Fowler, the persecuted Lancastrians found a secure hiding place for several months.

But of late their safety had been compromised by the appearance of riders at Abbey Cwm Hir bearing King Edward's royal warrant for the arrest of all those mentioned in the bill of attainder, and in this bill were particularly reported the Earl of Oxford, his son, though a mere boy, and Master Vaughan.

Perhaps the most extraordinary part of Rosamond's revelation was the fact that Sir Andrew Trollop, having obtained the reversal of his attainder, was now endeavouring to curry favour with the Court by turning spy and informer, and had appeared at Abbey Cwm Hir, evidently for the purpose of tracking those denounced and endeavouring to effect their arrest.

Under these circumstances Master Vaughan determined to escape if possible to France and had left Radnorshire with the Countess, her son, and Rosamond. But this was not easy to do, and for several days they had been wandering among the woods and villages of Herefordshire, avoiding the principal towns, and sheltering at night where best they could. Rosamond's knowledge of the country was greatly in their favour, and for some days they had avoided a party of soldiers at Ledbury by taking up their abode at a small hostelrie in the village of Woolhope, a wild district in the centre of the forest of Haughwood.

Here they might have remained in safety, but Master Vaughan was anxious to go to Bristol and see about a vessel wherein they might escape to the Continent. It was therefore resolved that he should find his way as best he could; and that, in the mean time, Rosamond should conduct the Countess and her son to our manor-house as being more defensible and less likely to be searched than Master Berew's.

Their only means of conveyance was one wretched Welsh pony between them, and to avoid Ledbury they had to make a circuit by the remote village of Marcle. Here they met with a great fright, for in a narrow trackway they were passed by a party of horsemen bearing the pennon of the Mortimers and making for the castle there, but who fortunately took no notice of them, save telling them to stand out of the way. On they plodded through the thick copses below Hatfield Camp, when in crossing the Gloucester trackway they again heard the rattling armour of troops and the sound of the clarion.

Rosamond determined upon abandoning the pony and striking through the woodlands for the almost impenetrable recesses of the Howling Heath above Broomsbarrow. Here, cowering in a quarry, surrounded by dense gorse and thicket but sheltered by an oak, she left the noble lady and her boy while she walked on, half dead with fatigue and terror, to beg asylum from my mother and myself for a few days for a worn-out woman, whose only fault was that she was the wife of one of King Edward's enemies, accompanied by her proscribed son.

Insisting that Rosamond should go to bed immediately, I started for the Howling Heath taking with me a party of men bearing a litter, whereon the unfortunate Countess might be carried, and a palfrey for her son.

On arriving at the quarry in the thickets was a scene I shall never forget. On the mossy roots of a giant oak sat the lady, her head bowed over the face of her son, who was lying at full length upon the cold ground, his head resting on his mother's knees, while a moon flickering through dark clouds showed dresses soiled with mire and torn with thorns. At my approach the Countess rose to her feet, and I could see that she was of commanding stature and of dignified mien. The boy, too, bore himself with courage, and laid his hand upon the small dagger which was attached to his girdle, as he sprang from the turf and stepped before his mother.

I reassured them by saying, "I bring you good tidings, lady. Rosamond Berew is safe at that home to which I would, by your leave, conduct you."

"Home," sighed the lady, "alas! when shall we reach home again! Nevertheless, good Sir, if you are the trusty friend of Rosamond Berew, we cannot do better than seek your hospitality and succour, for we are stricken deer, well-nigh hunted unto death."

We lost no time in parleying, so leading them through the thickets to the bottom of the hill, where I had left the litter and the palfrey, we crossed the flanks of the Chase End and proceeded by the Hawthorns homewards.

It was now past midnight, and notwithstanding her fatigue, Rosamond had insisted upon assisting my mother in her preparations for our unhappy but distinguished guests.

I now had an opportunity of seeing distinctly the features of the Count- ess of Oxford. I thought I had seen them before, as she was carried by the light of the moon. There was a foreign accent, too, in her speech, which struck me as peculiar, and which I had heard on another occasion. I could now doubt no longer. This was the lady and the youth we had conducted to the White Friars at Hereford.

Seated in the great armchair by the chimney, in the panelled room, her face pale with sorrow and wasted by suffering, there was yet an expression of pride and energy which bespoke a man's courage beneath a woman's form. Beautiful she undoubtedly was, but it was the beauty of a Boadicea or a Clytemnestra.

The youth was a boy of promise. He might have been expected to have quailed with all he had undergone, as he could not have been more than ten years old, but on the contrary, in aspect and mien he looked far older than his years, and young as he was displayed a most chivalrous attention to his mother.

Having replaced their wet and soiled garments in the best way we could, and seeing them to their chambers after they had partaken of refreshments, I went forth so as to meet the serving men, as they came at dawn of morning to their daily work, and make arrangements that no one approached the manor without due information; giving orders that the drawbridge was not to be lowered without my especial command.

Neither the Countess nor her son ventured to leave the house across the drawbridge ; nor did I encourage their doing so, as I did not care to be compromised with King Edward through harbouring fugitives so especially proscribed.

Before many days had passed away, Master Vaughan made his appearance before the drawbridge disguised as a Bristol woolstapler; all his love-locks shorn off, and accompanied by a serving man, who led a couple of strong horses for the purpose of carrying wool bales from Birtsmereton to Bristol, and which I need hardly say were altogether imaginary. I told him that I thought he was running more risk than our guests, for I could not believe that so gallant a knight as King Edward would wreak his vengeance upon women and children.

Master Vaughan replied that the executions after the battle of Towton had been most vindictive; that Edward had only just removed the heads of his own father and young brother from the spikes above the gate of York; and that the son of the Earl of Oxford would be safer across the seas, while his mother would rather die than be parted from him. He had made arrangements with the captain of a Bristol trader to sail for France as soon as he could escort them across the country in safety, where they would all remain in refuge until happier times.

He also told me that no time should be lost, as it was quite true that the double traitor Trollop had sought immunity by volunteering to bring in proscribed fugitives, and that he was the leader of a party of riders who were sent into Radnorshire and Herefordshire for the express purpose of arresting King Henry – who was believed to have escaped to Wales – Queen Margaret and the Prince, and the families of such as Exeter and Oxford.

One difficulty Master Vaughan feared, and this was the passage of the Severn at Gloucester. He had reason to believe that the bridge there and the fords above and below were well watched by spies, and I therefore undertook to ride over and see our old friend Master Walred, and obtain through him a safe passage across the bridge and through the town, for my friend the Bristol woolstapler, his wife and son, without being subjected to the unnecessary scrutiny of the sentinels.

After making every arrangement possible for the safety and comfort of our guests, and giving Hasting strict injunctions to watch well for any indications of spies, I started early in the morning for Gloucester. I had not ridden farther than the green near the church of Berew when I fell in with Sir John Carfax, accompanied by a couple of strange riders who wore the livery of the House of York.

He stopped me at once with the information that he was engaged in the service of King Edward in endeavouring to arrest some of the most malignant of his enemies, who had been traced as far as Marcle, and were supposed to have taken refuge in Malvern Chase; also that a large sum was offered for their capture. He thought it possible that they might be secreted in the little monastery of Pendyke, which he intended to search thoroughly, and was on his way with the men-at-arms for that purpose.

Sir Andrew Trollop, he said, was closely searching the castle of Branshill and the woods in that direction. After giving him a hint to search Gadbury Camp, its thickets, the grange of Hasfield, the lodge at Fordington, and the grange at Eastington, I rode as fast as I could for Gloucester.

It was no easy matter to arrange, even with the aid of Master Walred, for the safe passage through the city. It took me the whole of the day and night came on before I was able to return. Still, by the aid of friends at the Castle, and well paying the warders, I settled that Master ap Rice, the Welsh woolstapler, and his family, should be allowed to pass through without let or hindrance, especially as I undertook to bear them company.

On my return home I found that my mother had received a visit from some most unwelcome visitors, and that she and Rosamond had been put to their wits' end to protect our guests. Early in the afternoon Sir John Carfax, accompanied by a strange knight and a number of soldiers, rode to the barbican and demanded admission to see me or Mistress de Brute without delay. On Hasting holding a parley with them he declined to let down the drawbridge until he had received orders from my mother. In the meantime Rosamond had surveyed the party through the crenelles of the gatehouse and at once recognized Sir Andrew Trollop as the leader of the soldiers. What was to be done?

It was hardly likely that suspicion could fall upon me of harbouring King Edward's enemies, as I was well known to be devoted to his cause. Still, the knights requested a personal interview, and a refusal would be almost unprecedented, as the troops were undoubtedly those of the King, and led by his officers. There was only one thing to be done. The drawbridge must be lowered, Sir John Carfax and Trollop admitted, and the Countess, her son, and Master Vaughan must be shut up in the secret chamber. It would be close quarters, but nothing was left for it. They might insist on searching the house with the King's warrant, and no other place was safe.

My mother touched the spring of the secret door, and in a moment all three were safely ensconced within the narrow space which was to be their refuge in this dilemma.

There is no doubt that Trollop had ascertained from Sir John that I was absent from home, or even his impudence would hardly have induced him to face me in my own home after what had happened. As it was he entered, with his usual pompous bearing and self-assertion, and, having seated himself at my mother's invitation, stared at Rosamond and informed them that he had come in the name of his Majesty King Edward to demand my aid and assistance in searching the Chase, around our district, for certain malignant rebels supposed to be harboured by other malignants and abettors. With this he exhibited a parchment roll signed by the King's own hand.

My mother replied that I was absent from home and would not return before night, and that she had no doubt I would pay every attention to his Majesty's commands.

Fortunately Sir John had directed Trollop's attention to the shields and armorial bearings above the panels, and they were examining the devices of Vaughan, and Blount of Eye, when Bessie Kitel entered looking like a damask rose, and made her curtsey to the assembled party. She at once saw something was wrong, and therefore proceeded to assist Rosamond in entertaining the guests, while my mother attended to the spicing of the hippocras with mints and honey.

Bessie had never seen Trollop, and had little idea that she was making herself agreeable to my most bitter enemy. Sir John was as usual profuse in his attention, but the beauty was too indignant at a man who could so easily turn his tunic inside out, to receive those attentions with anything but disdain. Indeed, Rosamond told me afterwards that she could not help laughing at the expression of Sir John's puckered countenance when Bessie pointed to the shield of Baskerville and asked if it was not that of a 'very perfect, gentle knight, full of truth and honour, and faithful unto death'.

After examining the *azures* and *gules* of the armorial devices, Sir John proceeded to compliment my mother on the size of her ducks, and Trollop was evidently examining the room with curiosity, when the young Lord in the secret chamber gave a violent sneeze, so sharp indeed that it startled every one.

Rosamond, with a woman's aptitude, at once rushed to the casement, and said, "There is Tom fallen into the moat; we must help him or he will be drowned!"

Every one of course rushed forth to assist in rescuing Tom; but the drawbridge was up again, and by the time they had gone half round the moat, and reached the spot where he was supposed to have tumbled in, Thomas had disappeared, with no more, according to Rosamond's theory, than a good fright and a wetting.

After this the knights took their departure, much to the relief of our entire household, for nobody liked Sir John, and sneezing in the secret chamber was dangerous in such company. On my return at night the Countess begged that there should be no unnecessary delay with respect to their journey to Bristol, for she had heard Sir John's peculiar squeaking voice through the panels, and recognized it at once as that of one of Queen Margaret's court attendants in former years. It was a voice she would know anywhere, and the voice of one who loved to espouse the winning cause. She feared the chance of meeting him, as he would recognize her at once.

It was therefore determined that we should proceed to Bristol at midnight; there was a moon, and it would be well to pass through Gloucester before daylight. I particularly wished Rosamond to remain with my mother, but her uncle pressed her not to desert the Countess in this her emergency. She had been of immense service to her and her young son; he therefore entreated her to assist him in seeing them safe across the Channel.

"It did not" he said, "involve any great self-sacrifice." She was safe, and there was no charge of rebellion against her. The captain of the vessel was his friend, and would undertake to see her safe to Bristol, where I could meet her in the course of a few weeks. All this Master Vaughan urged, and to his entreaties the young Lord added his beseechings, while the Countess looked imploringly but said little.

So it was settled that Rosamond should bear them company for a few weeks, although it was much against my desire, and I could not lay aside the dismal forebodings which would cross my mind at such an adventurous proposal on the part of her uncle. Had I known the objection he had, as a Catholic, to his niece marrying one of my opinions, and his determination if possible to prevent it, Rosamond would never have yielded to his importunity, and we should have both been spared some years of anxiety and sorrow.

The journey to Bristol was performed without much fatigue or danger, owing to the precautions I had taken at Gloucester and those already made by Master Vaughan at Bristol. I accompanied the vessel down the river Avon and told Rosamond that preparations would be made for our marriage early in the ensuing year.

There was no necessity for our longer delay. She had lost her aged grandfather, and Silent John and Master Vaughan were her only near relations, and both would be glad to see her comfortably settled. She made no objection save that we were both very young and my mother thought we had better wait awhile; objections which I merely laughed at and thought most ridiculous.

But the time came when I was summoned by the captain to go ashore if I would not be carried with her to the shores of France and so I had to say farewell, bitterly regretting I had not made arrangements to accompany her on this chivalrous journey for the sake of those who differed from us in everything we believed to be right and true.

The Countess expressed her gratitude for all we had done on behalf of herself and son and promised to take as much care of Rosamond as if she was her own child, until an early opportunity occurred for her return. Master Vaughan said little and appeared to take it all as a matter of course, treating all we had done, and all Rosamond's devotion to the care of these noble refugees for months, as if we were highly honoured by the opportunity.

I confess I was irate at his coolness and self-sufficiency, making an inward declaration that when we were married, Master Vaughan

Chapter Twelve

should never again compromise us with rebels, even if it were Queen Margaret herself and her royal son.

I pressed Rosamond to my heart in the little cabin which had been prepared for the reception of the Countess, and who had the good taste to remain on deck during our last interview. The last I saw of her beloved form, for some long, weary years, was standing on the poop of the vessel, her hand in that of the youth, side by side with Master Vaughan and the Countess of Oxford. I had a long ride before me and not a pleasant one. Owing to circumstances I could not control, my betrothed wife was borne away to a foreign land, and for the sake of those who were really neither more nor less than our born enemies.

On my return home, I found that Sir Andrew Trollop and his men had gone northwards to the forest of Wyre in pursuit of fugitive Lancastrians, and that Sir John Carfax was as anxious as ever to gain the favour of King Edward by denouncing the wounded Calverley, who was crippled for life at Branshill Castle.

Having heard reports of this cowardly proceeding, I intended to ride over and see my wounded friend, when one morning he made his appearance riding down the avenue towards the manor house. He was still much crippled, and could only proceed at a foot's pace and was attended by his forester, who often had to guide his palfrey down the steep paths. A sadly different fashion from that of the daring horseman, who was accustomed to gallop down the Gullet or dash into the Severn by Wainlode.

Assisting him to dismount, I conducted him to the house where my mother and Bessie Kitel were consulting together on household arrangements. We entered the room suddenly, and without preparation, and as this was the first time Bessie and Calverley had met since the battle of Mortimer's Cross, it was a trying ordeal for both.

All Bessie's roses fled at the sight of the tottering invalid and crippled man she now beheld, instead of the hale and noble looking fellow we once knew him. She sat pale and motionless with her eyes fixed on him, and an expression and twitching about the lips which made me fear she would become hysterical and cry aloud with sorrow. Calverley was calm, composed, and manly, and paid his personal devoirs to my mother right gallantly. But when he turned to Bessie it was with a kind of hopeless manner, as if to say, "I am no longer a fit companion for the young, and blithe, and brave, but a broken-down man whose lot it is to face what is left of life alone. You won't find me pressing my company upon those who should choose their associates from the healthy and the uninjured. We have ridden our last ride together."

Bessie somewhat recovered herself, and muttered some indistinct expressions about his recovery, but she was so occupied in checking an outburst of tears, that her manner was constrained and cold, and she did not appear to sympathize as heartily as she should with so old a friend and neighbour. So Calverley was cold also, and haughty withal, and soon ceased addressing her to talk to me on the business which brought him over. We left the room to walk in the garden by the moat, when he took his leave, refusing my pressing invitation to return for refreshments. My heart ached for the brave fellow, knowing how bitterly he must feel the ruin of all his ambitious hopes as a knight and a soldier.

On returning to the room in which I had left my mother and Bessie, my mother asked me to leave them, but not before I had seen Bessie lying like a statue in her arms. I went forth wondering if Roger Calverley intended to separate himself through pride from the girl who, I felt sure, would love him unto death.

Months passed by, and King Edward appeared to be so firmly established on the throne that we all hoped the curse of civil war had passed away. Rosamond wrote, but it was in a constrained manner, and there was evidently something she wished to tell me, but thought it inexpedient to commit to a parchment that she had to entrust to the Lancastrian captain of the Bristol ship. Nor did she say when she hoped to return, and already I was mourning for her absence.

Bessie Kitel seldom came to Birtsmereton after that interview with her lover, and looked pale and harassed; no longer the ever-smiling lass of our happier hunting days. She passed much time, too, with the old Sub-Prior of Pendyke, learning to read and write; clerkly accomplishments which she had hitherto much neglected. So we thought she would become a nun.

I now had determined to appeal myself to King Edward respecting the attainder of Calverley; when one evening an armed knight attended by his esquire rode up to the barbican, and I at once recognized the bronzed fine face of Robin of Elsdune.

Chapter Thirteen

RIGHT GLAD was I to welcome my trusted friend once more, and well did we regard each other with that gladsome look which none can mistake when old and dear friends meet in uncertain times and circumstances. Robin avoided ornament in dress, but the uniform of the Archers of the Guard was so rich and handsome, that it set off his figure to great advantage, while the calm and steady bearing and the gentle though determined look was as unchanged as ever. His demeanour to my mother was that of one who might have been bred in a Court, but without that affectation which spoils the gentleman.

Our greetings over, Robin presented me with a letter written with King Edward's own hand, offering me a commission in his army higher than I had any right to expect, and commanding my immediate return with Robin to Windsor, that I might make myself acquainted with the duties of my post.

I now learnt that Margaret of Anjou and her son, after a long hiding, had escaped to France, where she was endeavouring to incite Louis XI. and the Duke of Brittany to espouse her cause, and in the name of King Henry offered Calais to the cautious and cunning Louis. Henry of Lancaster had been conveyed to one of the strongest castles in Wales, and King Edward seemed securely seated on the throne, with the great Earl of Warwick as his adviser, minister, and general, while the Lancastrians were too crushed to rise in fresh revolt.

I begged of Robin to give me a couple of days to make my preparations for attendance upon the King, when I promised to return with him to Windsor. In the mean time I related to him all that had occurred through Trollop's appointment over the soldiers who were charged with the arrest of fugitive Lancastrians; his impudence at coming to my own house in my absence, and the intimacy he had of late struck up with my nearest neighbour, Sir John Carfax.

Nor was this all. The succession of Edward to the throne had done nothing as yet to remove the disorders of the times and restrain the lawless violence of petty barons and needy knights. Complaints had already reached our neighbourhood of the despoiling of houses by the men under this very Trollop, and of many insolent exactions in the name of the Crown, not only from Lancastrians, but from those who throughout had favoured the House of York.

This conversation had hardly taken place before Hasting informed me that Sir Andrew Trollop was now staying at Castlemereton with Sir John Carfax, and that both of late had been seen examining the defences of Branshill Castle from the hills above. So convinced was I of this man's treacherous disposition, that this announcement caused me some alarm. I knew his hatred of myself. and his persistent endeavours to injure me. Yet here he was again lurking in our immediate neighbourhood, and just as I was leaving home for an indefinite period.

I almost felt inclined to send my excuses to Windsor, at least for a time, but Robin assured me Trollop would not dare to undertake any conspiracy against one so much a favourite with King Edward, while a personal representation of the lawlessness committed in remote districts would be most advantageous to us all.

Before I left Birtsmereton, I took the precaution of leaving my mother in charge of Hasting, telling him to look well to the drawbridge and defences, and to strengthen our little band of archers with some hinds who were good bowmen, and who could come each night to sleep within the walls.

I also wrote to Calverley, informing him that the quondam Yorkist, Trollop, who turned Lancastrian at Ludlow and nearly killed me at Kingsland field, was now Yorkist again and on a visit to Sir John Carfax at Castlemereton. I begged of him, through his foresters and woodmen, to keep an eye on them both, and if he perceived the slightest trace of any plot to injure his yeomen and franklins, or mine, to spare no trouble or expense in sending to me at Windsor. I also entreated Bessie, for my sake, to return to Birtsmereton nightly to sleep, even if she passed most of the day at her own farm.

We were now enabled to pass a long evening together, and Robin had some opportunity of judging of the superior attainments and education of Bessie. It was pleasant to listen to her as she talked of Master Chaucer or Master Lydgate, and the poem of Piers Plowman: She could now read, and could quote Chaucer from memory, and she was venturesome enough to promise to write to me at Windsor, though I laughingly declared that the Sub-Prior of Pendyke would hold the pen. My mother was ever busy with her tapestry and listening to our rattle, while she watched me with a look of deep affection, and glanced at Robin from time to time as if she would judge with her own eyes if he were faithful and true.

Chapter Thirteen

The times of which I write were not as the peaceful times of Henry VII, but so full of danger were they that one's heart must needs be heavy at parting with those near and dear. So my mother wept as she folded me in her arms, and tears filled the eyes of Bessie. She too gave me her kiss at parting, and I felt that she was in sad and secret trouble for her wounded knight across the hill, who had left her without saying one kind word, or giving her one kind look. She sobbed out something about "bringing back a sound heart", even if I returned "with a wounded body", and as I kissed her forehead I whispered, "All will yet come right; the fiercest storm will pass away, and God will give us sunshine."

So Bessie smiled amidst her tears, as if a vision of happier times had come before her, and that there should yet be gladness at Kitel Keep. Robin, having made his salutations, was becoming impatient, so we rode away, my horses following under the charge of Tom of Gulley's End, and we crossed the drawbridge on the road to very different scenes, and very different company.

A steady ride for two days across the flat wide country on the summit of the Cotswolds, then by the beautiful Thames at Maidenhead, brought us to the noble castle of Windsor, first founded by Norman kings, then the favourite home of several of the Plantagenets, and the birthplace of the gallant Edward III. The royal banner floated over the great Keep, and numerous men-at-arms and sentries paced to and fro on the battlemented walls.

King Edward was in the great Horncourt, engaged with the stout Earl Warwick[1] in examining some war steeds. He then wore no gown or flowing surcoat, the effeminate garb of courtiers in times of peace, but the tight fitting tunic, which became him well, and showed the splendid symmetry of his powerful frame. His voice, too, rang like the trumpet accents I had heard upon Kingsland field, as he shouted to riders and steeds as they were going through their paces.

When we rode up with the mud and stain of travel, he came forward and gave us both a cordial welcome. He then spoke of us to the Earl of Warwick, who, stately as the King himself, smiled and bid us welcome, saying I had made a good beginning on the field of Kingsland.

Seeing that we required refreshment, King Edward commended me to the care of Sir Robin, to rest awhile, and commanding me to seek his presence in the Winchester tower in some three hours.

I was astonished at the magnificence of the Castle, which was originally a mere hunting seat of the Conqueror, and the grand buildings of which a hundred years before de Wyckham was the architect, and Edward III the king. Twelve glaziers had employed their skill on the new buildings and collected vast quantities of glass. The Keep, built on a vast artificial mound, and surrounded by a deep moat in the centre of the Castle, is a noble object, and the view from the summit commands the windings of the river Thames, the wild forest, the green glades therein, the nestling hamlets, and, in the eastern distance, the great city of London.

Quarters had been prepared for us in one of the Norman towers which had been spared when Edward III built the present magnificent fabric. In one of the chambers, tradition reports that Queen Eleanor, the consort of King Edward I, gave birth to one of her children, and that King John occupied another during his contest with the Barons. It might have been so, but they seemed to me cold apartments for kings and queens.

Robin then conducted me to a great dining hall, where courtiers and officers were engaged in the necessary occupation of eating and drinking. Of the refection itself the least said the better. There was indeed abundance, enormous masses of beef and mutton, and whole barrels of ale stood at the end of the hall. The contrast to the well-cooked capons and delicious meats, conserves, and sotelties of my mother's own making at our manor was very great, and not conducive to appetite. But a soldier is ever accustomed to rough living, and I mention this for the instruction of my daughters, who as good housewives may thus learn that the meats at a king's table may be badly served, and that a gentleman with a good housewife is better off than a king with bad cooks.

In these early days of King Edward's reign, the Court, whether at Windsor or in London, was of very different character to the later periods after his marriage with Dame Elizabeth Gray. It was now more like an armed camp, and had not yet become the haunt of men who should have been women, and women who should have been men.

When I entered into the presence of the King, he was holding council with the Earl of Warwick and other lords. He had that fire in his eye and pride of mien, which ever distinguished him when war or danger was imminent; entirely different from his manner in times of peace and luxury, and later, alas, of sensuality. His quick eye caught my entrance, and he motioned to me to remain stationary while he listened to those nobles who were privileged to speak and express their opinion on the subjects of debate.

The topic now discussed was the presence of Margaret of Anjou at the court of Philip, Duke of Burgundy, who had so long been the ally of the Lancastrians, and who had sworn solemnly to support Henry of Lancaster. With her was the Duke of Exeter, Lord Oxford, de Breze, and other proscribed exiles, while the Duke of Somerset was in England and, in spite of his recent submission and pardon, was suspected of being in correspondence with the Queen.

When the council broke up, the King came to me with that frank courtesy which won for him so many hearts, especially those of women, and giving me his hand bade me welcome as an old and tried friend. He then bade me tell him all my experiences since we last met, of the death of my father on Kingsland field, my own escape from Sir Andrew Trollop, and my subsequent illness.

"By my halidome, Sir Hildebrande," said he, "if I had known that Trollop had been the man who thus struck you down, I never would have signed the release of his attainder. It went hard with me to do it, after his chase of myself in your Malvern forests, but his sister wept and moaned, and I am ever too easily persuaded by the sighs of a fair damosel. However, Sir Andrew Trollop had better mind his future conduct, and he never enters my presence as long as I am King of England."

About this time Edward fell desperately in love with the beautiful Elizabeth Gray, who was the daughter of Jacquetta of Luxemburgh, the widow of that great Duke of Bedford who was once Regent of France. After the Duke's death, the Duchess married Sir Richard Widville, who was known for his learning and association with learned men.[2] The King kept this amour a secret even from Robin and myself, though we suspected from his frequent absence on secret expeditions that there was a woman in the case.

Early one morning, in the month of March 1464, the Earl of Warwick entered the antechamber of the King's apartments in the Winchester tower, where I was engaged in studying the models of some arquebusses and culverins, and thinking that our archery would ere long be superseded by these wonderful machines for war. The stout Earl had little sympathy with the gallantry which could induce a monarch to ride from Windsor to Grafton Regis to visit a fair lady. He asked bluntly for the King, and his countenance changed when I said that he had ridden the previous evening, attended only by a single esquire, for the Duchess of Bedford's manor of Grafton.

"Then do you mount and ride to Grafton too, Sir Hildebrande," said he, "and tell King Edward that this is no time to listen to the lute of Dame Elizabeth Gray. Tell him that his bitter enemy, Margaret of Anjou, is again in arms; that Somerset has thrown off the mask, and has marched with a large force to join Percy in the north; that the army of the Lancastrians is again in the field and his crown in jeopardy while he is going through love passages at Grafton."

"Nay," he continued, "say nought of this foolery of amours, but entreat of him to lose not a moment in showing himself, what he can be, if he likes, one of the most gallant soldiers and ablest captains of the age. Say also that I will at once send troops under the command of my noble brother, the Lord Montague, to prevent if possible the junction of the forces of Somerset with those of Percy and Sir Ralph Gray, for if these once join, the Lancastrians may yet reinstate the pious Henry at Windsor or the Tower of London."

"Even now," he continued, "I should like to take it on myself to bid Sir Robin and you march northward with our archers to join Lord Montague, but I may not deprive the King of his body-guard without consulting him. By St George, these women are the ruin of kings. Ride, Sir Hildebrande, for the honour of our King and the safety of his crown!"

I was not long in preparing for this ride of nearly forty miles across the whole of Buckinghamshire to Grafton Regis on the borders of Northampton. I mounted Kingsland, and accompanied by the faithful Tom, as my esquire, we first drew bridle for a short delay at Wendover among the chalk of the Chiltern hills. The birthplace of that great historian, Roger of Wendover, who wrote a chronicle from the creation of the world to the reign of Henry II.

When we arrived at Stoney Stratford, I felt sure that the King must be more than usually enamoured to have journeyed so far across such a country, by trackways so deep in mud and through such dense woodlands. Grafton Grange was then but a mean place for the residence of so great a lady, once the wife of the Regent of France; but it was much improved in later years, when Sir Richard became Earl Rivers, and when his son, the Lord of Scales, succeeded to the honours and estates of his father. It was somewhat larger than our moated grange at Birtsmereton, but wanted our beautiful oaks, our avenues of elms, and our fish pools. Above all, it wanted our Malvern hills and wooded glades, although there was more than enough of dense forest around the manor-house.

On our arrival late in the afternoon, we rode up on our tired and mud-bedraggled horses as King Edward and Dame Elizabeth Gray were ascending the stone steps to the mansion. It was evident that they had been engaged in gathering the earliest flowers of spring, as the King carried in his hand a large bunch of the nodding snowflake, primroses, and the sweet white violet. He was annoyed at my sudden appearance, but after conversing with me aside, he recognized the importance of Earl Warwick's message for, turning to Dame Elizabeth, he said, "We must ride to Windsor, fair lady, at tomorrow's dawn, and, in the mean time, let me present to you my good esquire and faithful friend, Sir Hildebrande de Brute."

The lady bowed her acknowledgments, and I had now for the first time an opportunity of looking upon the form and face of her who was destined to play so great a part in the future of King Edward and of England. Several years older than King Edward and both a widow and a mother, she did not look so, but with beautiful golden hair, blue eyes, and complexion of the loveliest pink and white, she seemed the very poesie of beauty. At first sight I was entranced by this lovely vision, but a longer acquaintance somewhat diminished her attractiveness to me, for there was not a trace of the intellectual expression which so distinguished her father, Sir Richard Widville. Her mind was fashioned like her mother's, who was notorious afterwards for her superstitious tamperings with the necromancies of Friar Bungay.

Having made myself presentable, I was right glad of the excellent supper which awaited us, at which I made the acquaintance of Sir Richard and his son Anthony Widville, both of whom I found to be learned men, and who contrasted most agreeably with the courtiers who had lately been my associates at Windsor.

The King occupied himself the whole evening, as might have been expected, with the ladies, but principally with Dame Elizabeth Gray. It was not until late that he bid me attend him to his bedchamber and then it was, as I assisted him to undress and lay aside the numerous ornaments he had worn, that he entered into the question of the rising of the Lancastrians, and enquired particularly about the mood of the Earl of Warwick.

He laughed heartily when I mentioned that he had thrown out hints about neglecting business for love passages, saying that the stout Earl was cold as a stone as regarded beauty or the softer influences, and was never happy save at the head of troops or in his seat at the council chamber. He alluded to my conversation with Sir Richard Widville, and laughingly said he hoped I had gathered instruction from the wise heads of both father and son.

He said not a word about Dame Elizabeth Gray, or her mother, who at the supper table asked me 'if there were not many parlous witches on the Malvern hills?' To which the King replied that 'they were as thick as hazel nuts in the groves at Grafton'. Once too afterwards, she took me aside and mysteriously presented me with a small box of salve, a sovereign remedy for heartburn, and was the 'ointment of the stars'. It looked like hog's lard.

The King was in the saddle soon after daylight, though he lingered awhile in the grey dawn of the morning with Dame Elizabeth Gray, who somehow managed to be dressed ready to hand him the stirrup cup. We rode as rapidly as the road would permit, but the King did not seem in the vein for conversation. He was moody and absent, and this was not surprising, for he had promised before he left Grafton to contract a private marriage in a month's time with Dame Elizabeth.

He was doubtless contemplating the effect this would have upon his future, or whether it would, as it proved afterwards, affect the stability of his crown. It was the first day of April, and we had nearly reached Windsor, when he exclaimed, "By St Fool, Sir Hildebrande, it is 'All Fool's Day,' and I have forgotten to make you look for a ghost behind you, or to send your Tom of the Gullet, as you call him, on a fool's errand." The thought crossed my mind that perchance he was himself returning from a fool's errand.

Once at Windsor, I expected that King Edward would be himself again and active as usual, now the trumpet of war was sounded. We heard that Henry of Lancaster had been released from his confinement in Wales, and had joined the rebels under the Duke of Somerset, Sir Ralph Gray, and Sir Richard Percy. But instead of putting himself at the head of his army and marching northwards, the King ordered Sir Robin to march to the aid of Lord Montague, and himself remained at

Windsor and commanded me to go to Doncaster. Again, early in the month, he went off to Grafton.

On the 25th of April, Lord Montague defeated Percy at Hedgely Moor in Northumberland, scattering the forces of the rebels; thus the King left this battle to be won by Lord Warwick's brother instead of himself. My orders were to remain at Doncaster with the archers of the guard until the arrival of the King. I was therefore in a fever of apprehension at this waste of time and opportunity, especially as tidings came of a large muster of rebellious Lancastrians at Hexham in Northumberland.

At last Edward reached Doncaster, but he was very scantily attended and we wanted more troops. He was also so ill that he had to take to his bed, and a leech was sent for. Robin of Elsdune was now sent on to the front with orders to join Lord Montague at Wooler, while I remained with King Edward, never leaving him day or night until he rallied. But we missed the celebrated battle of Hexham on the 15th May 1464, while Lord Montague gained a complete victory over the Lancastrians, which ended in the execution of the rebellious lords who were taken prisoners.

When the King was recovering from his illness at Doncaster, he did me the honour of taking me into his confidence, and telling me how, while we had been so anxiously expecting him before the battle of Hexham, he had contracted a private marriage with Dame Elizabeth Gray on the first of May, and how he intended before long to acknowledge his nuptials before the world, but that for state reasons it must be kept a profound secret for the present.

We had not returned from Windsor many days, when a messenger arrived from my mother, entreating me to obtain leave of absence for a time, as there were various reports respecting the lawless deeds of a set of ruffians, who now infested our forest of Malvern Chase, and who had been bold enough to attack the grange at Eastington, where they had levied a considerable sum of money, under threat of setting fire to the farm homestead. I at once communicated these tidings to King Edward, who told me to lose no time in riding down to Birtsmereton and, if there was any necessity, to apply forthwith for aid and soldiers to put down these lawless deeds and punish the offenders.

On my arrival at home I found the accounts which were forwarded to me at Windsor had not been exaggerated. A body of marauders had of late frequented the forests of Wyre and Malvern Chase, and had not only levied 'black mail' from travellers, but had broken into the houses of several franklins and farmers and committed robbery with much violence.

They had robbed some of the monks belonging to Great Malvern Priory of their shoes and money. They had attacked Master Lachmere as he rode from Worcester in the broad daylight, and eased him of his purse, his boots and his buskins, as well as his palfrey. More than once they had been seen at the hostelrie of the Robin Hood at Castlemereton but, while they had sacked the granges at Welland and Longdune they had left Sir John Carfax unmolested, though they might easily have driven off some of his cattle or harried some of his tenants.

I determined to consult with Sir John, notwithstanding my prejudice against him, as to the best method of bringing these scoundrels to justice, not doubting for a moment that he would lend every assistance in his power in such a cause. There was Master Marten too, his tenant, who lived at Castlemereton in a little house without any defence but that of a small moat, and who was known to be a man of ready money. What more likely than that he should be plundered, perhaps murdered, for the sake of his gold Richards.

While thus reflecting what action I should take, we received information that a body of outlaws at least a hundred strong had pillaged a farmer's dwelling-house at Welland on the previous night, and had also murdered a poor franklin as he was returning home from Upton-on-Severn, and left his rifled body in the middle of the trackway.

It was now evident that this was something more than a roving body of outlaws, and would have to be met by forces of greater strength than our village archers. These too had been sadly thinned by the slaughter at Mortimer's Cross; and Hasting could not now summon a third of those who shot at the trials on the mere of Longdune. There was now no Kitel of Pendyke with gallant crossbow men; and Bessie was a lone woman with only serving men and hinds to protect the Keep.

Calverley, though now amnestied, was a suspected Lancastrian, and could not venture to keep more men than were actually necessary for the protection of the castle of Branshill. Still, something must be done and, as Sir John Carfax had some archers within a short distance of his keep, I determined to ride over and try to induce him to unite with our men, and to hunt down or drive away these marauding murderers.

I found Sir John standing on the high steps before the entrance of his keep, and with him was Master Marten. The knight was rather confused when I told him my business, and said that all his people were busy haymaking, and there was little doubt the marauders would now go to other parts of their own accord. He nevertheless promised, on my pressing him, to summon together as many men as could be spared; a promise he never fulfilled.

He then proposed that an interview should be sought with the leader of this gang of outlaws and, as had been done in the Forest of Dean in a similar instance, to effect a compromise with the gang and induce them to carry their depredations to a distance by the contribution of monies, to which he and his friend Master Marten would gladly subscribe. As I spurned such ignominious counsel, Sir John renewed his promises of aid with his Castlemereton 'lambs'.

I now despatched Hasting to Calverley to ask him to send what men he could spare, and to enquire at the holstelrie of the Wind's Point for any information that could be given respecting the numbers of these marauders and their movements.

My next plan was to ride over to the farm cottage at Welland, where the murdered farmer now lay dead. I had some difficulty in finding the house, as it lay in a desolate spot bordering upon Welland glade, close to a melancholy swamp through which flows a shallow brook rising in the Malvern hills. As I approached I heard the sounds of lamentation and mourning. Fastening my horse to the paling in front, I rapped and entered, having to bend low to avoid the cross beam.

So dense was the smoke that for some time I could not see, and there were only two small apertures for light, rudely filled with cow-horn. The body lay on a wooden truckle, and the sad wife and her children, with the exception of one neighbour, were alone in their sorrow, performing as they best might, the last sad offices for the dead. The corpse had been robbed of most of the clothing, and even the rough wooden clogs had been taken from the stockingless feet. These poor garments, and a groat, were all the booty the robbers had obtained, and for these they had murdered the young farmer and left desolate his widow and three children.

I sat down by the broken-hearted woman and said what I could to console her, but what are words in tribulation such as this? I gave her what substantial aid I could from the monies I had with me, and bid her to come to Birtsmereton as soon as she had laid her goodman in the grave, that we might give her some help for her poor children. She knew nothing of the perpetrators of the foul deed, but her neighbour had seen a dozen strange men, all armed, cross the trackway from Upton to Ledbury, on the evening of the murder. One was clad in a steel cap or morion, with a thick brown leathern jerkin, and he carried a large mace or bludgeon, while by his side was a big sword.

From her description they appeared to be some of those wandering men-at-arms, who after the late Lancastrian defeats roamed about the country ever ready to plunder and, not unfrequently as in the present instance, to commit the most unprovoked murders, especially when disappointed of booty.

I had heard enough to induce me to ride across the country to Kitel Keep to persuade Bessie in her unprotected condition to come to us at Birtsmereton until such miscreants were punished; which I determined should be the case, even if I applied to King Edward for aid, but this I did not wish to do in the case of a few paltry highwaymen and outlaws.

I rode at a gallop across the green glades and, entering a thick part of the forest near the great elms of Castlemereton, made for the crest of the hill above the meres known as Hill End. Here I encountered a series of sloughs which brought my gallop to a walk, when, at some distance at a cross trackway, I saw Sir John Carfax walking side by side with a tall man clad, as the woman had described, in a steel cap and a thick brown leathern jerkin.

As this was a common dress in these troublous times, when every man had to mind his head with his own hand, I thought little of it, but shouted to them to stop. Instead of doing this, they walked on at a quicker pace and disappeared in a bye path of the forest, so I pursued my way, though I would gladly have told Sir John what I had heard and seen at the farm cottage in the Welland glades.

I found Bessie quite ready to come with me, and we rode back by the monastery of Pendyke and the Underhill of Berew, to let the inhabitants of both places understand that night-hawks were abroad in the Chase, and that they would do well to prepare for emergencies. When Hasting returned, we learnt that Calverley promised the aid of several men-at-arms on hearing from me where to assemble, and that he proposed to ride over on the morrow to consult on the measures to be taken. Hasting had also learnt, from the host at Wind's Point, that a number of armed men had from time to time been seen to cross the pass, and that they generally disappeared in the dense thickets of Newer's Grove. He also heard from Prior Alcock that for a month past the forest below Malvern Abbey about the Rhydd ford had been the haunt of a body of outlaws who had committed numerous depredations of an alarming character.

At one time they robbed a yeoman's grange on the banks of the Severn, and the following week they appeared in the wild distrct through which the Leddon runs, and had there plundered the Bishop of Hereford's seneschal, and sent him home to the palace of Colwall tied to his horse with his face towards the tail, deprived of his purse, his shoon, and his breeches. They appeared to have a kind of policy in their depredations, as they generally spared the property of Yorkists, and harried the homes of any unfortunate Lancastrians. No doubt thereby they hoped to escape the notice of the Crown authorities, who were often too ready to wink at any lawlessness which befel the opposite party.

During my absence from home, in attendance upon the King, my mother had induced Mary Bolingbroke to come from Elsdune to bear her company; but the rumours about the outlaws did not prevent Mary from roaming among her old haunts and seeking those who lived in humble cots among the forest glades, and owed many a cure of 'the rheumatics' and of 'the quavers' or ague shakes, to her pharmacy of herbs.

On my return home, Mary Bolingbroke had intended returning to Elsdune, but she had been induced to stay to meet her friend, the great Worcester herbalist, who came every July to the hostelrie at Wind's Point to gather certain plants in the wild and dense parts of the forest. There was the herb Paris, famous for rheumatism, and toothwort for toothache, and the wood vetch, the seeds of which were a sure remedy against the cholic. None of these grew near Elsdune, or even at the Devil's Garden at Stanner rocks, so Mary wished to take back with her a hoard for winter use. For days together she and the Worcester herbalist had been roving, gathering their much treasured plants among the slopes of the Malverns below Wind's Point.

I was anxiously expecting Calverley, who had not fulfilled his promise of riding over, and Mary had not returned, though far beyond her usual hour, when a small boy came running up to the drawbridge bearing a slip of parchment, which he said "A great man on a big horse" had given him to take to me.

By this missive I was horrified to find that Calverley had been seized by these miscreant outlaws, as he was riding along to our manor by an obscure forest trackway across the Swineyard pass. Calverley was directed to say that, if in three days from the writing of that scrip, five hundred gold Richards were not placed in the Hermit's Cave, and by a single person, without any follower or movement of men-at-arms from the surrounding villages, his decapitated head would be found in the Hermit's Cave, and his body committed to the Severn stream.

He concluded by saying that the heavy fines exacted by the Crown on the reversal of his attainder had left him well-nigh penniless, and asking me if possible to raise the money on loan. Without an hour's delay I sent off Tom of Gulley's End to Windsor, where I knew that Sir Robin of Elsdune was in attendance, to whom I wrote a brief account of the circumstances in which we were placed, and requested him to explain the whole matter to our royal master, and the damage which these miscreants were committing to private property.

The next thing was to consult with my mother about the amount of ready gold we could muster, and we were alarmed to find we had not two hundred rose nobles between us. After the drain of these times of civil war, I knew it was unlikely that Bessie Kitel or John Berew could furnish a hundred gold pieces, so I determined not to alarm them. I thought of pledging some land to Master Marten, when Mary Bolingbroke entered in a high state of terror and excitement produced by the adventures of the day.

She had gone early to the pass of the Wind's Point and after waiting some time in vain for the herbalist, she determined herself to search Newer's Grove for the herb Paris she so much wished to obtain. When there she heard loud shouts for aid, and the sounds of a struggle, as if several men were engaged in rifling some solitary individual. Feeling alarmed, she made at once for the steep slopes of the Malverns above Waum's Well and succeeded in reaching the Hermit's Cave, which tradition says has more than once afforded a night's shelter to both Owen Glendower and Sir John Oldcastle.

Mary had not been long in the cave when she heard persons approaching as if about to enter, and she hid herself underneath some fern heaped up at the back of the cave, and lay there trembling with fear lest she should be detected. Lying still as a mouse. she saw Sir Andrew Trollop enter in deep consultation with Sir John Carfax. She then heard that one hundred outlaws were engaged in different depredations, and that some Lancastrian of importance had fallen into their hands, and Trollop said he owed him an old grudge.

They then discussed the amount of the sum to be fixed upon as ransom. Trollop wished it to be one thousand gold pieces, but Carfax declared that sum could not be found in all the country round, save perhaps in the money-bags of Master Marten. She heard Trollop swear a deep oath that the victim should be slaughtered if the money was not forthcoming at the exact time specified,[3] and he insisted on the necessity of Sir John watching every movement in our neighbourhood and reporting it to him accordingly. At this crisis a bugle horn sounded, and these two precious scoundrels left the cave and disappeared in the depths of Newer's Wood.

I was astounded at this revelation. Trollop, I knew to be capable of any villany, but that our own near neighbour, a belted knight, could stoop to such practices against another knight and neighbour, would have been incredible, but that I knew such things had been done in other parts of England; though they were hitherto unknown in our own remote and peaceful Malvern Chase.

I rejoiced greatly that I had sent Tom of Gulley's End to Windsor, but he might be delayed in many ways, and he might meet with outlaws himself. The King and Robin of Elsdune might be away and some days might elapse before aid could reach us. I could obtain aid from Worcester or Gloucester, but my movements and those of my men were watched, and the slightest indiscretion might hasten the death of my friend. If I roused the immediate neighbourhood we could not find fifty men to contend with a hundred trained soldiers fresh from the battle-field. The only resource left to me was to apply to Master Marten to lend me the money upon our land, and as Sir John Carfax set his men to watch me, I set Hasting and my men to watch him.

A Reconstruction of Kitel Keep

Chapter Fourteen

HASTING volunteered to endeavour to trace the rendezvous of the outlaws and the prison house of Calverley. He preferred to go into the forest alone, with no weapon but his dagger, and clad as a simple woodman. Thoroughly acquainted with the most intricate paths, the bold forester departed for the recesses of Newer's Wood, whistling a tune as if merely in search of a heron or a stag.

I set spies to watch every glade and trackway towards Castlemereton Keep, for any tidings that could be obtained of the movements of Sir John Carfax. The knight was reported to be at home, and had been seen going daily to Master Marten's; while several strange men had been observed going to and from the Keep, and even prowling about the glades; asking questions of the hinds respecting the difierent families in the neighbourhood.

Taking an unfrequented path, I found myself at the little grange of Master Marten. He was in his garden, and the house was covered with roses, ivy, and honesty, which he and his serving-man were tending and entwining among the gables. Everything around was in perfect order with a fine display of flowers in the garden, for Master Marten was a travelled man and had brought seeds and plants from foreign parts, which had never before been seen in all the Chase.

It was not with pleasant feelings that I approached him, as I knew him principally as the friend of Carfax and I had doubts about the terms of the loan. He seemed right glad to see me as I walked across the drawbridge, admiring the taste with which he had turned the little stream to supply his small piscatorium or fishpool, and wondering at the beauty of the flowers.

He told me that Sir John had just departed and had taken great interest in the working of his drawbridge and the new bolts of his entrance door, thinking of having some made of like fashion for his own Keep. He then led me to a chamber admirably fitted up with every modern improvement and placed me in a chair equal to any in King Edward's palace at Windsor, while there were goblets of pure silver upon the tables. He had heard of the presence of the outlaws in the Chase, and the murder of the farmer, and had consulted with Sir John about his defences, when the knight informed him there was no fear, so close as he was to his own Keep and under the protection of his own 'brave lambs'. He was nevertheless much startled when I told him of Calverley's seizure by the outlaws, and the consequences which would follow if the ransom was not sent to the Hermit's Cave by the hour named.

Knowing his intimacy with Carfax, I concealed his conduct in the transaction; but Master Marten at once offered to advance the ransom at his own risk, while he absolutely declined to take usury for monies lent for such a purpose. In short, he acted like a generous gentleman rather than a money-lender. So thanking him heartily, I quaffed his health in a stoup of canary of the richest flavour, far better than any we had in our own cellar.

I had taken my leave and gone a short way on my return, when I remembered what Mary Bolingbroke said about the money-bags, so I went back and entreated Marten to bring his monies and movable valuables to our manor, where he could remain in safety until the Chase was freed from these outlaws. I told him that I had intelligence which convinced me that a man like himself, known to have ready money in an unprotected house, would not be safe, near as he was to Castle-mereton Keep. I cited Calverley as an example, who, crippled though he was, had been seized and carried off within two miles of his own castle. He thanked me, accepted my invitation without hesitation, and by night he and his property were safe within our walls.

This sudden thought was most fortunate, for the same night a band of the outlaws ransacked his premises. They shamefully ill-treated the poor gardener when they found Master Marten was gone, half-roasting him before the fire, which they made in the garden of the oak furniture. I have no doubt the house itself would have been burnt to the ground, but that they knew it was the property of their ally and associate at the Keep.

On my return I found Bessie in a very excited state, for the capture of Calverley had transpired and the poor girl could not conceal her terror. When I told her that Master Marten had promised to advance the ransom, I tbought she would have embraced him, so heartfelt was her gratitude. Still, I determined that paying the ransom should be our last resource. If such a precedent was established, who would be safe in the future? It would be a premium on the worst of crimes. Yet I did not see at present how it was to be avoided, for no one knew whither Calverley had been transported, or the lurkingplace of the outlaws.

Chapter Fourteen

In the vast woodlands which stretched to the forest of Wyre beyond Kidderminster, there were many places where bands of men might lurk for days together, and make forays on private houses at a distance from their regular rendezvous. I therefore looked with anxiety to the exertions of Hasting, hoping to receive some tidings of the place where our friend was hidden.

Another day passed away, and time was becoming precious, but we were indefatigable in strengthening our own defences and arming our own men. The women worked night and day feathering arrows and grinding pike heads on the stone, while my mother and the damsels welted every jerkin with padding, and the smith refurbished every morion.

We were all hard at work when Hasting appeared from his foray and gave me a signal that he wished to speak to me alone. He had found some of the outlaws in the depths of Newer's Wood beyond Waum's Well and, pretending to be a woodman ready to join their band as a recruit, he had actually been enlisted among their numbers, promising to supply all local information as to the best way of attacking Master Marten's, Kitel Keep, and other places not likely to be well defended.

He gradually learnt that Calverley, when dragged from his palfrey at the Swineyard Pass, was blindfolded and taken to a lonely house beyond Cowleigh, where Sir John Carfax met Trollop, who proposed that the unfortunate prisoner should be conducted to Castlemereton Keep. The crafty knight thought, and thought rightly, that no one would suspect he was incarcerated so near to his own castle, and that any rigorous search would be conducted in very different quarters.

The outlaws had settled that a beacon-fire should be lighted on the hill above the Hermit's Cave if the ransom were not forthcoming at the hour named. The signal of smoke ascending was to be the death warrant of the prisoner, to he executed by the band, who were to assemble at the Keep and who would then leave the neighbourhood, at all events for a time, to carry on their depredations elsewhere.

It was now midnight, and twelve o'clock next day was fixed for the surrender of the ransom and the assembling of the outlaws at Castlemereton, with the exception of the band who remained to watch the cave and the pass of the Wind's Point. Was it now possible to avoid this ignominious acquiescence to a set of thieves and robbers led on by the double traitors Trollop and Carfax?

We thought over and weighed well all the circumstances before us, when the bold idea struck Hasting that it was not impossible to turn the tables on Carfax by seizing his Keep with our own men and rescuing Calverley, who was imprisoned there, before the arrival of the outlaws. Carfax would probably be away with the outlaws and, if he was not, we could imprison him in his own dungeon, as he had sent most of his 'lambs' to assist in a night foray against Master Hornpiper's. Once in the Keep we could defend ourselves against Trollop and his men until aid came from Windsor.

We now heard a tap at the door of the antechamber, and found that it was Bessie, who finding that Hasting had returned, could not rest without enquiring if tidings had been heard of Calverley.

It is difficult to say at which we were all most astounded, the knavery and deception of Carfax or the boldness of the outlaws. Calverley in the dungeons of Castlemereton Keep! It seemed impossible. Bessie was half-distracted at the emergency, but she thought that Hasting's plan of seizing the Keep was safer than trusting to the delivery of the ransom at the cave, lest some mishap should occur or Trollop turn treacherous after receiving the monies.

One of my scouts gave a hail at the drawbridge, and we learnt that Sir John had just arrived at Castlemereton, unattended by any of his men or any of the outlaws, so we made our preparations for the expedition as soon as daylight should dawn.

The question was how to persuade Sir John to let down the drawbridge and steps up to the Keep, and we agreed not to show our-selves in any force, as he might be as suspicious as traitors generally are. It was therefore determined that Hasting should take one dozen archers and, proceeding at the back of the meres, come upon the Keep by the thick woods of Castlemereton banks. Forming an ambush close to the fish pools near the Keep, they should rush out on a signal from me and act as circumstances would allow.

I was to walk unattended as if for private consultation with Sir John and to persuade him to come forth, at least as far as his own drawbridge, when I was then to collar him, giving a signal to Hasting with my horn, and to prevent the elevation of the drawbridge when the Keep would be won. Bessie entreated to be allowed to accompany me, saying that Sir John, as a gallant, must come forth to receive a lady, and that she knew exactly where the dungeon door was, in which there was little doubt Calverley was immured. Also it would be important that he should be free to use his limbs when succour came.

In the grey dawn of morning Hasting led our archers by the roundabout paths it was necessary to pursue, and I took the precaution to put my steel cuirass beneath my jerkin, with a cloak to hide my trusty battle-axe; while Bessie bore a bow and a sheaf of arrows as if we were going after a clump of wild ducks in the meres. We set forth when we thought Hasting was in ambush.

It was about eight o'clock in the morning of the first of August that we made our appearance in front of the Keep, and the sun was pouring his rays upon mountain, glade, and forest, and the new tower of the church, but just finished. No scene could look more peaceful or more unlikely to become a scene of slaughter and carnage than around this village church and ancient Norman Keep.

The church bell was going for matins, and here and there villagers might be seen wending their way to prayer, and yet within a few miles, houses and barns had been fired; men killed attempting to defend their hearths and homes; a poor gardener maimed and ill-treated within sight of the church; a farmer murdered for sheer spite and cruelty because he had no monies in his pouch; one of our principal proprietors of land and wealthiest of gentlemen in jeopardy of his life; and two belted knights turned into robbers. Such was the change which civil war and its consequent lawlessness had brought upon our once peaceful Malvern Chase.

Blowing my horn, it was not long before Carfax himself appeared on the summit of the steps. On seeing me alone with Bessie, he at once descended and appeared at the barbican with an aged warder, who proceeded slowly to lower the drawbridge as Carfax smiled and simpered at the appearance of the lady of his love.

No sooner had Sir John met us on the lowered bridge, than, to use the language of baiters, I took the bull by the horns, and seizing him by the collar, I blew a loud bugle blast. I then said, "As a magistrate and officer-at-arms of His Majesty King Edward the Fourth, I here arrest you, Sir John Carfax, for treasonable and unknightly practices against his Majesty's liege subject Sir Roger Calverley, whom, by false and traitorous correspondence with outlaws and robbers, you now hold incarcerated in your Keep of Castlemereton."

The coward looked ready to sink into the earth as I held him fast by his collar, when Bessie rushed past us and snatched the keys from the trembling hands of the ancient warder. She then ran up the steps which led to the entrance doorway, while I held a stern grip upon Sir John, threatening to hurl him headlong into the moat if he stirred or resisted. By this time Hasting and our archers reached the drawbridge, where we bound Sir John's arms and legs, and carried him up the steps into his own stronghold.

As Hasting said, all the men-at-arms save the old warder, were out on the night foray with Trollop, so we hastened to garrison the Keep against their return. Bessie had found her way to the dungeon door, outside of which she was holding a conversation with the imprisoned Calverley, for she could not unlock it; a feat which we soon compelled the warder to perform, releasing our friend, while in his place we safely locked up, tied and bound, the quondam esquire of Margaret of Anjou. Fearing, too, lest he might shout through the single crenelle to the outlaws when they appeared across the moat, we gagged him with his own kerchief.

Calverley was indeed surprised when he learnt that he was imprisoned in Castlemereton Keep, for the outlaws had not released his bonds or taken the bandage from his eyes, until he was shut up in this dark and dismal dungeon. He knew that he was in the hands of the false knight, Trollop, and his myrmidons, but, like ourselves, he had not the remotest suspicion that Carfax was an associate of the robbers. He believed from the long time he was led about bound on horseback, that he was taken to some forest wilds at a distance and would be murdered in cold blood if the ransom named was not placed in the Hermit's Cave as dictated by Trollop.

As the outlaws would probably not assemble at Castlemereton much before mid-day, the time for the surrender of the ransom, we set to work to investigate the resources of the Keep for means of defence. We found strong cross-bows or arblasts, which would throw their bolts two hundred paces with deadly effect from the summit of the Keep and from all the crenelles; many of these arblasts commanded the trackway up to the church.

Our archers we placed opposite the crenelles, and we sent two to the summit, where Calverley, who was well used to this kind of artillery, had Bessie by his side to hand the quarrels, while the archers wound the windlasses. Then he sent her, in a most unromantic manner, to search in the larder for a manchett of bread, as Sir John had not gone near his prisoner himself, or permitted any of his men-at-arms to do so, and he had not tasted food for many hours.

Thus hour after hour passed away, and there was no sign or sound of the presence of armed men. The height of the sun in the heavens told us it was mid-day, when three notes on a bugle horn were heard in the forest trackway leading from Welland, and shortly afterwards a dense smoke arose from the hill above the Hermit's Cave, known as the Herefordshire Beacon; the signal that the ransom was not forthcoming and for the death of Calverley.

The woodlands around the church and keep are so dense on all sides, save up the little dingle on the west leading to Master Marten's and the mill, that we could see no one, although we at last heard the trample of horses in the trackway above the church. In short time Trollop, followed by a dozen riders, rode slowly down the trackway towards the drawbridge. I had ordered every man to remain hidden, and all at the Keep was still as death.

Sir Andrew again blew three loud notes on his bugle horn, but no reply was returned and the drawbridge remained as motionless as ever. He then shouted his war cry, "Trois-loups", and throwing his bridle rein to one of his companions, approached on foot opposite the barbican, immediately above which stood Hasting opposite a crenelle with his deadly bow.

An arrow now struck the traitor in the region of the heart, which must have been fatal but for his armour of proof underneath his jerkin. At the same time I let fly another at his steel helmet, the vizor of which was closed, but this arrow did not rebound, and he rushed back holding his head in his hands, as it had struck between the bars of his vizor and driven out several of his teeth. I now shouted "De Brute to the rescue!"

We were hardly prepared for the number of men the robber knights had mustered under their command for purposes of plunder, for at least two score horsemen rode down the trackway by the church, and there were numerous footmen, among whom were included the Castlemereton 'lambs'. Calverley was busy with the arblasts on the tower and, as every arrow told from the sides of the Keep, men fell fast, while wounded horses galloped to and fro.

The horsemen sought refuge behind the church, where they dismounted and, accompanied by the footmen, surrounded the Keep on all sides. So close were they that their shafts came through every loophole, and it was impossible to look through one without standing a chance of being transfixed. As no one had a shirt of mail but myself, I sent all to the summit of the Keep; two of our men being already wounded.

Many of their footmen had now occupied the thickets on the east side by the fish ponds, while others, climbing on the shoulders of their fellows, surmounted the palisades and walls on the west, though several fell in the attempt, until at last a rush was made from the side of the fish ponds and a few managed to obtain access to the outer court. Arrows against stone walls are of little consequence, and we were well sheltered, while the besiegers evidently began to fear the effect of our deadly archery.

I had gone to the summit of the Keep and was talking to Bessie and Calverley while I wound an arblast, when to our horror an arrow whizzed so close to Bessie's head that it grazed her cheek, and we now saw that Trollop with several bowmen had ascended the church tower, the heights of which commanded the Keep and rendered it dangerous for Bessie to remain there a moment longer. By this time some of the outlaws had brought down timbers and boards to the side of the moat, which they threw in, endeavouring to construct a raft by which they could cross, while Trollop, descending from the church tower, directed their labours, but took care not to expose his precious person more than was necessary.

At last some of the bolder outlaws crossed the moat on a pile of timber, but the steps to the doorway had been drawn within, and they now found that to attempt to enter the Keep was hopeless without they had recourse to fire, and that would be a long and tedious process.

But the scene was soon to change into a very different aspect. The sound of a trumpet was heard at the bottom of the hill below the Keep, and with loud shouts of "Elsdune to the rescue!" a large body of horsemen galloped up the trackway from Birtsmereton. We could now see Trollop running as fast as his legs would carry him up the hill past the church, and in a few minutes there was a general flight among the outlaws, and cries of terror from those who fell beneath the swords and battle-axes of the men-at-arms Robin had brought from Windsor.

Lowering the steps from the Keep, and the drawbridge, our own men also gave chase, and in a few minutes the flight or death of the outlaws was the result. The thief, Trollop, managed to reach his horse and get clear away, while many a braver and better man rolled in the dust. Few of the horsemen ever regained their steeds, but some escaped by flying through the Welland woodlands. The footmen ran for the forest, but some were overtaken and brought in as prisoners by our archers, when Sir Robin gave orders that they should be immediately hung, and suspended from the walls as a terror to like evil doers.

Robin now appeared amongst us with his usual calm demeanour and a hearty greeting for us all. He congratulated Calverley on his happy deliverance, and shook hands with the brave Bessie, whose cheek was still bleeding from the effects of the arrow discharged from the church tower. We now learnt that Tom of Gulley's End had found Robin at Windsor, and he had immediately made King Edward acquainted with the proceedings of the outlaws.

Similar scenes had been enacted in Yorkshire and other parts of the kingdom, so the King determined to put down such lawlessness with a high hand. He therefore despatched Robin, with a considerable force, with orders to extirpate the robbers root and branch. Thus the Archer reached Birtsmereton with two hundred men-at-arms, and on learning that we were at Castlemereton, rode on at once to our assistance.

The sight outside the moat was a sad one for Bessie, as more than a score men lay dead on the trackway, but they richly deserved the fate which they intended for others. We had now to explain to Robin the strange history which compelled us to occupy the Keep in order to rescue our friend Calverley, and the humiliating guilt of Sir John Carfax and his detection by Mary Bolingbroke.

King Edward's orders for the extirpation of the outlaws had been most peremptory, but moved by the tears and entreaties of Bessie, the Archer spared the life of Carfax until he had undergone a regular trial. Had it not been for her beseechings, he would have hung there and then above his own barbican. The miserable wretch came forth from the dungeon cringing and cowering, a more pitiable object than the dead men around him.

Robin deprived him of every token of his knightly rank, and then sent him bound behind a stalwart trooper for the gaol and dungeons at Worcester, where he is said to have died in a few months from gaol fever. The Keep was filled with property which this man had received as the confederate of outlaws and brigands. Since that time we have had isolated instances of robberies and even murder, but no band of outlaws has ever again ventured to assemble in our Malvern Chase.

Robin begged of Calverley or myself to take Bessie away, as these scenes had well-nigh proved too much for her. I thought it a good opportunity to leave them to their own explanations, so offered to remain and assist in making arrangements for the burial of the dead and in manning the Keep with the troops who were now to hold it in the name of the King. Robin also arranged for masses to be said for the souls of those who had fallen, and Master Marten was liberal in his donations for this purpose. He offered, too, to take the old warder and provide for him, as he could water his flowers and let down the little drawbridge until the end of his days.

We met that evening around the supper table with grateful hearts, and in very different mood to that in which we assembled the previous day. Calverley had left for Branshill Castle before my return to reassure his mother by his presence, but there was something about Bessie's face and manner which told me, without a word of explanation, that all estrangement had passed away, and that he had said to her those words which an honourable man tells to the girl he loves; the more especially if he thinks that love is returned.

The time arrived when we had to return to Court, so, leaving my mother to superintend our home matters, and entreating Mary Bolingbroke to remain as her friend and companion, while Calverley and Bessie both promised to attend to her welfare, I proceeded with Robin to Windsor to rejoin our corps of Archers of the Guard.

We found that the Court had removed from Windsor to the Tower of London, and we passed through some strange scenes before we reached our destination.

No place in the world can be more unlike our forest homes and our Malvern Hills and Chase than the Strand in the city of London. The narrow streets of houses, mostly of wood and wattle, have holes in them, which are dangerous for a horse or a foot passenger. Then there are numberless booths with pert 'prentices standing at the doors shouting, "Cock pie, hot trotters, fresh chitterlings, hog's puddings, hot peascods, and boiled beef!" while vielles groaned, pipes whistled, and harps twanged before the hostelries and public buildings.

Now and then, as we rode past an entry, we caught a sight of the river Thames, covered with boats and barges; and down the streets rode horsemen, some in armour, others in leathern jerkins and steel-morions. Even the foot passengers were armed, and all the merchants walking forth on their daily business were followed by armed servitors.

Riding slowly, Robin led the way by narrow, noisome city lanes to the magnificent Tower of London, where has happened so many an event in the history of our kings, and queens, and nobles. The royal banner floated over the great White Tower of the Normans, and painted barges, filled with barons, knights, and noble dames, swept down the river to the gate of St Thomas. Other courtiers were pacing up and down the great courtyard, dressed in court corsets and supertunics, waiting for audience and the royal summons of the King or Queen. It took us some time to see to the stabling and care of our horses, and dress ourselves in Court costume, before we faced the impertinent pages, who were to conduct us to the presence of royalty.

The King was in the great hall, surrounded by his officers of state, such as the Earl of Warwick, and Lords Mantague and Hastings. He received us with that frank and courteous manner which made him so popular, and was so different from the shuffling, weak address of Henry of Lancaster, or the proud bearing of Margaret of Anjou. He questioned us closely respecting the raids of the outlaws on Malvern Chase and denounced the conduct of such knights as Carfax and Trollop as a curse to the people and dangerous to the crown.

But the truth was that at this period the feudal barons were nearly as lawless and cruel as those of the time of King Stephen, and it was King Edward who changed the character of the nobility, by introducing those who had risen to wealth by trade and commerce, thus destroying the influence and pride of hereditary and needy lords and knights. Times had changed, and, instead of reviewing troops or drilling archers, Robin was made Groom of the King's own chamber, and had the high honour of attending on his person, as well as to the decorations ot his bed-room.[1]

As personal esquires of his Majesty, we were presented to the Queen, who received us with that studied supercilious manner which she mistook for dignity; a manner she wore through life, and ever made her unpopular and disliked. By her side was her mother, Jacquetta, Duchess of Bedford, soon to be the talk of England as a 'parlous witch'. This lady hardly vouchsafed to recognise me, so much was she taken up with a dirty friar, whom I was told was Friar Bungay, the great necromancer. It was Friar Bungay who, in after years, was said to conjure up the dense fog on the day of the battle of Barnet, and which resulted in so great a victory for King Edward.

My sojourn at this period of my life at the Court gave me the opportunity of seeing much of London and its noblest buildings. In the noble Abbey of Westminster, which is finer far than are those of Theocsbury or Gloucester, I have stood by the tombs of Edward the Confessor and those of the Plantagenet Kings. I visited the Cathedral of St Paul's, where John of Gaunt, the Duke of Lancaster, protected Master Wycliffe from the Bishops, and told them he would humble their own pride. I visited too the Lollard's Tower at Lambeth, where so many a wretch who believed as I and my father believed, was imprisoned for heresy. And there, on the bare stone walls, are carved the names and devices of some of the victims, and the rings by which they were chained, as if they were howling wild beasts of prey.

But nothing in all London astonished me more than the elevation and power of the great Earl of Warwick, to whose mansion I was often sent on business or messages of courtesy. Warwick House was as much guarded by men-at-arms as the Tower itself. Indeed, the retainers who frequented the court-yard and guarded the approaches to the mansion consumed six oxen every morning for breakfast.

My children were to live in times when retainers were not allowed to the nobility of England, and the Earl of Oxford was fined[2] ten thousand pounds for assembling a number of men in liveries to do honour to King Henry VII. What would they think of the power of that Baron, afterwards termed 'the King-Maker', the last of the great barons of these times, who maintained thirty thousand retainers at his different castles.

The Earl of Warwick never forgot our meeting at his castle of Hanley, and ever said "Welcome" when I sought his presence. With all his hospitality to his friends and retainers, he appeared to me to be simple in his dress and tastes, nor was the furniture of his London residence so rich as might have been expected. He seldom wore velvets and satins even at Court, and he never looked like a popinjay or an overdressed woman, which many courtiers did. His stately figure, almost as tall and stout as that of King Edward, was always clad with some mark of the warrior, in polished steel inlaid with gold, sometimes as a placcard, sometimes as a cuirass, which sparkled beneath a surcoat.

Clerkly learned he was not, for his writing was somewhat like Bessie Kitel's signature before she took lessons with the grey goose quill, and though he had writings on the laws by Sir John Fortescue, I never saw him reading them. He never failed, though, to question me about the condition of the people; the complaints of the Lollards; the work done by the lower clergy, who had much sympathy with the common people; and the possibility of granting greater freedom to the oppressed classes. But with all this it was evident that the Earl of Warwick would support the Barons and the feudal system.

Towards the close of 1464 came the coronation of the Queen, and her uncle the Duke of Luxemburg arrived In England with a retinue of one hundred knights and esquires to do honour to the coronation of his niece. Still, the Countess of Warwick and some of the other great ladies kept aloof, and offence was taken by the Queen's party.

Already I was becoming heartily tired of a Court life, and longed to find myself back in our woodlands among those I loved, instead of being surrounded with dames and damosels in brocaded skirts, satin sacques, and silk modes, or by courtiers 'lithping and piping' like a sick girl with the measles. I longed, too, to look upon a modest face, instead of being stared out of countenance by some Court dame, whose character was more flimsy than her bodice, and who never spoke a kind word for an absent friend.

It is impossible to describe the magnificence af the coronation feasts, tournaments, and public rejoicings, and the King commenced his future policy of encouraging trade and commerce by making four of the London tradesmen and citizens Knights of the Bath, which excited much sneering and discontent among the Lords, who called them 'Knights of the Tub'. Neither shall I attempt to describe the marvellous rich dresses worn by the Court dames and gentlemen on this occasion. One appeared to vie with another in extravagance of ornament and attire.

But the sight in the Abbey of Westminster was very magnificent, as the gorgeous throng of nobles, knights, and beautiful ladies assembled around her whom the King had raised from the condition of a knight's daughter to the proud eminence of Queen of England. Show and ornament were displayed even in the platters upon the tables and the food thereon; but the Court cooks thought overmuch of the finery and the rarity, rather than of the wholesome character of the provisions.

Fried porpoises there were, with stewed seals and sturgeon,³ but none of these can be rendered good eating by tinsel and glitter, and more than once, when seated opposite to a porpoise, I wished for one of our larded capons at Birtsmereton.

I was ever accustomed to look upon hunting and hawking and such like sports as manly exercises, requiring some nerve and skill, so I was little prepared, when in attendance on the Queen at a great hunt in the parks at Windsor, to see the sport of venery reduced to a contemptible pastime, if pastime it could be called. The stags and other wild animals were driven by a great concourse of people into paled enclosures, where sheds were erected from whence lords and knights, bishops and abbots, all clad in hunter's gear, shot them down with their arrows, and thus avoided any labour or risk in the chase.

I looked upon the whole matter with contempt, and so did the noble Earl of Warwick, for he said, "Pardieu, Sir Hildebrande, but this is sport for women, not for men. What think you? Can you yet show us a stag of ten in the Chase of Malvern, or have you a wild boar left amidst the thickets? I should like right well some day, to bring my Countess to her Castle of Hanley, and see a stag hunt from the crests of your hills."

All now seemed settled and peaceful, and the King and Queen appeared to be on excellent terms with the powerful family of the Nevilles. Nevertheless, my position as equerry to the Queen gave me opportunities of observing that jealousies would arise from the relations of her Majesty being ravenous for titles, rich wives, and places at Court.

Her father was now created Earl Rivers, and made Treasurer; and then the Queen affianced the heiress of the Duke of Exeter to her own son, Thomas Gray, which gave offence to the Earl of Warwick, who wanted the heiress tor his nephew. Her brother, John Widville, married the old Duchess of Northumberland at the age of eighty-two, a most scandalous match.

In short, Queen Elizabeth's Court was full of selfish family intrigues, and I hated it most heartily; the more especially as King Edward gave up all personal attention to warlike pursuits, and occupied himself in the pursuit of pleasures. Matters went from bad to worse, and the matchmaking and match-breaking continued until five of the unmarried sisters of the Queen were mated to the heirs of dukes and earls.

In the year of grace 1461 the Earl of Warwick went to France to negotiate the alliance of Edward's sister, Margaret of York, with one of the sons of Louis XI of France, and considered himself grossly insulted when the King allowed his sister to accept the proposals of the Count of Charolois. Neither could he tolerate the abridgment of his influence at Court, while King Edward detested the interference of this great Baron who had placed him on the throne.

During all this time my heart was sore at receiving no tidings of Rosamond Berew. For a year or two she sent an occasional letter enclosed with others from Master Vaughan to his tenants at Hergest. In these she expressed hopes of a speedy return and her sorrow at being so long absent from her home and those she loved. It was evident that the letters were written under the superintendence of others, and that she was not allowed to say where they were written from. At last they ceased altogether, and for a long period I knew nothing of her welfare, or indeed if she was still among the living. Once only she alluded to the Countess of Oxford, and this allusion had been partially erased.

In the mean time the Duke of Clarence, King Edward's next brother and heir to the throne – for as yet the Queen had no son by Edward – fell in love with the Lady Isabella, the beautiful daughter of the 'stout' Earl of Warwick, who once more presented himself at Court, where he was hailed with great enthusiasm by the common people.

The King and Queen did all in their power to prevent this marriage, but to no purpose, for the Duke of Clarence was married to the Lady Isabella at Calais, in the month of July 1469, and this marriage was the cause of extraordinary events and circumstances which shook the throne of Edward to its very base, and brought about some strange adventures in my own existence.

The Black Bear, Warwick

Chapter Fifteen

GREAT CHANGES had taken place since Rosamond went away with Master Vaughan and the Countess of Oxford, owing to King Edward resuming all grants made by the Lancastrian kings; 'pretensed kings', as they are styled in the first act of King Edward's Parliament.

He now transferred many lands, privileges, and offices to his own supporters, and numerous Lancastrians forfeited their properties. Castlemereton Keep was transferred to Robin of Elsdune; I received sundry grants of land to be enclosed from the forest, and, through our entreaties, Branshill Castle was saved to Calverley, but with a diminished estate. He had married Bessie Kitel, and they were leading happy useful lives.

But all were not so fortunate as Calverley, for the same year 1469 in which the Duke of Clarence married the Lady Isabella Neville, I received a commission from the Parliament to visit Sudeley Castle and Winchcombe, and report upon its condition and the general state of the Manor of Sudeley. I therefore gladly took the opportunity of re-visiting the old home below the Malverns, and consulted with my mother as to what steps it was possible to take to find out what had become of Rosamond Berew, for nothing more could be learned from Hergest save that Master Vaughan was still beyond the seas.

The very day before I started from home on the Sudeley commission, Sir Roger Calverley rode over, as he wished to consult me with respect to a letter which he had received, signed by Master Vaughan's own hand and sealed with his own seal. This letter, sent from Hergest, called upon him to 'render every assistance in his power at a rising of the Lancastrian party, which would shortly take place, and when thousands of Englishmen would rally round the standard of King Henry, their lawful and right righteous King'.

But Calverley had accepted King Edward's amnesty, had pledged his word not to foster rebellion, and had been allowed to retain his Castle. He was not a likely man to commit a breach of good faith, and would join in no conspiracies against the House of York. He wished, too, particularly to show me the letter of Rosamond's uncle, for in it the name of Sir Andrew Trollop occurred as one of the principal leaders and promoters of this rebellion. Thus this worthy, after his escape from

Castlemereton, when he endeavoured to plunder a Lancastrian, had gone round again to the Lancastrian party, and thus completed the circle of treachery.

The messenger who brought the epistle from Ledbury to Branshill Castle declared that he was paid to deliver it into Sir Roger's own hands by a dark-visaged knight or gentleman, fully armed, who rode at the head of a score of Welshmen, who drank gallons of small beer, and could not speak a word of English. This was no doubt Master Vaughan.

It was evident that he had returned to England, and was engaged in some wild scheme of rebellion, but to me the great question was, what had he done with his niece? Had he brought her to Hergest while engaged on this hazardous project? This was hardly likely but, happen what would, I must see him and learn the history of her whose loss I had now mourned for years. When I had attended to the commission on which I was sent by the Court, Master Vaughan should account to me for his abstraction of my affianced wife.

Attended by Hasting and Tom, I started for Sudeley Castle on a bright July morning. We were all well armed, and our way led us through the town of Theocsbury. We crossed the Severn at the Lower Lode, and rode past the Castle of Hamme[1] or, as some call it, Holme Castle, which occupies the rising ground above the Swilgate stream, and faces the Abbey.

Hamme Castle is a very ancient one, having been built in the days of William the Norman, and was the principal residence of the first Earl of Gloucester, the natural son of Henry I. It was often the residence of the de Clares and Despensers, and it was the Lady Constance Despenser – the widow of that Earl of Gloucester who was executed at Bristol by Henry IV for his fidelity to King Richard – who set free Mortimer, the young Earl of March, and his brother from their imprisonment at Windsor, in the year of grace 1405.

Although the great estates of the Despensers had passed away to the Beauchamps on the marriage of Isabel in 1411, Hamme Castle was occupied in these days by a widow of her cousin-german, an elderly Dame Despenser, who lived in great seclusion. This lady we now met walking up the rising ground towards the new Park[2], from the town, and she beckoned to me as if she wished to speak to me. I dismounted, and she told me that there was great disaffection to the House of York in and around Theocsbury, and that well-known Lancastrians, such as

Sir Gervais Clifton, with Master John Throgmorton and others, had been lately seen in the town, and had been heard talking treason against King Edward. It was then agreed that I should return to Hamme Castle after my survey of Sudeley Castle, and remain a few days with Dame Despenser, in order that I might ascertain to what height this disaffection to the Crown was likely to be carried.

On our arrival at the south entrance to the town, we found a concourse of people opposite the Abbey gateway, and others assembled in the new bowling-green Playing at closhes and tennis[3], both of which games had been prohibited by the King, as interfering with the practice of archery. This prohibition was very unpopular, and instead of being greeted with courteous salutations, as we rode through the streets, I and my followers, who wore King Edward's cognizance, met only with averted faces and scowling looks. Nay, some at the Bull Ring ventured to hiss, but Hasting had ever a mortal antipathy to the sounds of geese or snakes, and it was dangerous to hiss in his presence.

Nearly opposite the Cross in the centre of the town is the Tolsey; a noble structure of wood, in the midst of a number of poor dwellings of wattle and clay. The upper stories are fine gables projecting over the lower, and the chamber where the merchants meet is a room of great size. There are several good merchants' houses in Theocsbury, for they make much money by their mustard, their wool hosen, and their corn and cider, which they send in boats both up and down the Severn. At the Tolsey, we passed Master Payne, who was known to be disaffected towards King Edward, and, although he saluted me as I rode past, was evidently expatiating with great warmth to some Theocsbury scriveners.

A sharp gallop took us into the wild open country between Winchcombe and Theocsbury, for the most part destitute of trees, but covered with gorse and thickets about Gretton. Soon we reached the famous abbey and town of Winchcombe, situated under the Cotswold range and the seat of a mitred abbot. Here Offa, King of Mercia, built a nunnery, but on the misbehaviour of the nuns, Kenulph, King of Mercia, built an abbey for three hundred monks. Here, too, came Henry III, when such was the grandeur of the festivals that Matthew Paris says 'he fears to describe it, lest he should be accused of being a liar'. The abbey and monastic buildings are very grand, and well worthy of their high repute. We found Abbot William Winchcombe surrounded by workmen who were building a fine large church for the use of the parish, to the west of the abbey itself[4].

The Abbot was noted for his hospitality, and good care was taken of both riders and their steeds, while I still have remembrance of a pasty of lampreys for which the monks of Winchcombe are famous, and with which they console themselves on the strictest fasts[5]. This pasty, washed down with good red Burgundy, is a dish for a king.

The Castle of Sudeley stands well above Winchcombe and the stream which runs through it, and I could not but admire the size and grandeur of the buildings erected by Lord Boteler, especially the Portmare Tower, so called from the French Admiral whom he took prisoner. It was melancholy, too, to think that this old warrior, who served King Henry V in his wars in France with twenty men-at-arms and sixty archers on horseback, could not remain quiet, but must hatch plots against the King.

Ralph Boteler, Lord of Sudeley, had been a famous soldier, and also an admiral on the sea. He pulled down the old castle, which was built in the time of King Stephen, and erected one of great magnificence in its place with the money he obtained from the spoils of war. At the same time he was a bitter Lancastrian, and fought at St Alban's against Richard Duke of York in the Wars of the Roses. During the first years of King Edward's reign, the Lord of Sudeley had not been interfered with, but he was suspected by the King of treasonable designs – indeed, there was no doubt that he tampered with malcontents; so it was determined by the Council to seize his manor of Sudeley, and to transfer it to the King's brother, Richard Duke of Gloucester.

Having acquainted Abbot Winchcombe with my commission, and told him how I had been sent to report upon the condition of the Castle and the surrounding lands, he offered to accompany me over the domain, which he said was a place well fitted for the residence of a royal Prince. Lord Boteler had gone to London, where he was summoned before the King, and we found only a few domestics in charge of the Castle. It is, indeed, a noble estate. There is a large park filled with stalwart oaks and elms, and a lake well stocked with fish, while every sort of improvement is displayed in the apartments.

We were taking our survey of the fine buildings and standing in the court-yard, when three armed men, who from their dress were evidently knights, descended quickly down the steps from the doorway of the Portmare Tower. They were followed by a black boar-hound, which seemed to me like the celebrated hound of Hergest. They quickly disappeared through the various courts, and the Abbot like myself wondered who they could be.

On enquiry from the warder and domestics all we could learn was that these knights had come with letters and keys of Lord Boteler's, and had been engaged for some hours in examining parchments in the Portmare Tower. One of them, however, in the hurry of departure, had left a riding thong of peculiar make, and this I recognized as belonging to Master Vaughan. The hospitable Abbot would have received us for the night, but I thought it would be as well to know more of the Lancastrian manifestations about Theocsbury, so we received the Abbot's blessing and set forth upon our return.

On the summit of the rising ground which descends towards the village of Gretton, we saw in front of us the knights I had noticed leaving the Portmare Tower, and with them were at least a score of riders with spears erect. I determined to diverge from the trackway, and, taking a somewhat more circuitous route, to gallop into Theocsbury before they reached it. Nevertheless, as we arrived at the entrance known as Barton Street, we found the clump of spears were before us, so I begged of Hasting to ride on and see whither they were bound, and, if possible, to ascertain who they were.

Near the Cross at Theocsbury is a fine new hostelrie with the tabard of the de Guyse, and their device of the Swan, and at this hostelrie the men-at-arms halted, but apparently for a short time only, as they called for manchetts of bread and flagons of ale without dismounting.

Hasting was seated on his horse, calmly looking on at a crowd of people in a great state of excitement and shouting "Down with all tyrants!" but who the tyrants were we were left to imagine. As I rode forward Hasting held up his hand, as if in caution, and coming to my side said, "The Earl of Pembroke whom we beat at Mortimer's Cross, and that false knight Sir Andrew Trollop."

The whole party now rode away amidst the shouts of "Long live King Henry!" This was rank treason, and I was just in time to recognize the saturnine features of the traitor Trollop. My first thought was to follow them, but our horses were tired, and we were but three against a score, so we rode quietly through a scowling mob to the Black Bear of Warwick.

Here I learned from the host that within the last few days several hundred troops had ridden northwards up the hill by the Mythe Twt and the Keep said to have been inhabited by King John, when he was Earl of Gloucester, and built the long bridge across the Avon[6]. Leaving our steeds under the care of Tom of Gulley's End, Hasting and I now wended our way to Hamme Castle.

This once powerful stronghold has become much dilapidated, and since the manor passed away from the Despensers to the Beauchamps has been suffered to fall into decay.[7] In former days numerous were the great men and high-born dames who assembled within its walls, but now all was cold and comfortless.

The walls are of vast thickness, and the stairs are of stone, as indeed are the roofs of the chambers. The widowed Dame Despenser lived there upon no great means, with a few worn-out serving men and some Theocsbury wenches, who seemed but a mockery among chambers that had been often occupied by kings, and among mouldering turrets which, could they have spoken, would have re-echoed the war cry of some of the noblest barons in England's history.

Still the Dame Despenser kept as much state as her circumstances would allow, and we were received in due form by a hoary-headed chamberlain before we were ushered into her presence. The lady was of most dignified demeanour, and with somewhat of pride of lineage.

A most bountiful supper was laid in the King's Chamber, and as I led her to the dais she gave me an account of the royal visits at Hamme Castle, and how King Henry III had banqueted in the King's Chamber on his return from Hailes Abbey. We were regaled with beef and the mustard for which Theocsbury housewives are held in repute, and with tankards of the famous cider of Styre. Here, too, were jorams of the lesser lamprey, a most savoury dish stewed in cider with a sprig of rosemary and cloves. With these was a noble salmon, fresh from the Severn's wave, with souse and a roasted lamb.

Dame Despenser was pleased to enquire as to my experiences of the Court of King Edward, and to allude much to the services rendered to the house of Mortimer by 'the Lady Constance of blessed memory'. She enquired, too, respecting that delicate subject, namely, the bruited witchcrafts and necromancies attributed to the Queen's mother, the Duchess of Bedford, and before I could reply, she gave us a full and true account of the history of the noted Witch of Eldersfield.

She had herself received the information from Master Payne, who had heard it from the monk, Father Bore, and he had it from the Abbot of Theocsbury's own serving man, who accompanied his master to Gloucester when the ecclesiastical commission was summoned in the chapter house to examine into the sorceries of this witch. And the good Dame's voice dropped to a whisper as she described "how it was supposed that Master Snakes had met the witch, when tracking her in the old crypt of the Abbey of Llanthony, and that she had fled at him, throttled him, and sucked his blood."

"It was known that he went forth in search of her, and he was found bloodless, and with all the appearance of having died a death of terror. The witch herself had never been seen since in human form, but a big black cat still frequented the woods of Eldersfield, and howled and caterwauled the live long night."

Having listened to this veracious account, I proposed retiring to rest, and we were conducted to the chambers which were once occupied by King John, and that which was the favourite domicile of the Red Earl and the Princess Joan d'Acre when they visited Hamme Castle. Verily in those days lords and ladies cared far less for creature comforts than we, who are not satisfied if the rushes in our chambers are not changed every other day, and must have our wine cups handed to us after we are in bed. The tapestry with which the walls of these chambers were hung was mouldy with age, and it was difficult to tell which was Noah and which was Pharaoh's daughter in the designs said to have been worked by Eleanor de Clare. The beds wanted stuffing with fresh bed straw, and the furniture was of the most antique character.

We had not undressed when there was a noise at the barbican, and then a trampling of feet and unbarring of doors, from which it was evident there was some unexpected arrival since we left the supper-room. In a short time a serving man came to my door to say that Dame Despenser would be glad if I would go below stairs.

I lost no time in complying with the request, when to my surprise I saw the Queen's father, Earl Rivers, resting against the splay of the window, looking worn and anxious, and covered with mire. He was relating to the good Dame how he was dying for his life, having escaped from a most disastrous battle, fought near Banbury, in which the forces of King Edward had been surprised by a great rising on the side of the Lancastrians, and were utterly routed.

The victorious army was in full pursuit of the fugitives, and he quite expected the result would be the overthrow of the King and the restoration of Henry of Lancaster. He said, also, that he narrowly escaped at Worcester falling into the hands of Jasper Tudor and Sir Andrew Trollop, who were on their road to Northampton. Jasper Tudor had gone north, but Trollop had returned south, and might be expected at Theocsbury any moment, whither several like himself had already fled. Among the fugitives were the Earl of Devon and his own son John Widville, who had married the ancient Duchess of Northumberland.

We had now to consider not only what to do to shelter Lord Rivers, but what course to take ourselves. Theocsbury was no safe place for Yorkists in such an emergency, as I had learned from the events of the previous evening and the conduct of the rabble, ever ready to hound on the bloodhounds of war on the losing side. Hamme Castle, too, would be the first place the Lancastrians would search, for the Despensers ever favoured the White Rose and the House of York and Mortimer.

After a brief consultation we determined to leave the Castle, although it was in the dead of night, and go to the Black Bear of Warwick, to mount our horses and escape for our lives, none of which were worth a moment's purchase if we fell into the hands of Trollop and his men-at-arms. As we passed down to the street we met other fugitives, some hurrying towards the sanctuary of the Abbey, and others to the little church in St Mary's Lane, both of which the Lancastrians might be expected to consider as sacred, and as yet the sacredness of such refuges had been broken by neither party,

It was not until we reached the Black Bear that I learnt from Lord Rivers the full account of the total rout of the royal army at Edgecote under the command of Sir Richard Herbert, who had been made Earl of Pembroke in place of Jasper Tudor, when Tudor was proscribed by the Yorkists. The Lancastrian army was commanded by Lord Fitzhugh, Sir John Conyers, and Robert Hulden, and were now in pursuit, determined on slaughter and revenge.

It was no easy matter to arouse the household at the Black Bear, or Master Tom of Gulley's End from his couch. It was necessary, too, to obtain refreshment for Lord Rivers, as we had left Hamme Castle too hurriedly to allow of his partaking any there. We also feared that some of the Lancastrian army would soon arrive at the hostelrie. Hasting in

Chapter Fifteen

the mean time had informed Tom of the strait we, as well as Lord Rivers, were in. The horses were at the door when Tom came to me and said he knew of a sure and safe refuge, within a short distance, and where a man might remain a month with little chance of detection.

This was at his cousin's house in the parish of Fordington,[8] a wild and desolate spot known as Slop's Hole, on the borders of the forest towards Chaceley. I knew the place from hunting, and a more secluded place for refuge it was impossible to fix on. Surrounded on the south and west by morasses, the only approach was from the north, and this was by a forest path, deep in winter time with slush and mud, and at the bottom of which was a small grange protected by moat and drawbridge.

I quite agreed with our horsekeeper that this would be a good place to conduct Lord Rivers, at least for a time, until we could make farther arrangements for his safety. Lord Rivers now mounted his worn and tired steed, and we rode unmolested through the streets, though the people had begun to stir through the flocking in of fugitive Yorkists, and crossed the Severn at the Fordington Ferry. Here I paid the ferryman to cut the rope of his boat and let it drift down the river, while he promised that it should take at least two days to recover it.

Having seen Lord Rivers safe at Slop's Hole, and promising to return before long, we rode rapidly homewards, as I was most anxious to put our manor-house in the best state of defence possible, knowing that if Trollop had but time and opportunity, nothing would delight him so much as burning our home above our heads.

The sun was just rising on a beautiful August morning as we rode by Swinley Green and its great oaks and up the steep hill on which rises Kitel Keep on one side and the church of Pendyke on the other. All looked as secure and peaceful as in days of yore, when we hunted the stag in the forest, or flushed a bittern in the mere of Pendyke. The Malverns gleamed with a ruddy glow and the grey towers of the village churches peered from the trees by the side of our homesteads.

But the curse of civil war was again amongst us, and a man in my position, who had been active in the service of the King, could not lie down at night without feeling that before morning he might be attacked by some marauding band, who called themselves followers of King Henry, in search of rebels and malcontents. It was therefore with great joy that I found on my return that Robin of Elsdune had arrived at Castlemereton from Nottingham.

He was sent by King Edward with the hopes of again raising troops who would flock to his standard as they did before the battle of Mortimer's Cross, now nine years ago. Then I learnt that, after the terrible defeat at Edgecote, the King had advanced at the head of some troops as far as Nottingham, but his army was weak and depressed, so the King sought refuge in the strong castle of Nottingham, from whence he had despatched a letter to Calais, beseeching his brother the Duke of Clarence and the Earl of Warwick to come to his assistance. This letter reached Calais just after the Earl of Warwick's brother, the Archbishop of York, had married the Duke of Clarence to the beautiful Lady Isabella Neville, the great Earl's daughter.

With regard to raising troops in our neighbourhood, circumstances were altogether altered. King Edward had been several years upon the throne, but nothing had been said or done for those who followed the Lollard's faith. The stout Earl Warwick, too, was now the popular idol, and his name as a redresser of wrongs was in every man's mouth. But Lord Warwick had his ambitious views; and his devices for advancing the power of his own family were as deeply laid as those of the Widvilles.

Yet, although it would not have been easy to raise troops to battle for King Edward's crown, we could ever rally aid for the defence of our own homes and hearths from any sudden raid. Robin and I had taken good care that our own hinds were well practised in the use of the bow and the pike. The Birts Street and Rye Green archers were the best cross-bow men in the country, and they would join us at an hour's notice. We were also a long way from the great trackways by which troops were moved, so that it was unlikely that Trollop could bring large forces to attack us, until the Lancastrian successes were much more developed.

We now arranged to place watchers in all the villages round, so that a line of communication could be kept up day and night as long as the danger lasted. All was quiet for two or three days, so I felt more assured for the safety of my beloved ones at home, and it was agreed that I should ride to the ferry at the Lower Lode to reconnoitre, and also enquire at Slop's Hole after the welfare of Lord Rivers. As yet we had not heard of any Lancastrian forays on our side the Severn.

At the Lower Lode ferry I found the Abbot of Theocsbury, Abbot Strensham, who had passed the previous night at his Court house at

Fordington, which he generally made his summer's residence, and from him I learnt that Theocsbury was being well searched by the victorious Lancastrians for all fugitive Yorkists, that several had been taken and sent as prisoners to Banbury, others were executed on the spot.

The good Abbot was most sorrowful at the apparently endless bloodshed of these civil wars. He was too simple-minded to enter much into politics and questions of inheritance, and too good not to feel bitterly the loss of valuable lives on both sides of the contending parties.

When I rode up he was waiting for the ferry boat, and received me with that hearty manner and genial kindness for which he was remarkable. Abbot Strensham was not one of those priests who love to exhibit themselves in fine garments of velvet and spangles, but his dress indicated his clerical profession, and he looked like an English gentleman as well as an ecclesiastic.

He was not rich in this world's goods, for he was generous beyond his income and had poor relations whom he did not think it right and manly to ignore. With this he had commenced buildings and restorations of great cost within the Abbey, but which he was not destined to see completed. But his heart was in the work, and it was pleasant to see him wandering among the tombs of the barons, watching the workmen, or giving information to some stranger on the age of the tower or nave, or some mortuary chapel raised to the memory of the dead.

Few were so full of historic lore as Abbot Strensham, and he could descant on themes of which the generality of the clergy, as a rule, are profoundly ignorant, they being usually occupied upon questions of dress and postures, ceremonial processions, gluttony feasts, and such like pageantries. He was talking cheerily, as was his wont, to the ferryman's wife, and telling her about the swallows as they flitted to and fro across the waters, or the martens as they fled chirruping from their nests below the eaves of the ferryman's hut; and how in the autumn they would take their flight to more sunny climes.

On my enquiring what news there was from Theocsbury, he pointed to the Lancastrian banner which now waved just below the lofty spire which rose proudly from the Norman tower[9] and said that he was anxious to cross over as soon as possible, to see that the sanctuaries were not invaded or profaned. The ferryman, it seems, had gone after his 'elver putchins',[10] and the boat had not returned.

I was standing conversing with the Abbot beneath the shade of some great oaks, when Sir Andrew Trollop rode up to the opposite side, accompanied by a score of armed riders. They tried the ford above the ferry, but the water was too high with the August rains. He then shouted for the ferry-boat, and raved at the ferryman's wife, who could only point down the river in the direction of the absent boat. He now shouted the words "Slop's Hole!" and asked where was the next ford. The ferry woman pointed up the river, and he galloped off, accompanied by his men.

Hearing the words Slop's Hole thus shouted across the river, I felt sure that Trollop had discovered the locality where Lord Rivers was hiding, and was even now endeavouring to cross the Severn to arrest him. Bidding a hasty adieu to the good Abbot, I sent a lad from the ferryman's hut with a message to Hasting and Robin that a troop of Lancastrians were crossing the river, and then rode as hard as I could for the retreat of the Queen's father.

We had little time for explanations, and to make matters worse, Lord Rivers' horse was dead lame. The honest franklin recognizing me, at once offered the use of his own steed, and there was nothing to be done but accept it. I begged of him in the mean time to lose no time in taking the nearest forest path to Birtsmereton, as Trollop would most likely hang him when he found Lord Rivers had escaped. Fortunately he was a bachelor, and had only a couple of hinds about the premises whom he could take with him, so he consented to follow my advice.

He had a singular way, too, of impressing Slop's Hole upon the memory of Lancastrians, and one which some of them will remember to their dying day. Before fastening the door he shut up every crevice in the little ante-chamber, and taking a hive of bees from the stool below the eaves of the dwelling, he upset them in the middle of the room, retiring precipitately himself. Having done this he smiled grimly and disappeared in the forest among the Swinley glades, followed by his serving men.

Trusting to my knowledge of the forest rides by Cors Hill, I thought it would be easy for us to escape to Gloucester, where we could obtain shelter until this Lancastrian storm had passed by, so I struck off by an intricate horse track, and followed by Lord River, rode for the woodlands of Cors, avoiding the trackway, which, as long ago as the times of the Romans, led from Gloucester to Upocessa, now Upton.

Alas! we soon found that the franklin's steed was 'as slow as a badger', and that it was impossible to ride beyond a slow trot. Still, I hoped, notwithstanding this serious drawback, that it would be impossible for any one not well accustomed to the country to follow us by the paths I took, for the most part through dense woodlands.

We had not ridden above a couple of miles before we heard the sound of a horn and the deep chested note of a sleuth-hound. We were toiling up the hill of Cors, when looking back I could see the flash of spears among the trees, and that our pursuers were rapidly following us along the route I had selected.

I entreated Lord Rivers to give his horse the spur, and turning sharply to the right tried to gain the more open trackway; but it mattered not which way we turned, or which direction we took, there was the challenge of the sleuth-hound, which evidently had been set upon our track at Slop's Hole. The farther we went the slower did the franklin's horse become, and it was evident to us both that Trollop and his riders must soon overtake us.

There was but one thing to be done. We had now gained the trackway by Hartpury, and I insisted upon Lord Rivers changing horses and riding Kingsland, as hard as he could for Gloucester. He refused at first, but on my telling him that I could escape myself on foot through the woodlands, he at last consented, and rode off at a pace few horses were likely to overtake. I now left the useless horse standing in the middle of the track, and dashed into the thickets, running as rapidly as I could for Hartpury, where I had a right good friend and true who would have lost his right hand rather than have surrendered me to the Lancastrians. But Trollop laid the sleuth-hound upon my trail, and, while he sent half a score of his followers after Lord Rivers, followed the hound and me with the like number of his men.

I had not run far before I was obliged to defend myself against the dog, with my dagger, standing with my back against an oak tree like a stag at bay. Fortunately I had a strong leathern glove on my left hand, and getting hold of him drove the weapon to his heart as he flew at my throat. But hardly was the struggle over when I was dragged to the ground by the men-at-arms, who quickly overpowered me, already half exhausted, and bound me hand and foot.

"You have not escaped me this time," said Trollop, "and I will take care you do not have the opportunity again."

I made no reply, knowing it would be useless, when this double traitor gave orders to his men to hang me by the neck from a large oak which was near at hand, and quickly, as he wanted to be off after 'the traitor Widville', whom he doubted not was the man in front.

I expected that every moment would be my last, and visions passed through my brain of Rosamond, and my dear old mother left alone in the world, with hopes that Master Vaughan and our sure friend Robin might be their friends and protectors when I was gone; when one of the men-at-arms, who seemed to have some authority, spoke to Trollop aside, and after his expostulations the rope was taken from my neck. Trollop then gave orders that I should be roped, saying, "Be it so, perhaps it would be better to send him straight to Banbury or Northampton, where the example of hanging a traitor will be more public, and they may stick his cursed head over one of their gateways. I will see him off myself from Gloucester under a strong guard. Now ride to the front, and catch this newly-fledged lord who is so light of heels."

I was now placed on a horse behind one of the troopers, my arms being bound tightly behind my back, and my feet strapped under the horse's belly, a most painful condition; amounting indeed to torture, and heavy drops coursed down my face with the torment. This the gallant knight heartily enjoyed, and he smiled and made jocular remarks as he drew the knots tighter with his own hand.

Turning to the guide who had accompanied them from Theocsbury, he enquired the way to Gloucester, and rode on in front, leaving me in this wretched condition behind the trooper.

The rest of the riders he commanded to gallop forward, and await him at the western gateway. Weary now seemed that well-known road which ascends the trackway above Hartpury, and on the crest of the hill looks upon the noble city of Gloucester.

I had looked upon this view when I was a happy boy riding by my father's side on the old palfrey that was my first steed, and when all in the world seemed young and fresh and beautiful. I looked upon it now as one whose days were numbered, and who would soon have to meet my God, and serve him, I humbly trusted. in another sphere, perhaps in one where there should be no more killing and slaying, and hunting one another to the death. I felt no fear or terror, but sorrow that I should have to die in so ignominious a manner rather than on the battle-field.

These thoughts and many others ran through my brain, when I heard the gallop and snorting of a horse immediately behind us. I was so fettered that all I could do was to turn my head half round, and see my good esquire Hasting mounted on our gallant Mortimer, ride to the head of the trooper's horse. In an instant a blow from his battle-axe felled the trooper in front of me from his seat, and in the next Hasting was engaged in a hand-to-hand fight with Trollop.

Trollop was some twenty yards in front of us when the trooper went down, and attempted to defend the impetuous charge of Hasting with the spear at the end of his battle-axe. He might as well have attempted to stop the rush of a bull or the charge of a wild boar. Then I heard a crash of iron against iron, and saw the recreant knight fall to the ground as falls the ox stricken by the butcher.

Hasting now galloped back to where I sat helpless upon the trooper's horse, and a few seconds, with the edge of his dagger, sufficed to set me free. So tightly had I been bound, that when I scrambled from the horse I could not stand for some minutes, and my arms were as useless as my legs. After a time I rallied, and we proceeded to examine the unlucky trooper. He was stone dead, indeed it was unlikely he should have lived a minute after that crushing blow.

Trollop lay at full length on his face on the green sward, now deeply stained with his blood. The bridle was still in his left hand, and the well broken charger stood by him motionless. But the cruel man had ridden his last raid, for when we turned the body over and unfastened his helmet, hardly a feature of his face was recognizable. Hasting had struck him with tremendous force and driven in the bars of the vizor, crushing the head as if it had been an egg.

We drew both corpses to the side of the trackway, and left them where they lay, for we knew not how soon the men-at-arms under Trollop's command might not return to see what had become of their leader and his prisoner. I mounted Trollop's steed, and we galloped away for Birtsmereton, my gallant friend telling me, as we rode, how he had the good fortune thus to rescue me.

Robin knew I was going to Slop's Hole, and being anxious to learn what had become of Lord Rivers, asked Hasting to ride over and see if he could be of any service with our archers. Hasting met the franklin and his men on the road, and learnt how they had amused themselves with seeing from the summit of some trees the discomfiture of the riders who entered among the infuriated bees, and listening to the wild oaths of Trollop, who seemed to have been severely stung. They then saw the party following upon our trail and supposed I was making for Gloucester. Hasting now rode for the trackway, and galloped in pursuit, and in the hopes of seeing or helping something of us.

Thus was wrought out for me, in a most unexpected manner, this merciful deliverance from my inveterate foe; the only personal enemy I ever had in the world – for a soldier's foe on the battle-field cannot be deemed a personal enemy.

Payne's Place

Chapter Sixteen

THE FATE of Lord Rivers was less fortunate. He escaped as far as Gloucester, and left my horse Kingsland, as agreed between us, at the New Inn stables. Finding a number of Lancastrian troops at this city he, with his son Sir John Widville, fled to the Forest of Dean[1], among the wilds of which they hoped to obtain refuge. For some days they hid in the old scowles,[2] but at last were taken prisoners and sent to Coventry, where they were both beheaded.

Hasting seemed to think very little of his performance in my behalf, saying "It was good luck," but he could not escape from the gratitude of my mother, and the way in which she said "God bless you, Master Hasting". He was also much pleased by my presenting him with Mortimer, the best horse I ever possessed. A battle-axe which Sir Robin had used at the battle of Towton was given him by the Knight of Castlemereton and Elsdune, with many a hearty handshake.

While this was taking place in our neighbourhood, King Edward had retreated to Olney in a very precarious condition. Herbert, whom he had created Earl of Pembroke, was dead; the Earl of Devon had been executed at Bridgwater; and his own father-in-law, and brother in-law, Earl Rivers and Sir John Widville, had been beheaded by the insurgents. Others of the Yorkists were dead or scattered, fleeing for their lives, or hiding themselves in remote places.

It was now that the extraordinary power and popularity of the Earl of Warwick became manifest.

He arrived in England from Calais, after the summons of the King, accompanied by his son-in-law the Duke of Clarence. On reaching Olney they found Edward regularly beset, and the rebels preparing to attack him. But such was the great Earl's popularity that, after he had held an interview with Sir John Conyers and the other leaders, the insurgent camp broke up and dispersed, while the King accompanied Earl Warwick to his strong castle at Middleham. Here the King remained some time as a guest, some say as a prisoner, but I do not think this likely, for he soon returned to London and reigned as before.

These strange episodes happened in the year of grace 1469, and five years after the King's marriage, but he had as yet no son, and the Duke of Clarence was still heir to the crown. Court matters seemed peaceful again; solemn oaths were interchanged, the royal brothers were reconciled, and there was general feasting and forgiving. Sir Robin and I were again summoned to the counsels of the King, but I entreated of Robin to make my excuses, save if war broke out again, for I had an idea, from my former experiences as the Queen's equerry, that I should soon be involved in Court manoeuvres and intrigues, crafts and artifices.

Besides this dislike of again living a Court life, I had determined to seek Master Vaughan and learn what had become of my lost Rosamond. I revisited Elsdune and Hergest, and again I found that nothing whatever was known of Master Vaughan. A few of the Welshmen whom he had taken with him had returned to their mountain homes, but all they knew of their chief and master was that he was engaged in several of the skirmishes which occurred about the time of the battle near Banbury, and had been seen badly wounded riding with Sir Andrew Trollop through Worcester. They thought it was probable he was dead, as the shadow of a black hound had been seen more than once in the glades of Hergest, a sure sign of the decease of the head of the family.

In this year of grace 1469, was fought the great fight of Nibley Green near Stinchcombe, among the Cotswold Hills, and which was more fatal to those concerned than even our struggle at Castlemereton Keep. It arose out of the disputes and claims for the possession of the Castle and Barony of Berkeley between Thomas Talbot Lord Lisle and Lord Berkeley.

It was on the 19th of March that Lord Lisle, who was only twenty years of age, and had recently married Maud, the daughter of that William Herbert who was made Earl of Pembroke instead of Jasper Tudor, sent a challenge written in his own hand to Lord Berkeley, and dared him to come forth 'with all his carts of gunnes and bows and other ordinance', and 'to try between God and their two hands all their quarrel and title of right'. The following day Lord Berkeley returned answer to this challenge, and summoned Lord Lisle to 'faile not to morrow to be at Niblyes Green at eight or nyne of the clock'.

So, at sunrise on that March morning the two noblemen met, and Lord Berkeley commanded an army of some thousand men. Lord Lisle's army was not so strong, but they marched in order from Nibley Church and attacked Lord Berkeley on the great green of Fowleshard, near a rough wood where Lord Berkeley's men lay hidden.

The fight was very bloody, but Lord Berkeley's party gained the day, being much the most numerous. Lord Lisle was shot by an arrow, his vizor being up, through the face, and he was also stabbed by Black Will of the Forest of Dean. Lord Berkeley then led on his archers to Wooton, where was the manor of Lord Lisle, and sacked and pillaged it right fervently.[3]

The yule log had burnt and smouldered all through the night of Christmas eve of 1469, and this was hailed as such an excellent good omen that mother declared we should have tidings of the lost one. It would take too long to tell of the Christmas feast, and the songs of olden times, with all our merriment and revelry.

Suffice to say that it took our dames and damsels with their wenches, a month to prepare for it, and that not a poor person within hearing of our church bells went either dinnerless or supperless to bed.

New Year's Day of 1470 arrived, with its interchange of presents and hopes for 'good luck and good gear for all the new year'; while the wasshael was replenished from morning to night. There were more carols and more feasting and dancing, but at last we settled down to our usual home life. Then came St Valentine, 'when every lover kissed his maid, and every maid her John', and the snowflake was eagerly sought for as a lucky posy by anxious lovers.

It was on St Valentine that I had occasion to ride over to Theocsbury and, on my way to the Lower Lode, I passed the good Abbot Strensham, who was standing at the gateway of the Abbot's Court at Fordington, and entreated me to dismount and go to the Court and see a painting on wood of most excellent limnering. This was a portrait of King Offa investing a pilgrim with the staff and ring, and had been found, hidden away behind the altar in the little chapel.

The Abbot surmised that it was of great antiquity. He also invited me to inspect the new works of the Lady Chapel at the Abbey, and accompanied me across the ferry on my way to the town.

When I had stabled my horse I went down to the Abbey and found Abbot Strensham in the cloisters attending to some guests who were evidently personages of consequence. I now recognized, to my great surprise, the Earl of Warwick and his Countess, Anne Beauchamp. They had visited the Abbey from their castle at Hanley, as the Countess was desirous of seeing the tombs of her mother, Isabel Despenser, Countess of Warwick, and of her brother, the Duke of Warwick.

The Earl gave me a soldier's greeting, and the Countess a courteous recognition. This lady possessed a gentle voice and manner, far more winning than the sharp tones of Elizabeth, Queen of England. She was a right gentle lady. We lingered until the Abbot conducted us to the western view of the noble nest window with its great Norman arches, and the grandest in all the Abbey.[4]

While we were thus engaged, the Earl enquired if the Abbot had heard of the infamous conduct of the Queen's mother, the Duchess of Bedford, in employing sorcery against his life, and having a waxen figure made which by wicked witchcrafts should cause him to die by slow and lingering disease.[5] Abbot Strensham replied that the accusations of witchcraft against the Duchess were the common talk of the country, but that he was glad to see that the Earl looked none the worse for the necromancy, which often recoiled upon those who had recourse to such abominable devices.

Declining the hospitality of the Abbot, the Earl of Warwick invited me to accompany him to his barge, which was waiting on the Severn to convey them on their return to Hanley Quay, as the Countess wished to grant me certain privileges of chase in her manors of Hanley and Welland. As we walked through the town he told me that the jealousies and animosities of the Queen's family against himself and his relations were so manifest, that they tended to produce great misunderstandings between himself and the King.

At the corner of Tolsey Lane we met with Master Payne, who recognizing the stout Earl, was most profound in his salutations, and we were soon surrounded by a delighted crowd eager to welcome their illustrious visitors, while the welkin soon rung with shouts of "A Warwick! Long live the Earl of Warwick!"

Crossing the wide Holme meadows to where the barge lay on the Severn waters, Earl Warwick said that it was his intention to challenge me to a day's stag hunting in the Chase at Hanley, but that he had been summoned unexpectedly to a great entertainment to be given to the King and the Duke of Clarence by his own brother, the Archbishop of York, at his Manor of the Moor, in Hertfordshire. Still, he hoped the time would come when we should have a gallop together among the glades and woodlands of our Chase.

By this time we neared the barge, which was well fitted for the accommodation of noble ladies, as there was a kind of dais at the prow sheltered from the sun or from storms by curtains of silk and damask, such as I had often seen on the Thames. Four towing horses, richly caparisoned, and with riders in the Warwick liveries, stood ready harnessed for hauling up the river. But I ceased to look at these on beholding a fair young face, wreathed in smiles, and peering through the curtains as we approached the river bank.

Then, bounding from the barge's prow on to the shore came one of the most fairy-like figures I have ever beheld. This.was the Lady Anne Neville, who, not being strong, had remained on board the barge and now came to meet her parents, looking like a lily of the valley, which cannot bear exposure to a hot sun or a bitter wind.

Her father presented me as "A stalwart knight who fought at Mortimer's Cross", and she gave me a sweet smile and a curtsey before she cast her arm round her mother's waist and assisted her across the wooden platform to the barge.

I thought at the time how little this noble girl was fitted to battle with the stern ambitious men with whom her lot was cast. Earl Warwick took the tiller with his own hand, and shouting to the prowman to look well ahead, the horses started, at first slowly, up the stream, hundreds of people running by the side of the barge and cheering vociferously.

I walked along the shore for a short distance, removing my cap from time to time in adieu, until the barge passed by the red cliff of the Mythe Twt, when I received a wave of the hand from one of the greatest statesmen and soldiers England ever possessed. It would have been better for him, as events turned out, if he had not gone to meet the King at that feasting of the Archbishop's, where he was enticed into a conspiracy which was unworthy of his fame and character.

I was returning slowly to the hostelrie when I was accosted by Master Payne of Bushley and the fertile meads of Pull, who begged of me to accompany him to his little grange, Payne's Place, as a Lancastrian gentleman lay there badly wounded, who had enquired after me and how far it was to our manor.

On reaching the timbered lodge of Payne's Place, which stands by the quaint old church with its Saxon relics, where it was built among the wild bushes on the ley, I found, to my great surprise, that the wounded soldier was Master Vaughan. He had been with the insurgents in the late fight, thinking the rising would end in the restoration of Henry of Lancaster, and had been struck by an arrow but, making light of it, he rode southward with troops, until his wound rankled to such an extent that he was compelled to halt at Theocsbury, where he would have died had not Master Payne, finding he was a Lancastrian, acted like the good Samaritan, and removed him to his own house and under his own care, where he lay lingering for weeks and weeks.

Master Vaughan's wound had again rankled and festered, so that he was now in a high fever, and lay in a very precarious condition. For several days he was quite delirious, and I feared he would die without being able to tell me what had become of my beloved Rosamond. I rode daily over to see him, and passed a good deal of my time watching by the sick bed of one whom I soon found had done me most grievous wrong.

At last he rallied for a time, recognized me, and I could see was not a little confused at my presence. Then little by little he told me of the miseries many of the Lancastrians had undergone for six long years, ever since the great defeat at Hexham and the marriage of the usurper Edward of York. He told how King Henry had wandered about for weeks in a half-starving state until he was taken a prisoner to the Tower, and how the Queen and her son roamed from place to place, fell among a band of robbers, and at last escaped to France.

But not a syllable did he say about his niece, or the Countess of Oxford, until I pressed him to tell me what had happened to them among all this misery and indigence. Even then he avoided the subject, and told how one Philip de Comines[6] had himself seen the once proud Duke of Exeter 'serving for his livelihood as a running footman'.

After this he appeared exhausted, and lay back upon the couch, closing his eyes and begging of me to leave him quiet for the present. Nor was it for three days that I learned how, fearful for the eternal welfare of Rosamond owing to her Lollard predilections and youthful training by her grandfather, and my belief also in 'the heresies of Master Wycliffe', he had consulted with the Countess of Oxford and had placed his niece in a convent in the south of France, where he hoped she might eventually be converted to a true faith and her future salvation.

Many years have passed away since these revelations were, little by little, dragged by questioning from Master Vaughan, but it is impossible to express my indignation at the time, or the bitter way in which my heart was wrung by such treatment of my affianced wife.

I knew perfectly well that her custody in this convent was against her will, and that could she have escaped she would have begged her bread to the sea-side, and endeavoured to return to us and her own home; but it was evident she was a prisoner, and might remain so, and undiscovered for the rest of her life, without I could learn from her uncle where she was immured.

I now knelt by the side of his couch and told him how long we had loved each other; how we had been brought up together from our earliest childhood; how anxious we were to lead together good and useful lives, and besought him, for the sake of a merciful God, if he hoped to obtain mercy himself, not to sacrifice the happiness of two persons connected with him by the ties of relationship and the old friendship of years, and all for the religious opinions of erring men and misguided priests; but he only turned uneasily on his couch, avoided my earnest gaze, and said feebly something about 'to-morrow'.

But that to-morrow never came to him. I sat by him all that night, the fever again rose to its full height, and before midnight his spirit passed away as he was talking and gesticulating to an imaginary hound, which nothing would induce him to believe was not endeavouring to jump up upon the couch.

It was a sad spectacle next morning, as the corpse of this gallant gentleman lay distorted, and the morning sun burst full upon it, another victim of these accursed wars. And mine was a sad heart, as I knew not whether I should ever again see, or even hear of the beloved of my heart in this world of sin and suffering.

I did all that was left to be done for the body of Rosamond's uncle, and he was laid in the church of Kington, near to the home of his youth and maturer years, and where he might have lived for many years honoured and respected, but for the conflicts and disputes of the Wars of the Roses. He had been knighted by King Louis of France, and now lies beside his wife, with the escutcheon of Sir Thomas Vaughan. Verily, I had cause to curse the day when English men and English women could be thus separated and persecuted through priestly quibblings about their common Christianity.

It was quite evident from Master Vaughan's manner before he died at Payne's Place that he had still great hopes for the Lancastrian cause, but it was not possible to ascertain on what foundation those hopes rested; and as King Edward appeared to be safe on his throne once more, I dismissed the idea of danger from my mind. and was busy making arrangements to go to the Continent, search out the Countess of Oxford, and endeavour to learn from her where Rosamond Berew was imprisoned in the south of France.

The Ides of March of the year of grace 1470 had now arrived, the time of warnings and omens. Ever since the days of the Romans have these March Ides been notable for visions, warnings, omens, and portents. The village maidens hate to see a single magpie, as that bird seen alone in the early morn at this time of year is fatal to all hopes of their wedding for another twelve months; whereas two in company are a most loving sign. The croak of the raven, too, as he wings his way towards the Malverns, is ever a bad token if heard during the Ides, and makes the wenches turn the left way in their beds to try to undo the unlucky spell.

A strange omen was also reported from Theocsbury. A damosel was searching for spring violets and the early primrose among the glades in the New Parks, then at Lincoln's Green where now is the Field of Blood she came on bunches and clusters of crimson daisies.

I thought little of this at the time among the many wonderments which are ever told on the Ides of March, but after the great battle I remembered how daisies were the emblem flowers of Margaret of Anjou, and how she ever wore them worked in noble stitchery upon her bodice.

Another warning of those war-begotten times happened at the old Saxon grange and mill called Bury Mill, beneath the hanging groves of Hazeldine at Redmarley. Mistress Alice Shipside,[7] who lived at the Grange, was a learned lady, and though she loved well to play at tennis and was famous at closh bowls, loved still better the lore of scrip and the grey goose quill. Nay, she had written a poesie of romaunt with her own fair hand. She knew well, too, how to interpret a token or a manifestation; and so her friends Miranda and Dorothy Paunceforte entreated her to try the test of March mistletoe.

The 'kissing boss' of Christmas had been carefully saved until the Ides, and was put upon the blazing hearth in all solemnity at the hour of midnight, each damsel hoping and praying for a fair omen. But alas! instead of the steady, fervent, glowing blaze of the future lover, the boss burst forth not only in those sputterings and spitterings which warn the damsel against cross and ill-tempered swains, but in forty thousand death sparks, frighting the omen seekers, and a sure sign of future and grievous battle.

My mother, too, had received several omens. Some portended marriage, for 'bells upon the wind' were heard in the early morn, and she had searched, too, for the four-leaved shamrock. Others portended death, for a piece of wood like a coffin had shot out from the fire, and winding sheets had been seen in the rushlights.

But of all the ominous forebodings none seemed to promise such disastrous results as that unlucky entertainment of the Archbishop of York to King Edward, which the Earl of Warwick left his hunting seat at Hanley Castle to attend.

The illustrious guests had assembled at the Archbishop's Manor of the Moor, at the end of the month of February, and as the King was washing his hands for supper he received information through an attendant that the Earl of Warwick and the Duke of Clarence had conspired to seize his person, and that an armed band was lurking near the house.

Leaving his supper and his host the King got secretly to horse, and riding all night reached Windsor Castle alone, furious at such treachery. The Duchess of York, the King's mother, had endeavoured to patch up a reconciliation, but from that hour Edward never again had faith in the Earl of Warwick or any of the Nevilles.

In a few weeks the King manifested such open hostility against his brother Clarence and the great Earl, that they in their turn took to flight and, embarking at Dartmouth, sailed with their ladies and a number of adherents to Calais. There was now an open breach which was never likely to be healed.

And yet Edward seemed little concerned at this crisis. He followed his sport, his feasts, and his gallantries, and although warned by his brother-in-law, Charles the Bold, 'to put his kingdom in a state of defence', he took no precautions, and summoned no fresh troops to his standard.

Yet another omen of future war burst upon us. In the month of June the fallen Lancastrian Queen, Margaret of Anjou, and her son the Prince of Wales, met the Earl of Warwick at the chateau of Amboise, and forgave the Earl the long years of humiliation of which he had been the principal cause. Soon, too, this extraordinary reconciliation was ratified by the marriage of the Prince Edward to the beautiful Lady Anne Neville, whom I had seen so lately in all her virgin loveliness by the Severn shore at Theocsbury. Well indeed might Master Comines write of this marriage, 'An unaccountable match this, to dethrone and imprison the father, and then marry his own daughter to the son'.

But I shall ever believe that the stout Earl knew well enough that Edward would never forget that attempt to arrest his person at the Archbishop's supper; that he also knew the weak and flimsy character of his first son-in-law, the Duke of Clarence, and so determined to fly a new hawk at the quarry of ambition.

Still King Edward made no sign, but acted as if he cared nothing for Warwick or anything that happened across the seas. It was a most hazardous negligence, as time soon discovered.

Our corn had ripened beneath the August's sun; we had partaken of the codlings and cream, garnished with the willow herb; had netted our partridges and leverets in the early September; and I had arranged to sail for France in a merchant's ship to search for Rosamond, when I received a message from Dame Despenser, begging of me to wait upon her at Hamme Castle without delay.

On riding over, I found that she had tidings to communicate, which came upon me, as it did upon thousands of others, like the crash of a thunderbolt. It was that the Earl of Warwick and the Duke of Clarence had landed on the 12th of September in Devonshire, and already many thousands had flocked to the standard which they had raised in the name of Henry of Lancaster. Already the populace were tossing their bonnets in the air, shouting "God bless King Harry!"

While this was going on, King Edward was in the north, drawn thither by a feigned revolt, and there were no troops to meet Earl Warwick and prevent his marching on London. What the end of all this would be no one could foresee, but it behoved every one who supported the White Rose of York to be up and stirring, and every soldier that could be enlisted must be rallied to the standard.

Dame Despenser was ready to do all a woman could, out of a poor purse, to aid in levying troops in and around Theocsbury, but she had little interest with those who would take up the bow and spear in such a cause, being more affected towards the clergy, to whom she was ever hospitable. Indeed, as far as circumstances allowed, she assayed to follow the example of Robert, the first Earl of Gloucester, who centuries before lived much at Hamme Castle, and was wont to invite the Abbot and his monks to dine with him every Sunday in the year.

Thus a Sunday never passed without some ecclesiastic being the guest of this hospitable lady, at the well-nigh ruined edifice, once the proud home of the great Earls of Gloucester. It was said that the good Abbot never missed the Sunday's dinner, as long as the least lampreys were in season, or as long as the salmon was pink and crimped.

Here, too, often came Master Holdhard, the chirurgeon – for Theocsbury could boast a real chirurgeon – a man of mark and learning. From Master Holdhard I gathered that little good was to be done at Theocsbury itself in recruiting for King Edward. Indeed, it was doubtful whether the common people cared for either king, for the Earl of Warwick consumed more mustard at his daily banquets than ever did the courts of King Henry or King Edward, and mustard here meant politics and patriotism.

Nevertheless I went to the Bowling Green and played closh bowls with several gentlemen of the neighbourhood, and to the Tolsey, where I met Master Payne and Sir Gervais Clifton; but these were both Lancastrians, although neither as yet had heard of the landing of the Earl of Warwick.

Having met with little encouragement at the Bowling Green, I applied to the host of the Black Bear of Warwick, and from information I received from him, was induced to take a boat up the river Avon to Twyning Fleet, where the Danes are said to have turned back after the burning of Theocsbury and the pillage of the Saxon granges and church of Bredon. At Twyning and Bredon I was enabled by promises and money to enlist about half-a-score archers, but here as everywhere the cry was "A Warwickl A Warwick!" and I perceived that the stout Earl might, if he would, become King of England, as far as the populace was concerned.

The aspect of affairs was such that I rode homeward anxious and depressed, but determined, come what may, never to desert the cause of my royal Master, while inwardly cursing the family squabbles which again seemed likely to bring the best blood of England to be shed like water.

Still no message came from Robin, and no summons from the King to march with what troops I could assemble. Everything was in a state of uncertainty, at all events to us who lived in a remote district, until, on the 29th of September, came the sad tidings, by a special messenger of Robin's, that King Edward had found all resistance hopeless and had fled for his life to Holland with few attendants. Indeed, such was his haste and so great his straits, that of this adventure Master Comines has written, 'The King, having no money, was forced to give the master of the ship a gown lined with martens, and to promise to do more for him another time, and sure so poor a company had never been seen before'.

The King-Maker, as the Earl of Warwick was now called, was now in possession of all England, and with his son-in-law, the Duke of Clarence, entered London in triumph on the 6th of October 1470. He then released King Henry, whom he had himself committed to the Tower five years before. So all the people shouted "God save King Henry," and declared Edward of York a foul usurper, in the presence of his own brother Clarence, and had great processions with praise and thanksgiving to the Virgin, as is ever the custom with mobs whenever there has been, or is likely to be, much slaughter and desolation.

The King-Maker was now really King, for Henry of Lancaster was too weak of character, although pious withal, to hold the reins of power in these troublous times. The Duke of Clarence was only a little over twenty-one years of age, and was trusted by no one who knew him. Besides, he was no longer heir to the Crown, for since Henry of Lancaster was king, Edward his son, the husband of the Lady Anne, was Prince of Wales.

Great, indeed, were the changes throughout all England, and thousands of Yorkists had to fly for their lives. Queen Elizabeth and her young daughters, with her mother the Duchess of Bedford, sought refuge in the sanctuary at Westminster; many fled to the wilds of Scotland and Wales; many to the Continent; but all were in a state of despair. The attainders of the Lancastrians were reversed, and every one who was dispossessed by King Edward expected to be restored to their lost honours.

My own position became serious. I had been attached to the person of Edward of York at different times for ten years, and received grants of three hides of land from the Chase of Malvern as his free gift. It was true I had a sincere friend in Calverley, but his claims were little known at Court. Still, through his aid and endeavours I made enquiries respecting the Countess of Oxford, from whom I hoped to ascertain something or other as to the convent where Rosamond was immured, and learnt to my infinite mortification that she had not returned with the Lancastrian refugees from the Continent.

While these enquiries were being instituted, with delays which were most provoking, Robin of Elsdune arrived from his home on the borders of Radnorshire, and announced his determination of joining his royal master in Holland as soon as he could find a ship. He invited me to accompany him, but I hardly liked leaving my mother in such troublous times. She, however, entreated me to hold firmly to the King in this his dire distress, saying that she was well assured that if my father was living he would be one of the first to follow him to the death

With some difficulty we found a ship, and crossing the seas to Holland, joined King Edward at the Hague. Notwithstanding our appearance, without a single man-at-arms but ourselves, and rather scantily supplied with money, the King received us in his usual frank and hearty manner, and we found him preparing four great ships in Walcheren, with money furnished him by his loving brother-in-law the Duke of Burgundy.

We passed our Christmas and the commencement of the new year of 1471 in that strange country where live the Hollanders. It is one continuous mere or marsh land, flat as a Shrove pancake, and traversed by great dikes and ditches, while their towns and villages are ever ready to be swamped by the overflowng waters.

Right glad, therefore, were we when the month of March arrived, and we embarked with a gallant little force of well-armed men and, facing a stormy sea, sailed for the shores of England. It is true that the voyage reduced us both to a condition unbecoming knights and gentlemen but, if it was any satisfaction, the King himself and several noble lords were as incapable as ourselves. My Lord of Scales, now Earl Rivers, King Edward's brother-in-law, looked like a trussed fowl, and his cheeks chattered like castanets; while the bravest knights went stumbling about as if overcome with strong drink, and retching fearfully like a consumptive cat.

On the morning of the 16th of March we safely landed our little army at Ravenspur, and then marched on York, where we found but a cold reception, and so crossed the Trent, when numbers flocked to the King's standard.

The strong walls and numerous gates and towers completed by Richard II bespoke the magnificence at Coventry, and the noble Cathedral towered over all;[8] but the inhabitants were hostile to King Edward, and had admitted the Earl of Warwick with great stores of ordnance, for which afterwards they had to pay the fine of five hundred marks. Thus King Edward was driven to lodge that night at Warwick in a hostelrie.

Now had the Earl of Warwick to suffer for destroying the prospects of his son-in-law, the Duke of Clarence, to the crown of England. This fickle young man, who was to have joined his father-in-law at Coventry, made his men put the White Rose of York over their gorgets, and deserted to his brother Edward with all his troops. On this the King threw himself, with his whole army, between the Lancastrians and London, marching to the capital, where his return was hailed with enthusiasm by all the citizens, who, forgetting the splendid hospitalities of Lord Warwick and the piety of King Henry, now shouted "God save King Edward!"

Queen Elizabeth, too, had added to the general joy by presenting her husband and his loving citizens with a Prince of Wales of the line of York, who was born in the Sanctuary at Westminster.

We had but a short time to enjoy all the popular demonstrations, for in two days after our entry we heard that Warwick had formed a large camp on Gladsmore Heath, about midway between St Alban's and London, and with him were many powerful barons. Robin and I were in attendance on the King, who arrived at the small town of Barnet during the afternoon of Easter eve, and occupied most of his time in bringing up his army almost close to the Lancastrians under cover of the night, while they thought to frighten us by a continual firing of carronades, as most of the artillery was in their hands.

It is much to my regret that I cannot describe the famous battle of Barnet, for I was not present at the struggle, having been sent by the King at midnight on the eve of the battle with despatches for London. On my return it was to look upon a stricken field; the dead and the dying. I gathered from others how the battle commenced between four and five o'clock on the morning of that Easter Sunday, though the mist was so thick that neither Lancastrians nor Yorkists could discern the forces of the other. This dense fog was reported to have been raised by the incantations of Friar Bungay, who was employed by the Duchess of Bedford to make a waxen Image of the Earl of Warwick. The Duke of Gloucester commanded the van; the King, with the Duke of Clarence, the centre; and Lord Hastings the rear. Robin was all day in close attendance as an equerry of the King.

Lord Warwick led the centre of the Lancastrians, with his brother the Marquis of Montague and Lord Oxford. The Duke of Somerset led the archers, while the Duke of Exeter was in the rear. The armies were so completely enveloped in the mist that whole corps of men-at-arms went astray, and although forty thousand Englishmen were engaged in deadly combat against each other, the slaughter was not to compare to that of Mortimer's Cross, still less to that of Towton.

The contest was furious and terrible between the central forces led by the King and those led by the Earl of Warwick and his brother, while the two wings of both armies appear hardly to have engaged at all. Lord Warwick and his gallant brother sent away their horses and rushed on foot against their enemies, dealing death on every side. The King's standard-bearer was killed by Warwick's own hand, and it was said that Warwick himself was struck down by the battle-axe of the Duke of Gloucester, who rushed forward through fog and mist,

Thus fell the stout Earl of Warwick, so famed for his hospitality, so royal in his tastes, and so popular that his absence was accounted as the want of the sun in the heavens, and whose authority was such, that kings were raised or deposed as he willed.

With the fall of the leaders the Lancastrians took to flight, and were much sheltered by the Friar's fog. The slain were somewhat over one thousand on both sides; but of all the great Lancastrian lords not one escaped, save the Earl of Oxford, and he joined Jasper Tudor, who had reached Wales and was raising another Lancastrian army.

Gladsmore Heath was a sorry sight when the fog cleared about midday, for the battle was won before ten o'clock in the forenoon. The bodies of the stout Earl and his brother lay side by side. Loving each other in life, in death they were not divided. They were borne home to London on a litter, and after being exposed in the Church of St Paul's for three days, were buried in the same tomb, at Bisham Priory in Berkshire.

King Edward's first act after the battle of Barnet, was to send King Henry back to his old prison in the Tower. There were thanksgivings at St Paul's and all the great London churches. The banner with the three suns floated from the battlements of the Tower; the trumpets sounded, all was rejoicing, and no one thought that another bloody battle was soon to follow before Edward was again seated firmly on his throne.

I and Robin occupied our old quarters in the Tower, and only five days had elapsed after the battle of Barnet when the King received information that Margaret of Anjou and her son Prince Edward had landed with a large body of French troops at Weymouth on the very day her ally Earl Warwick was defeated and slain. The King was prompt and vigorous; all the perils he had so lately passed through by sea and by land did but increase his energy.

It was necessary to attack this French army of Margaret's before Jasper Tudor should march across the Severn with his new levies, or she should join him on the borders of Wales.

We now marched to Windsor, where we remained several days, and the King celebrated the feast of St George.

Queen Margaret, after her landing at Weymouth, was entertained at Cerne Abbey,[10] between Sherborne and Dorchester, and thither came the Duke of Somerset and the Earl of Devonshire to hold consultation, as they were raising troops in the southern counties. At Windsor the King was well informed of the movements of the enemy, through his scouts and spies, and heard that bodies of Lancastrian troops had advanced from Exeter to Wells, and sent their riders as far as Yeovil, as if they would advance on Reading.

But the King believed this to be a feint, and that the real intention of Somerset was to join forces with Jasper Tudor somewhere on the line of the Severn. That he was right the following events proved.

On the 24th of April the camp at Windsor was broken up amidst the neighing of steeds and the clangour of mail, and again at the head of his army rode The Lion of York, the silver sun on all his banners, and the very housings of his war-horse sparkling with devices. Robin followed as his body esquire, and I was attached also to his personal staff.

We marched by Abingdon to Cirencester, where the whole army encamped in a large park; and from thence proceeded to Malmesbury, from which place I was sent with a body of archers to watch the movements of the Queen's forces and send back reports to the King.

We rode to the village of Bath, famous for its hot springs and Roman ruins, and from thence I sent scouts to the important city of Bristol, where they learned that the Lancastrian army was embarrassed by the presence of Queen Margaret, her son, Prince Edward, and daughter-in-law, the Princess Anne; also that they had been well received by the Bristol citizens, who furnished them with food, men, and money.

No sooner had the King assurance of the encampment of the Lancastrians before Bristol, than he led his army from Malmesbury to Sudbury, and encamped upon the hill which rises above this little town, and is distant about seven miles from Bristol.

It was now the first of May, and we all felt sure that a battle would be fought between Bristol and Sudbury, but the Duke of Somerset could not induce the Governor of Bristol Castle to espouse the cause of the Queen, and he feared being caught in the rear by the garrison, if he should there engage with the forces of the King. So, at midnight I received information that the Lancastrians had broken up their camp and were marching towards Berkeley and Gloucester.

Not a moment was to be lost, as the enemy's tactics were now apparent. They would endeavour to cross the Severn. When the scout brought this news I was between Bristol and the hill of Sudbury, and not more than three miles from the King's camp, so I galloped to his quarters in the town below, and found him sleeping on a low couch as peacefully as if in his palace at Windsor.

Most generals would have waited, at least for the dawn of morning, before arousing the officers and troops. Not so the energetic Edward. While I assisted him to buckle on his riding gear, the sentinels were calling the troops to arms, and by two o'clock in the morning he was in full march along the high ground of the Cotswold Hills, while the Lancastrians marched in the vale below. During the time he was dressing he conversed with me and Robin, gaily, about the movements of his enemies, and made a great point of overtaking them before they could cross the Severn, where Jasper Tudor was awaiting them with several thousand Welshmen.

Robin, as his most trusted esquire, had charge of his armour, which was placed upon a sumpter horse, while Robin himself bore the King's casque and lance. His favourite battle-axe hung by the side of his war steed and, before dawn, on that morning of the end of May, Edward rode forth upon the most extraordinary march in all these unhappy wars.

The whole army moved as silently as possible, and not a trumpet sounded. But I was not destined to accompany him, for I was sent on a business of importance into the vale. Bidding me select the swiftest horse in all his stud, the King commanded me to head the enemy, and if possible reach Gloucester before the advent of the foremost riders of the Lancastrians. The Governor of the Castle there was Richard Beauchamp, son of Lord Beauchamp of Powick, and I was to entreat him to hold the Castle at all hazards, and if possible to prevent the Queen's army from entering the city.

Conducted by a well mounted franklin I took the route by Alderley, Wooton, and Frocester and, while the Lancastrians were refreshing their men with good Berkeley cheeses and strong ale, we struck ahead of their advanced corps of scouts and came upon the Bristol trackway below Haresfield, and rode from thence rapidly to the Southgate of Gloucester walls.

It was not easy to obtain admission, for Richard Beauchamp was a staunch follower of King Edward's, and had given strict orders that no one should be allowed to enter the city without his leave. He had a strong garrison and was enabled to enforce his commands, otherwise the Queen had numerous partisans within the city who would gladly have received the whole Lancastrian army. Before I could obtain entrance, the Governor rode down to the Southgate to make a personal examination of myself and my companion, and, on finding who we really were, gladly welcomed us as friends and allies.

The whole city was in an uproar, for news of the arrival of the Queen and her adherents at Berkeley had already reached Gloucester, although nothing was known of the movements of King Edward. The scaffolding of the Cathedral tower was covered with men curious to see the advance of the Lancastrians, as were the towers of all the other churches, and the parapets along the city walls.

It was evident that the Abbot and the clergy with their followers would, if they had dared, have opened their gates wide to the Lancastrians; but Beauchamp had hoisted the banner of York, which now floated proudly in the morning's sun, and said he would hang the first man who talked of opening the city gates over the city walls, and Richard Beauchamp was a man to keep his word. Several citizens, therefore, who had been very busy running to and fro shouting "God save King Henry," from henceforth held their peace. At the Castle, I found the garrison to a man in favour of Edward of York, and they were a strong body of men-at-arms under a very determined commander. Beauchamp, however, privately informed me that he should not like to lead them beyond the walls and leave the Castle defenceless, so strong a Lancastrian party was there within the city.

It was about ten o'clock in the forenoon that a party of riders, with whom I recognized Sir Gervais Clifton, reached the Southgate, demand- ing admittance "in the name of the Queen of England and the Duke of Somerset". Richard Beauchamp himself gave a stern refusal, and they returned to their leaders; but by eleven o'clock the whole army was encamped before the town.

Lord Wenlock now rode to the Southgate, preceded by two trumpeters, and again demanded admittance, threatening, if it were denied, to assault the gates[11] and enter by force, which Richard Beauchamp challenged him to do, advising him to retreat, if he would not himself be assaulted by a shower of arrows.

While these interchanges of menaces were going on, a number of King Edward's fore-riders, who were far in advance of the main army, and were led by Sir Thomas Grey, appeared with banners flying, on the summit of Robin's Wood Hill, within two miles of the city, and the sound of their clarions was brought by the wind.

The Lancastrians now thought that King Edward had approached with his whole army, and feared, if they attempted to attack the city, that he would assail them in the rear, so they marched away in the direction of Theocsbury as rapidly as they could.

No sooner had they departed, than I begged the loan of a fresh horse from Beauchamp, and rode by the bridge across the Severn, making for Theocsbury, by the right bank, while the Lancastrians marched on the other side by Norton and Deorhyste through woods and noisome lanes. The road by Maisemore and Ashelworth is full of cumbersome paths and deep ditches, and, on the left, hills and dales, so that it was not possible to travel fast; moreover, I found that in front of me was a strong party of men-at-arms, under Jasper Tudor, reconnoitring, and nothing but my knowledge of the country saved me from being taken prisoner.

I came upon them suddenly, near Ashelworth quay, and seeing by the badges I wore, that I was one of King Edward's equerries, two of them gave chase, but my gallant horse soon left them, cumbered as they were with armour and gear, to flounder among the Hasfield ditches, while I quietly quaffed a flagon of Styre cider at Master Paunceforte's, giving him due notice that there were wolves ahead, and savage ones withal.

I learned from him that Jasper Tudor's army was reported to be at Newnham-on-Severn, and that the men-at-arms I saw were foreriders, with Jasper himself in their company. I drew bridle for a few minutes only at Hasfield and then took my way by Chaseley for the ferry at the Lower Lode. My friend, the ferryman, had heard and seen nothing of the Lancastrian army, but the Tudor riders had been there in the morning, and asked questions about the fords, lodes, and ferry.

Before two o'clock I was in the town of Theocsbury, and had given warning to Dame Despenser and the Abbot of the approach of Queen Margaret and her army. At Hamme Castle I found many of the citizens assembled, discussing various rumours. Some said that Gloucester had opened her gates to the Queen, others that a great battle was now going on at Apperley, with such like rumours, which generally fly abroad, pending all emergencies, in all towns and cities.

In the meantime, the Queen's forces, most of them foot soldiers, marched from Gloucester, with their left wing on the Severn, and their right advancing by Norton, until they came to the meres of Apperley, when they divided, and while one division – with whom was Queen Margaret, her son Prince Edward, and her daughter-in-law, the Princess Anne – marched by Combe Hill, the other traversed the muddy lanes and woodlands until they passed through the village of Deorhyste, and encamped upon the hill called the New Park[12], above Hamme Castle and Theocsbury.

Queen Margaret and the Princess Anne were borne in a litter along the trackway between Gloucester and Theocsbury, and while the left wing of her army, with Lord Wenlock and the Earl of Devonshire, took up their station on the hill, she passed the night with her son and daughter close to the trackway, near a place called Lincoln's Green, having declined the offer of shelter from the good Abbot.

With her usual courage, she resolved to share the same hardships as those who were risking so much for her and her son's sake. Neither would the Princess Anne leave her husband. There is no doubt that the Duke of Somerset might have crossed the Severn with his whole army, for they arrived before Theocsbury by four o'clock in the forenoon, but the men were beat and footsore, and he thought King Edward was much nearer to him than he really was.

He had been deceived by the fore-riders on Robin's Wood Hill, and feared an attack upon his troops before he could pass them over the Severn. Again, the men themselves were hungry and thirsty, and the provisions in Theocsbury were plentiful and good, and much easier to obtain on that side the Severn, whereas on the other there was but poor cheer, as the Abbot's cellar at Fordington was not well stocked, and Fordington was a poor place with few dainties.

In an hour after their arrival before Theocsbury the town was filled with men-at-arms who demanded provisions, and took them out in cartloads to their fellow soldiers, who, notwithstanding their weariness, were engaged in throwing up some entrenchments both on the hill and around the spot selected for the Queen's encampment for the night. Barrels of good ale and cider, with bread and meat, much refreshed them.

I was altogether uncertain as to the route the King would take, and it was nearly seven o'clock that evening when I recognized one of our own scouts, disguised as a country hind, passing the house where I had taken refuge to avoid the Lancastrian soldiers who well nigh filled the streets. This was at the new house with the gables and fine windows near the Church of St Mary's, and at the entrance of the narrow street leading to the Swilgate. He was well disguised, and pretended to be staring about him with country awe at such an array of armed men.

Beckoning him in to Master Holdhard's I found that the King was marching upon Cheltenham, a little village some seven miles distant as the crow flies, and, indeed, by this time must have arrived there with all his army.

I made up my mind to join him as soon as possible, but to ride was not easy, as the trackway was blocked by the Lancastrian forces, and the other roads were devious and difficult to find. We therefore decided to walk, and, altering my gear as best I could, we set off across the Swilgate drawbridge, over a wild unfrequented country, taking with us a nimble- heeled youth as guide, and in less than two hours I was standing in the presence of our gallant King, giving him the information I had gathered during this foray.

Chapter Seventeen

CHELTENHAM is but a poor village, nevertheless there are two hostelries, as people are apt to frequent them for the drinking, not good wine but strong waters, that is to say, waters which are unsavoury to the palate but strong to drive away meagrims, the cholic, and podagra.

It would have been impossible to have provisioned the army at this village had they not carried food with them from Sudbury on their sumpter horses, and found stores of provisions and whole casks of wines at Prestbury, a favourite hunting resort of the Bishops of Hereford[1], and where they kept much excellent provender.

King Edward had already made one of the most extraordinary marches ever known among generals and leaders of armies, having taken the high ground along the ridge of the Cotswolds intersected by many steep valleys. The day had been hot and the way weary, but no sooner did he hear of the position of the Queen's troops close to Theocsbury than the trumpets sounded to horse, and in a short time we marched by moonlight across a wide open country dotted with trees, thickets, and furze, to a place known as Tredington Common, where water could be obtained, and a certain amount of shelter for the night among the furze bushes and thickets.

Here we were not three miles from the place selected for Queen Margaret to pass the night, and it was certain that a battle would be fought on the morrow. The ground, fortunately, was hard and dry on the open common, but the lanes were of such stiff clays and stick-mires that one or two culverins had to be left behind.

The troops, too, had no refection for the night, save what they carried in their pouch bags and a barrel of wine from the Bishop's stores at Prestbury. King Edward addressed them before they lay down to rest for the night, promising that they should break their fast at Theocsbury on excellent good victuals. He passed the night himself at Fiddington Grange.

During the night spies were employed to ascertain, as nearly as they could, the exact positions of the Lancastrian army, but they did not accomplish much in the way of scrutiny.

As soon as the sun had risen on Saturday the 4th of May, King Edward marshalled his army and divided them into three battalions.

The Duke of Gloucester led the van, the King commanded the centre, and the Duke of Clarence with Lord Hastings brought up the rear and the reserves.

Robin and I, with two hundred picked archers, went to the front as skirmishers, my orders being to communicate with the King from time to time as to the movements of the enemy and their positions. A light mist in the early morning shrouded our silent advance, and favoured the King's army, allowing them to march unseen towards the Lancastrian camp. When the leading archers reached the Theocsbury trackway, we found a large corps strongly posted along the road, on the other side of which, and near to the trackway, was a small stronghold of fallen trees and dense fences of bushes. Here the Queen, the Prince, and the Lady Anne passed the night.[2]

Beyond was a position right hard to assail by reason of the deep ditches, hedges, trees, bushes and cumbersome lanes.[3] The right wing of the Lancastrian army was commanded by Prince Edward and Lord St John. The centre occupied the flat lands round the base of the hill, under the Earl of Devonshire, while on the crest, or New Park, was Lord Wenlock with the archers and a few culverins, but the Lancastrians had not the same number of big guns that the King had, some of which threw shot as large as a great apple.

By the time we reached the trackway, the heat of the sun cleared the mist away, and we found ourselves in front of a thousand troops, who at once took the alarm, and concentrating behind the hedges and bushes, gave us such a storm of arrows that we lost several men, and should have lost more, had we not dispersed at the blast of Robin's bugle, and fallen back upon the corps led by the Duke of Gloucester. The Duke, with his usual courage, attacked the forces in the trackway, but he found men as full of valour as himself, and every yard was desperately disputed.

The Duke of Somerset, who was on horseback in the trackway with several other riders in full armour, charged down upon us and, but for the thick hedge and ditch into which the Duke of Gloucester threw himself, he would have seen his last battle-field. For full half-an-hour the strife was renewed in the trackway, and round the Queen's encampment, while the King, standing on a slight eminence above the roadway, directed the assaults. Our men fell fast, for the Lancastrians were defended by their thick ambush of trees and hedges. On this the King

Chapter Seventeen

gave me directions to convey a message to the Duke of Gloucester to debouch to the right and make way for him to attack with the powerful troops of the centre, after he had poured shots with his great artillery into the Queen's camp and the surrounding defences.

It was not the position about Lincoln's Green that gave the King anxiety. He knew he could force it, but there was the corps of the centre within the Park, and the battalions on the hill, both of which might fall on us while we were engaged around the trackway. It was necessary to make a diversion, and before making his attack in person on this tough stronghold, he asked me if I was not well acquainted with the locality, and on my replying in the affirmative, he said, "If you, good Sir Hildebrande, with old Robin of Elsdune, will hold those Frenchmen on the hill in check for one single hour, we will win this battle by the help of God."

On reaching the Duke of Gloucester, I gave him the King's command to clear the trackway on the right up to the very gates of Hamme Castle, and hold the entrance to Theocsbury. I also told him of a plan I had, knowing the ground, of marching on the left with two hundred archers, and attacking the troops on the crest of the hill in the rear from the side of Deorhyste, and also in flank from the ferry by the Lower Lode.

I then begged of him to detach two hundred more archers and spearmen under the command of Robin, and send them by way of the trackway from Hamme Castle to the Lower Lode. Opposite the Lode were dense woodlands on hanging banks above the Severn, and by these Robin might attack Lord Wenlock and his corps of reserve on the crest of the hill, much about the same time as I did from the side of Deorhyste. The gallant young Duke, for he was only twenty years of age, shook me by the hand, and said, "A right good plan, most worthy knight. You lead your men, and Robin will back you as in days of yore."

By this time the culverins were making a great deal of noise, and doing very little damage, save that the Lancastrians liked them not, and left the trackway, concentrating their forces in the Park beneath the hill.

I now rapidly passed to the left, leading my men through woodlands until we could see the grey Saxon tower of the church of Deorhyste from the slope of the hill we were ascending. The noise of the culverins had ceased, and from the shouts and yells we could gather that the King was leading in person and forcing his way into the great close in the Park. I even thought I could discern his own powerful voice, and the shout 'En avant!' which I so well remembered years ago in the desperate charges at Mortimer's Cross.

We rested for a few moments to gain breath under some great oak trees on the slope of the hill facing Deorhyste, when I heard a shrill whistle which I recognized as Robin's, who was ascending the steep slope from the Severn through the woodlands. In a few minutes our forces were united, and with him was the Duke of Gloucester. He had left his corps under the command of the Duke of Clarence, as being the safer place, and of his own accord was our companion in the dangerous assault we were about to carry into the very stronghold of the enemy. Well do I remember that young warrior, for such he truly was, leaning against a tall oak, balancing the battle-axe he used with such a sturdy arm and tightening his armour for the fray.

We now marched up the southern slope of the hill and the din of battle arose louder than ever around Lincoln's Green, into which King Edward had forced his way. On the summit of the hill we found ourselves confronted by a strong body of Frenchmen, who defended the position with great bravery. We learnt afterwards that the Duke of Somerset had sent two or three messengers to Lord Wenlock with orders to lead his men down the hill to attack the King. This Lord Wenlock could not do, as he had to repel the onset of our archers upon his rear. Whereupon the Duke of Somerset galloped like a madman up the hill, and finding Lord Wenlock standing on the crest, reviled him, calling him "Traitor!" and with his battle-axe struck the brains out of his head.

At this moment, the Duke of Gloucester, ever to the front, dashed forwards, slaying the Frenchmen right and left, and cheering our gallant archers. The struggle was hard for a while around the great oaks on the summit, but at last, seeing they had been taken in the rear, and not knowing how small a body of men were attacking, the whole corps on the crest of the hill gave way, and rushed tumultuously down the slope towards Lincoln's Green and the Bloody Meadow.

We followed, driving them among the King's troops on one side, and among those of the Duke of Clarence in front of Hamme Castle. Everywhere they found themselves surrounded, and in a short time it was no longer a field of battle; it was a field of slaughter. After the Duke of

Somerset had killed Lord Wenlock, he saw his mistake, and tried to rally the flying Frenchmen; but all to no purpose, they rushed wildly down the hill, shouting "Treachery!".

The whole scene was changed; in every direction were flying men, and no quarter being given to the foreigners, not one of them that was taken was left alive. Some of the English troops from Devonshire escaped, but not many of these. Some fled through the park by way of Deorhyste; some hid themselves in ditches; a few swam across the Severn; and others were drowned in the attempt. A few found refuge in houses and the Abbey, others were drowned in the Swilgate stream, which was choked with corpses near the bridge by the Abbey.

When next I saw King Edward, he was standing, wearied with his exertions, on the rising ground to the west of Hamme Castle, looking down upon the Bloody Meadow, where nearly three thousand dead bodies lay in very small compass. His armour was covered with mud and blood, but he had taken off his helmet for air, and the flush of victory was on his brow. He ordered me to take a message to the Duke of Clarence, who was he thought, in the Bloody Meadow, and tell him to occupy the crest of the hill with the culverins.

I had proceeded a short distance, when he shouted to me, "Tell Gloucester and Clarence to find out what has become of Margaret of Anjou and her son, and make every effort to seize their persons, for if that woman escapes to those accursed Tudors across the water, we shall have to fight this battle over again."

The Bloody Meadow was a sorry sight, and just at the side next Lincoln's Green, lay the dead bodies of Sir John Delves, Sir John Leukenor, and Sir William Vaulx,[4] and the slaughter was still continuing near the Severn, where a noisome swamp had entrapped many who otherwise might have escaped.

Neither of the Royal Dukes could I find, for they had gone into the town, and I therefore prepared to carry out the King's commands respecting the culverins, which were now posted on the slope of the hill. It was no easy matter to induce men, after the heat of battle, to set to work to drag these instruments of warfare, but at last by dint of promises and guerdons I succeeded in doing so.

As we ascended the hill I met Sir Richard Crofts walking down side by side with a well-proportioned, handsome young gentleman, who was his prisoner and had surrendered on his parole. Would that I had known then that this was Edward, the Lancastrian Prince of Wales, as I might have averted the tragedy which was so soon to follow.

I had no sooner seen the artillerymen and their carronades posted on the summit of the New Park, than I mounted a horse and rode down the hill to the town.

As I was crossing a narrow trackway which leads to Lincoln's Green, I thought I heard a woman's shrieks proceeding from a peasant's cot some distance up the lane. On this I galloped to the spot, and there, struggling with two rough soldiers of King Edward's body-guard, was a lady whom they were endeavouring to plunder of a few gold ornaments she wore on her neck nd wrists.

Jumping from my horse I rushed into the small garden, where this scene was being enacted, and the men, recognizing in me one of their own officers, sprang over the hedge and disappeared among the trees of the park. The lady fell fainting into my arms, and, as I laid aside the long hair which fell in thick tresses across her face to give her air, I beheld to my utter bewilderment and astonishment, my long-lost love, Rosamund Berew.

As she gradually recovered, it was some time before she recognized me, so great was her terror and dismay at the perils around her. When at last she fully comprehended it was the Hildebrande of her childhood who held her in fond embrace, she laid her head on my bosom and wept tears of gratitude and joy. But this was no place for long endearments, or even for much explanation how she arrived there.

I could only gather that she had accompanied Margaret of Anjou and the Princess Anne on their landing in England, and had undergone with them the perils of the march, only to witness the utter disaster of the Lancastrian army before Theocsbury. She now entreated, after I had seen her safe within some friendly house in the town, or in the Sanctuary of the Abbey, that I would look to the rescue of the unhappy Queen and her luckless children.

Having placed my Rosamond under the care of a servant of the good Abbot, the next thing was to find what had become of Queen Margaret, and rescue her, and the Princess Anne, from falling into the hands of the rough and rude soldiers. I learned from John Baynton, one of the prisoners who had been in attendance upon them during the night, that both had gone up the park during the attack upon the stronghold near Lincoln's Green, and that when we took the hill with our archers, the

Queen was hurried away in the direction of the Lower Lode by a monk who had never left her side.

The Princess Anne had refused to leave her husband, until, at his urgent entreaties, she was carried in a half-fainting condition down the hill towards Theocsbury, where Baynton expected she must have fallen into the custody of the Duke of Clarence.

Hoping that both these unfortunate ladies had found a refuge and sanctuary in the Abbey, I hurried thither, and what a sight did I behold. The slain lay thick in the churchyard among the graves and around the Abbey walls, as some of the unfortunate foreigners who had been persuaded to join Queen Margaret in the hopes of plunder, thought that once inside they were safe.

On entering the Abbey, the noble arches of the nave resounded with the shouts of the savage soldiery, and the shrieks of those who sought in vain for quarter, while the pavement was streaming with blood. The mortuary chapels of Beauchamp and Despenser were thick with dead and dying, as many hoped for safety when within reach of their little altars. Vain hope, with men's passions aroused to frenzy.

The Abbot was standing in front of the high altar, exhibiting the sacrament of the Host, and entreating the Yorkist soldiers, in the name of the Most High God, to stay their butchery in God's House. The Duke of Somerset and the Earl of Devonshire, with the Prior of St John's, had sought refuge close to the high altar, and some fugitives were clinging to the robes of the Abbot and monks.

I did my utmost to stay the carnage, but my person was not known to the London troops, and I was nearly struck down through my endeavours to interfere. "The King gives no quarter!" was everywhere the cry, and the infuriated pursuers were proceeding to drag the fugitives from the shelter of the altar, when a voice like a trumpet call rang through the Abbey in the one word "Hold!".

It was the stentorian voice of King Edward himself, who now strode down the nave, his tall form and bare head towering above the crowd of officers and generals who surrounded him. Had a thunderbolt fallen amongst them the effect could not have been greater, for in a few minutes the shameless butchers had sneaked out of the doorways into the town, and were plundering the houses.

The King, addressing the Abbot, said that he entered the Abbey "to give God thanks for his great and glorious victory, and not to slay and kill. The sanctuary should be respected, and, the next day being Sunday, no one should be tried or arraigned until the Monday." Thus those who still lived were taken in charge by the Abbot and the monks, and were well cared for within the precincts of the monastery as long as they were under their care.

The dead lay in heaps, and I was leaving to obtain aid to remove the unsightly corpses,[5] when I received a summons to wait upon the King, who was now standing by the great doorway.

He enquired whether I had any tidings of Queen Margaret, telling me that the Duke of Clarence was in possession of the Lady Anne, who had been taken when flying for the Abbey. He then begged of me to spare no pains to capture the Queen and, as I was acquainted with persons in the town, to obtain aid and, if it were needed to search every house which was likely to afford her shelter.

During all that Saturday evening I was engaged in a fruitless pursuit. The Queen was not to be found in either the Abbey, or St Mary's, nor did I succeed in tracing that she had passed the Severn at either of the lodes, or gone through the town.

And now there happened the most sorrowful episode of this terrible war, and one which will ever stain the character of Edward IV. When the King departed from the staying of the slaughter in the Abbey, he took up his quarters at an old timbered dwelling house where lived Master Morley, a faithful adherent of the House of York, and who was in some fashion connected with the Despensers. This house is nearly opposite the Cross at Theocsbury, and the King chose to lodge there in preference to some of the nobler dwellings, as he was well affected to Master Morley.

The Duke of Clarence occupied a fine house with new casements and gables opposite the tabard of the Swan, and the Duke of Gloucester was lodged in the Tolsey. Robin and I had gone to our old friend the host of the Black Bear of Warwick, and were of some service to him in preventing the over-licence of the troops foraging for drink and provisions.

About six o'clock in the evening of that Saturday so fatal to the Lancastrians, having exhausted every effort to find Queen Margaret, I was going to report my want of success to the King, when I beheld a sight at the door of Master Morley, I would I had never looked upon.

A number of men-at-arms were placed before the entrance as a

Chapter Seventeen

guard, and through them I was going, with the pass-word for approach to the King's presence, when I saw the Duke of Clarence standing at the doorway supporting the senseless form of the beautiful Princess Anne. On seeing me he called me by name, and bid me lend him a helping hand, so we carried her, as she lay in a swoon, to the Duke's quarters, where she was handed over to the care of the women of the house in which he lodged. The only remark he made to me, as we returned to Master Morley's was, "Wild and sorry work this, Sir Hildebrande" for, as we reached the door, some men-at-arms were carrying the dead body of a noble-looking youth towards the Abbey.

Alas! this was the corpse of the Lancastrian Prince Edward. And well might the Duke say this was wild and sorry work, for future historians will repeat the report of these days, that he, with Richard, Duke of Gloucester, the Marquis of Dorset, Thomas Grey, and William, Lord Hastings, in the presence of the King, foully murdered Prince Edward in cold blood.

I was not present in the fatal room at the time the Prince was killed, but I may safely say that I will never believe that these noblemen themselves shed the blood of Prince Edward; and it is well known that, in these times, when a Tudor is King of England, any lie against the House of York is well received and duly circulated. What did happen I will truly write, to the best of my knowledge and belief.

After the battle was ended, proclamation was made that whosoever could bring forth Prince Edward alive or dead should have an annuity of a hundred pounds during his life; but the Prince's life was to be saved if he were taken alive.[6]

As I have already said, the Prince surrendered to Sir Richard Crofts, who it appears sheltered him for some time, when, not mistrusting the King's promise, he conducted his prisoner to the presence of Edward himself. The King then demanded of him "How he durst so presumptuously to enter into his realm with banner displayed?"

Whereupon the Prince boldly answered, "To recover my father's kingdom and heritage, from his father and grandfather to him, and from him, after him, to me lineally descended."

At which words King Edward said nothing, but with his hand thrust him from him, or, as some say, struck him with his gauntlet.[7]

Then report says, 'the above-named Lords stabbed the Prince to death with their daggers'. This, I say, I do not believe, and I will state my reasons. In the first place, I will leave it to the ladies of England to declare that no lady of the gentle disposition of the Princess Anne and so noble withal, would have married the Duke of Gloucester if she had beheld him murder her young bridegroom.[8]

Secondly, it was reported at the time of the Prince's death that the deed was done 'by some servants of the King, who thought that they would please their master'.[9]

Again, Master Fabyan, the Chronicler, who was living in London at this time, and who would have been certain to have reported such scandal of the Yorkists, if such had been spread abroad in his time, writes, with respect to the death of Henry VI, that 'the common fame went, that he was sticked by the hands of the Duke of Gloucester', but that the Prince was despatched by servants.[10]

Thirdly, the known characters of the Marquis of Dorset, and William, Lord Hastings, are altogether against the belief that these Lords killed the Prince with their own hands. No, I believe it not; and in these days, when I hear such reports of those who are gone down to the grave and cannot defend themselves, I lift up my hands and say, "How some men are given to lying!"

The following sabbath morning was a beautiful May day, and the sun rose on hill and dale, lighting up the spring green of the great Severn helms, the red cliffs of the Mythe Twt, and the great trees of the New Park; but such a Sunday morning Theocsbury never saw before, and I trust may never see again.

The Abbey had been cleared of the bloody corpses, all save that of the Prince, which lay exposed that all comers might see that the heir of Henry VI was dead, so his body lay upon a bier in the middle of the nave. And all day long tolled the death bell, and the dead were being buried in the churchyard, in a pit on the right hand of the great gate above which now rests an altar stone with a stone cross to mark the spot where lie some scores of unhappy Lancastrians.

During the whole of Sunday, the Duke of Somerset and the other fugitive Lords remained safe under the protection of Abbot Strensham within the precincts of the Sanctuary. I found means to send Rosamond Berew to my mother's care at Birtsmereton. The Duke of Clarence also obtained leave from the King to place the Princess Anne under the care of his Duchess, the Lady Isabella; but we could not hear or the whereabouts of the unhappy Queen Margaret of Anjou.

Chapter Seventeen

Theocsbury is full of narrow alleys and strange out-of-the-way places, but all these were searched in vain; so the Sunday passed away, and I had received no clue to her discovery, although a large sum was offered for her apprehension. On the Monday morning I received orders from the King to search the Abbot's house at Fordington, as there was some suspicion of the Queen having fled there for shelter. It was mere suspicion, for there were no signs of such having been the case. On my return I passed the great pit which was dug for those who fell on the battle-field, close to the turn of the trackway to the Lower Lode and where more than four thousand corpses of the foreigners and common men were thrown in heaps together.[11]

Then came the trial of the lords and knights, with other gentlemen and esquires who had taken refuge in the Abbey, at St Mary's, and other parts of the town. They were apprehended and brought before the Duke of Gloucester, as Constable of England, at the Tolsey in the midst of the town. After a long hearing they were all judged guilty of raising rebellion against the King, and were condemned to die; but some, among whom was my father's friend, John Throcmorton, whose arms are in our panelled chamber, King Edward pardoned.

Both Robin and myself strongly objected to the executions of these lords and knights, because hitherto the asylum of Church sanctuaries had ever been respected, and to these sanctuaries the King owed the preservation of his Queen, his children, and many friends whom the Lancastrians when in power left undisturbed in their sacred refuge.

The preparations for the execution were carried on all the Monday night, and a great scaffold was erected at the Cross in the middle of the town. At an early hour the space around was occupied by troops and spectators, who seemed little moved at the thought of the bloody scenes which were to follow.

Up to the last moment I hoped that the King would have pardoned many of the prisoners, even if he dealt rigorously with the Duke of Somerset and the Earl of Devonshire, who were ever his bitter opponents, and no doubt would have cut off his head had he fallen into their power. But Edward was ever of revengeful temper, and was still more so since the conspiracy of the Earl of Warwick and his brother, so he allowed the executions to be carried out, and even looked out upon several from the casement of the house of Master Morley where he lodged.[12]

The streets ran with the blood of nearly thirty Lancastrians of rank,[13] whose heads were struck off at Theocsbury Cross on this May morning. King Edward did not follow the example of Queen Margaret in setting up their heads and quarters in any public places, but permitted them to be buried; some in the Abbey, some in the churchyard, and some, as in the case of the Prior of St John, were transported for burial by their friends and relations.

This wholesale execution was but just concluded, when the King announced his intention of riding that afternoon to Worcester, and commanded me to follow with the archers. In half-an-hour I should have been in the saddle, but that Robin of Elsdune, who had been superintending the burial of the fallen on the battle-field, informed me that some men who were digging the great pit reported that a strange lady had been seen escorted by two monks crossing the Severn on the afternoon of the battle, in a fisherman's boat, just above the Red Bank at the Mythe.

It then struck me that Master Payne, who befriended Master Vaughan when sick and dying, was mayhap a person to run the risks of giving shelter to the unhappy Queen. I therefore begged Robin to inform the King that I had received what might prove to be tidings of Queen Margaret, and would follow him to Worcester after conducting the investigations.

I walked quickly through the town to the Mythe hill, where the nightingales were singing in the groves, and the yellow woad was blossoming on bright red cliffs, and crossing the river in a fisherman's boat, I walked over fine green meadows, with numerous skylarks carolling overhead, until I reached a narrow trackway which led to Rushley Church. Pursuing this I took the turn to Payne's Place, when opposite the doorway of the Orange was Master Payne himself, mounted on a tall horse, and on a pillion behind him was seated a lady dressed after the description of her who had been seen to cross the Severn in a boat by the grave-diggers.

Master Payne riding forward, without hesitation begged me not to interfere with the escape of the unhappy Queen of England, who was well-nigh distracted at the tidings of the murder of her beloved son, but to allow them to pass on unmolested.

While he was thus speaking the lady lifted her hood, which was drawn far over her face, and notwithstanding that time and sorrow had told sadly upon her great beauty, I recognized, in the fire of that eye, the remarkable expression of the Countess of Oxford, who ten years before had taken refuge both at Hergest and Birtsmereton after the battle of Towton. Lines of sorrow were deeply engraved upon that noble face, and she sat on her horse as if stricken dumb.

Payne now said, "You are too chivalric a knight to put the sleuth hounds of Edward upon our track. In God's name delay us not."

Overwhelmed at the sight of the sorrowing, broken-hearted mother, I approached and respectfully kissed her hand, entreating her to allow me to conduct her to the presence of the King, and offering to pledge my own life that hers should be spared. Master Payne sternly interposed, saying that Edward had broken his promise to Sir Richard Crofts, and falsified his own proclamation of safety for Prince Edward. He, too, had broken his kingly word to the Abbot and the prisoners in the Sanctuary, whom he pardoned on the Saturday, and then had them dragged forth to death on that very morning.

Alas! it was impossible to deny these charges, and my own heart was burning with indignation at these self-same deeds of cruelty. So come what may I determined to oppose their flight no longer, and they were soon lost in the woodlands which came down to Master Payne's dwelling, and the pleasant glades of Pull. Mistress Payne was in tears at the misery of the Queen, and the risks encountered by her own husband, but she insisted upon my entering the grange, and showed me a string of beads and a crucifix which the Queen had left as a memorial of her safe refuge. Yielding to the entreaties of her son, Margaret of Anjou had allowed herself to be conducted to this homely retreat, where she was well cared for until it was feared that search would be made by the King's emissaries. The room she occupied during three days of bitter anguish is called the Queen's Room to this day.[14]

By the time I reached Theocsbury, the King had left for Worcester, but Robin was to remain until the morrow with the archers, and await the return of some scouts who had been sent to find out the movements of the Welshmen under Jasper Tudor. My orders, too, were to march with the rear-guard.

We were glad to leave a place which would ever be associated in our memories with scenes of carnage and revenge no true soldier could look back upon without disgust. Robin was as indignant as myself at the murder of the Prince, and much did we lament on our ride to the city of Worcester that the King suffered himself to be swayed from his given word, and sent the Lancastrian prisoners from the Sanctuary to the block.

The young Duke of Gloucester, too, was exhibiting a ruthless disposition in early life, and Clarence had perjured himself over and over again. False to his brother in the affair of the Archbishop's feasting, false to his father-in-law before the battle of Barnet, who could tell where his perfidy would end?

"I would give my gold spurs," said Robin, "if that poor youth had not been stabbed to death in Edward's presence," and then, turning in his saddle for a last look at Theocsbury, he added in a low tone, "That is my last battle-field."

I knew what he meant, and fully sympathized with one who would sheathe his sword for ever, rather than draw it in a cause in which success was to be followed by cruelty and perfidy.

As we entered the city of Worcester the sun was setting behind the Malverns we both loved so well. Trumpets were sounding, crowds were cheering, bells were ringing, flags were flying from every steeple. King Edward was showing himself to the people, but he had lost the respect and affection of two devoted followers.

In Worcester we heard that Queen Margaret and her guide and protector had been taken prisoners at a place called the Old Hills. The unhappy Queen had an awful interview with the King, and a sad scene of recrimination ensued. This interview formed a bitter part of the cup which she was doomed to drink, as Edward reminded her of the skeleton heads of his father and brother, which, by her orders, were transfixed on spikes above the gates of York. He told her that he was much pressed by his advisers to set her head above the gates of Worcester, but that he never warred with women, and should send her to join her husband in the Tower.

Master Payne was confined in the common prison, and was condemned to be hanged, the following morning, as a traitor and accessor to the Queen's escape. On presenting myself before the King he gave me commands to wait upon Queen Margaret at the sanctuary of the Cathedral, and tell her to prepare to travel on the morrow to London ; and thus I saw this unhappy woman for the last time.

I found her gazing on the portrait of that son for whom she had sacrificed the lives of thousands, and who lay in the grave in the Abbey of Theocsbury, surrounded by the last holocaust of victims who fell for the Lancastrian cause. Over this picture she was moaning and wailing as I entered the gloomy chamber. She did not at first recognize me, but looked up as I knelt before her to deliver the King's command.

But what a look! What an expression of hopeless sorrow! The window of the chamber was open, and a glint of sunshine fell upon the chair upon which the Queen was seated, as if in mockery of such a scene of misery. She now rose, and turning to the window looked out for a few moments at the Cathedral Close, where sentinels and soldiers were pacing up and down, then, returning to where I was standing awaiting her reply, she drew herself up haughtily, displaying her commanding figure and, with some of the old fire in her eye, asked "Why Master Blackburn would not comply with her sole request, and send her to the scaffold?" "It is the one favour," she continued, "that Margaret of Anjou asks of the son of the Archer of Middleham".[15]

I was now leaving, when she said, "Nay! but I have one request to make of you before we part for ever." Then, taking a golden crucifix from her neck, she passed the chain from which it was suspended round mine, saying, "Give this emblem to your Rosamond in memory of Margaret of England. I shall never forget her care and solicitude towards my darling son long years ago, among the woods of Hergest and the hills of Malvern, or what she has since suffered for conscience sake."

I found the King at the Gueston hall in the Cathedral Close, surrounded by the royal dukes and nobles, who had assembled for a great banquet. As soon as he became aware of my presence he conducted me to an inner chamber and asked how I had been received by the Queen, and if she had any request to make that he could grant "without endangering his throne, and having all his best friends hung, drawn, and quartered."

He then added, "But by my halidome, Sir Hildebrande, you look as if you had seen a witch! Have you met with Mary of Eldesborough, or whatever she calls herself, as well as with Margaret of Anjou?"

I replied that the Queen seemed distracted with her sorrows, and was in no condition to ask for his royal favours, but that I had one to implore for the sake of olden times, and a promise of days gone by. I now knelt and showed him the ring I had worn since we were youths together, and he took my hand kindly, and pressing it said, "Ask away, good Hildebrande, Edward never forgets a staunch friend." I then entreated him to pardon Master Payne, who had been condemned to death for assisting Queen Margaret in her attempted escape.

He made no hesitation, but granted my request forthwith, saying laughingly, is that all? You may take half-a-score Paynes for the good services I owe you." He then called for writing materials, and with his own hand signed a free pardon, saying, as he handed it to me, "But, Hildebrande, you must attend our Court, and join our Council. We have plenty of work, and rewards, too, I trust, for such as you and our faithful Robin. Let us find you a noble wife." I bowed low, and begged to be allowed to retire, and for several years I never saw the face of King Edward IV.

Before dawn the next morning, I, with Master Payne, were on our road to Birtsmereton, for the King had given me as long a leave from my duties as his equerry and esquire as I chose to take.

On the 21st of May King Edward entered London in great pomp at the head of a large army; on one side rode the Duke of Gloucester, on the other the Duke of Clarence, all bare-headed and clad in splendid armour. The Sun banner of the conqueror preceded him, and floated proudly as he passed Queen Elizabeth and her mother, the proud Duchess, seated at a balcony in the May sunshine, the Queen holding in her arms the infant Prince of Wales.

Yet another dark episode clouded the fame of the conquerors with a blot no time may ever eradicate. On the morning which followed this noble entry, and when peace and pardon should have followed their rejoicings, Henry of Lancaster was found lifeless in the Tower, and, as Master Fabyan wrote,'Men said boldly that the deed was done by Richard Duke of Gloucester'.

In a few days after this happened, Robin retired to his Keep of Castlemereton. What transpired between him and King Edward I know not, but this I know, that nothing save falseness and cruelty would alienate the Archer from the cause of him he really loved, and I fear he did not acquit the King of conniving at Henry's death.

The Lancastrians as a party were annihilated, and peace once more settled over England. Disliking a Court life and disgusted at the deeds at Theocsbury, I, like Robin, determined never again to draw the sword for either the White Rose or the Red, especially as I now perceived that little hope could be entertained that King Edward would aid the

Chapter Seventeen

Lollards in obtaining freedom for worship, or in withstanding the demands of the ecclesiastics.

On returning home I found Rosamond safe under my mother's care, and overwhelmed with joy at her return to the happy scenes of our youth. I had much to listen to, and she had much to tell of all she had undergone, when for years she had been imprisoned in a convent away from all she loved, owing to her uncle's fear for her future salvation, and determination to prevent, if possible, her marriage with myself, a believer in the doctrines and teachings of Master Wycliffe.

On their first landing in France, after their escape from Birtsmereton, Master Vaughan had informed her that the so-called Countess of Oxford and her son were Margaret of Anjou and Prince Edward. For some time she remained in the service of Queen Margaret as a companion for the young Prince, and every means were taken to convert her from the faith she had chosen to that of the orthodox Church. But Rosamond steadfastly refused to listen either to the plead- ings of her uncle and the Queen, or to the sophistries of the priests; and it was then that Master Vaughan conveyed her to a convent from which there appeared to be no means of escape.

Nor indeed would she ever have been enabled to leave her prison house, but for the fortunate circumstance that the Earl of Warwick, being well acquainted with the lady superior, sent his daughter, the Lady Anne, there for a short time during his negotiations with Queen Margaret.

Rosamond was selected to attend upon this young lady, and so far succeeded in interesting her by her tale of sorrow, that the Lady Anne obtained leave from her father to request the lady superior to allow her to leave the convent as her personal attendant. In this way she accompanied Queen Margaret and her daughter-in-law to England, the Queen being really glad of an excuse to aid in the release of one to whom she was much indebted when herself a fugitive after the field of Towton.

In the sunny month of June I led Rosamond to the altar at our church at Birtsmereton. Bessie Calverley insisted that the wedding should be there, rather than at Berew, for in olden times the holder of the manor of Birtsmereton presented a rose to the Dukes of Lancaster[16] on the feast of St John the Baptist, and now my blushing rose would on this happy occasion be presented to me. On our wedding morning Bessie Calverley gave me good proof of her clerkly skill and sweet imagination in the following flowers of poesie:

> *I love the flowers which circle round*
> *Our Malverns far and free;*
> *The Heart'sease and Forget me not*
> *Are flowers I love to see.*
>
> *I love the yellow Buttercup,*
> *That sunny, springtime flower;*
> *And Daisy sparkling 'white and redde'*,[17]
> *Beneath the summer shower.*
>
> *I love the purple Heather Bell,*
> *Which o'er the moorland ranges;*
> *And Ivy clinging to the wall,*
> *Which like true love ne'er changes*
>
> *I love to see the yellow Flag*
> *By sparkling streamlets quiver;*
> *And the modest Lily of the Vale,*
> *Or Wild Rush by the river.*
>
> *I love the nodding Daffodil,*
> *Which blossoms on the mead,*
> *And Violet or Pimpernel,*
> *With humble Silver Weed.*
>
> *I love to see the Woodbine cling*
> *around our forest trees;*
> *And Honesty its tendrils throw,*
> *To every passing breeze.*
>
> *But oh! there is one flower I love*
> *O'er every flower that grows*
> *On mountain, woodland, hill or dale,*
> *Our own, our sweet Wild Rose.*

The church looked well worthy of being called God's House on that summer morning, and it was filled with wild roses from the thickets, and worshippers with grateful hearts. My mother wore a chamlet gown most beautiful to look upon; a gift from Queen Elizabeth, and the King sent me a wedding present of ten ells of fine cloth of colour violet in grain and, for lining, thirty bellies of minever.

Rosamond and Bessie wore gowns of fairest white linen, Rosamond's being worked with roses and Bessie's with white lilies, with silver girdles the presents of Calverley, whose own dress was fine enough for King Edward. Hasting and Master Thomas of Gulley's End wore their new fyne felt hats after the fashion of those alluded to in the London Lycpeny. We also gave to all our hinds, both at Birtsmereton, Berew, and Pendyke, smocks worked on the stomachers with the device of a rose, and to all their women new gowns and comfachers.

The Sub-Prior of Pendyke united us in the sacrament of marriage at our most earnest request, and he gave us a copy of the Gospels transcribed with his own hand from Master Wycliffe's Bible. The margins of the parchments were limnered over with shapes of stars and rocks, the wild birds of the air and the flowers of the field; for the old priest thought that such things in nature were the works of the Creator, and so pictured them with his quill upon the fringes of His Word.

As the years passed away Rosamond and I lived happy and contented lives in the old home under the hills. No son was born to us, but our daughters were ever comely from their cradles.

Two years after the fatal field of Theocsbury, Richard, Duke of Gloucester married in 1473 the Lady Anne of Warwick, the widow of Prince Edward; which should alone be sufficient refutation to the slanderous tale that he, Duke Richard, had any personal hand in the Prince's murder. Sir John Paston, writing to his brother soon after this marriage, says, 'The world seemeth queasy[18] here; for the most part that be about the King have sent hither for their harness'. In truth the brothers, Duke Richard and the Duke of Clarence, disputed about the Lady Anne's inheritance, and pleaded each his cause in person before the King in council. For several years the land was in peace and quietude, and the Duke of Gloucester, with the lovely Anne, resided at Middleham Castle in Yorkshire.

In the year of grace 1479, Isabella, Duchess of Clarence, died in a suspicious manner, and the nurse who attended her was condemned to death and executed for administering poison. No sooner was she buried in the Abbey of Theocsbury than Clarence proposed himself as a husband to Mary, Duchess of Burgundy, who had vast estates.

And now after this there befel one of those dark tragedies which ever and anon appear in the history of courts and kings. First of all two gentlemen of his household, and afterwards the Duke of Clarence himself, were accused of 'damnable magic', and 'of dealing with the Devil', in order to dethrone the King and disinherit the King's children.

Then this weak-minded Duke received sentence of death, and report says that he was drowned in a butt of that Malmsey wine he loved so well and quaffed so freely. His body rests by the side of his wife in the Abbey of Theocsbury, in a vault just opposite the effigy of the Skeleton Monk, and among the bones of those who were slaughtered on the battle-field and scaffold hard by.

It was in the year of grace 1482, and about the time of Midsummer, as I was fishing and watching the glimmer chafers in the great fishpool above our moat, with Rosamond and our loved Jacinth by my side, that a rider appeared before the drawbridge, charged with a message from King Edward, commanding me to attend him forthwith at Malvern Magna, whither he had journeyed accompanied by his Queen, his son the Prince of Wales, and the Princess Elizabeth. They had just arrived, the messenger informed us, on a visit to the Prior of Malvern, and came from Worcester in great privacy, attended only by Bishop Alcock, the tutor of the young princes.

I wondered greatly at the King's thus arriving at this lonely village in Malvern Chase. True it is noted for its priory, but King Edward never affected either churches or monasteries. Then the messenger told us how he had gathered, from some of the retinue, that the Queen would have the forest driven for deer for the pleasure of her princely boy, and would try a venture with her own cross-bow.

I was somewhat surprised, too, at this deer-driving at such a time of year, when the fawns were by the sides of the hinds, for the King was well versed in woodcraft; but I remembered from my experience at Court, how the Queen ever had her own way in matters of small consequence.

The sun was rising and bathing the heights of the beacon hills of Worcester and Hereford with golden light as I rode on the gallop by the green glades of Castlemereton towards the Priory of Malvern Parva. As I crossed the streamlet which flows from the pass of the Gullet, a bright blue kingfisher shot like an arrow up the waters, and a gallant stag arose among the ferns below the Wind's Point, and tossed his antlers as if in defiance. Taking the forest ride below the Holy Well I disturbed several hinds and their fawns but they soon disappeared in the woody dingles along the base of the hills.

Arrived at the Priory at Malvern I found that the Queen and Princess Elizabeth had heard mattins and were preparing to break their fast at the refectory. With them, besides Bishop Alcock, was Anthony Widville, now Earl Rivers, who was afterwards to conduct the Prince of Wales to Ludlow Castle and the Marches.

The King had gone forth early to fly some tercels of the Prior's at a hern or bittern, at Blackmere, a morass in the Chase between Malvern and Hanley, and generally a safe find. He was not disappointed, and returning in high spirits, received me with courtesy and cordiality, complimenting me upon my look of health and vigour. Verily, I could hardly return such greetings, for sack and canary, with wines of Spain and Burgundy, had much transformed the once handsome countenance of Edward of York.

The hall, refectory, and cloisters of Malvern remain much as they were built, in those Norman times, when King Henry I. confirmed the, grant of St Edward the Confessor; but the Priory Church has been renovated and the choir rebuilt.[19] Only the Norman nave remains of Wolstan's days. Tradition says that this noble church stands on the exact spot where the Prior of Deorhyste founded a little cell when he fled from the Danes, leaving his own church in flames, and sought here a refuge amidst wild woods and wilder hills.

Here, too, lived the pious hermit St Werstan,[20] who built a chapel to St John the Baptist, where he worshipped until he was slain by Welsh raiders, who had no love for copes and coifs, or monks and cells. It was somewhat singular, too, that the choir was finished, and the high altar and six other altars were dedicated, after the completion of the choir and transepts, in the year of grace 1460, the year before King Edward in his youth won his great battle of Mortimer's Cross, and it was before the high altar that he heard mass as he marched past the Priory on his road to Worcester.[21]

The good Prior and his monks did their utmost for festal cheer and the entertainment of their illustrious guests. The tables in the refectory groaned with the huge sirloin, and with savoury Midsummer fawns well stuffed with rosemary, while the wild boar's head was trimmed with sweet ciceley in honour of the King's venerable mother, Ciceley, Duchess of York.

I now learnt why I was summoned to attend the King. Queen Elizabeth wished to ascend the Malvern heights and behold with her own eyes, from these lofty crests, the Cathedral towers of Gloucester, where her royal husband first raised his standard; the city of Hereford, the scene of his revenge for Wakefield; the distant field of Mortimer's Cross; and the hill which rises above the spire of Theocsbury, and round which raged the battle which was his crowning glory. Edward himself wished to hunt with the Prince of Wales, as the youth was full of ardour for the chase, and to him a fawn was as good as a stag to older hunters, and as large.

Thus it was arranged that I should attend upon the Queen and the Princess Elizabeth and guide them to the Wind's Point, where palfreys would meet us, and refections; while at this pass it was probable that her Majesty might transfix a buck with her own bolt as he passed the borders into the woodlands of Colwall. Beautiful as the summer's morn looked Queen Elizabeth as she mounted the Prior's sure-footed palfrey, but still more lovely was her daughter, Elizabeth of York, then in her sixteenth year.

Fair as her mother, she was taller, with golden hair which flowed in long tresses down her back. Her demeanour, too, was more gracious and royal. She had not the Queen's ill habit of being fond and familiar one day, and cold and forgetful the next. The Princess insisted upon walking the whole distance to Wind's Point, and Bishop Alcock accompanied us, while the Prior, Earl Rivers, and a few others, joined the foresters, and started for the hunt and the thickets by the Holy Well.

I led the way past the solitary cell of St Michael[22] where a hermit met us and presented the Queen with a posy of roses, old man, and organy; he also invited us to view the portraiture upon the dingy walls of his cell, of an archer aiming his shaft at a hind, and supposed to be very ancient. Soon we reached the Well of St Ann, which is a hollow in the rock surrounded by fern and leafy foliage, and into which flows an unceasing streamlet of health-giving waters. Among the fern and yellow gorse arises a simple cross and a stone image of the blessed Ann.

Taking the Gullet above the well we ascended slowly, listening to the cuckoo's note, and the chiff-chaff of the willow wren, or watching the stone-chats as they perched upon the brambles. The Princess was delighted to see the yellow blossoms of Genista, the badge of her ancestor, the first Plantagenet, when we came upon a little streamlet weeping beneath the moss, by which grew the bright blue flowers of Forget-me-not, a flower which she laughingly declared was filched by that great usurper Henry of Lancaster, when he made the loving flower his floral symbol, his motto and watchword.[23] Then there was pink Herb Robert, the flower of the unhappy Robert of Normandy; and bright daisies in abundance, which reminded me of the broken hearted Margaret of Anjou, now far away in the French Castle of Damprierre, where, in a few months, she closed the sad pilgrimage of a troublous and most eventful life.

On arriving at the summit of the Beacon of Worcestershire, the glorious view almost startled the Princess Elizabeth, as she stood wondering at the hills of blue in the northern distance, where rise the Longmynds, Caer Caradoc, and the bold Clees. The Queen's eyes sought the westward, and were fixed upon the Black Mountains, the Gadir, and the peak of the Sugar-loaf, for it was westward the King told her to look for the site of Kingsland's battle-field.

Directing their attention first to Bredon's isolated hill, rising above the Avon water, I showed them the dark promontory opposite, beyond the bold tower of Pershore, and told the tale of Evesham's battle, and how de Montfort met the Plantagenet, and fell close by that Battle Well, around which raged the shock of fight, the clang of swords and spears, shouts of defiance, and the sobs of death.

Then nearer on, I showed them the Cathedral tower of ancient Worcester, where that false king, John, lies buried, and the city of which has hardly yet recovered from the burning it suffered from the troops of Owen Glendower, whose camp at Woodbury we could see crested with tall trees, and from which Henry of Lancaster had no small difficulty in driving him back to his mountains in Wales.

Northwards, and beyond Woodbury in the distance, we could see Round Wrekin rising against the bright blue sky, and beyond lies Shrewsbury, the birthplace of her Majesty's son, Duke Richard. Well did her Grace describe that battle-field, where Henry of Lancaster won victory from his stern foe the Glendower; where Percy died; and Douglas fell from the rock of Haughmond, and his horse lay dead below him.

Next, turning more westward, the bold Clees and the wooded Vinnals rose on either side, above the strong Castle of Ludlow, so often the residence of the bold Mortimers; the stronghold on the Marches, and the principal home for years of the King's father, Richard, Duke of York. More to the westward still, I was able to point out to the enquiring eyes of her Grace the hill of Shobdon, by which the Welsh marched to their doom at Kingsland. To an experienced eye, on a clear bright day such as this, the ridge above Avemestry is visible. And it was near these places, as the Queen well knew, that three suns were seen to rise on the first battle-field of the Lion of York.

Long did the royal visitors gaze upon this scene, and many questions did they ask; while much the Princess Elizabeth enquired respecting the bearing of the Tudors, and how Sir Owen fell a prisoner, and Jasper ran away. This led us to look upon the tall, grey spire of Hereford Cathedral and the waters of the Wye; when Bishop Alcock took up his parable and told of Herefordian lore and great antiquities. He discoursed upon the murder of St Ethelbert, when he came courting at King's Sutton to King Offa's daughter; and how a church of stone was built above the bones of the saint, and miracles without number were worked at his shrine.

He told of the pillage of the Cathedral, and, worse still, the murder of Bishop Leofgar by the ravenous Welsh, and the revenge of Harold. Much did he relate of good St Cantilupe, and how the Saint, who 'was a mighty hunter before the Lord', quarrelled with the Red Earl Gilbert about the right of chase, and caused him to dig the dyke close to which we were now standing.

He told, too, of the White Cross and the 'black dethe'; and pointed to the butts of bold Robin Hood, where Little John stood and allowed an apple to be shot off by an arrow from his head. The good Bishop was about to revert to the miracles worked at the tomb of St Cantilupe, but the Princess Elizabeth, somewhat irreverently, asked where lay the field of Theocsbury.

Turning to the southwards we could see the noble tower of Gloucester Abbey, now free from scaffolding, and the walls of the Castle, where first King Edward raised his standard. The Queen's cheek paled and crimsoned as I told of the great struggle round the camp of Margaret of Anjou at Theocsbury; and we could see the tears coursing down the face of the Princess as I alluded slightly to the death of Prince Edward, as if it had happened on the battle-field, through accident. Nor were they content until I had pointed out the hill of Wainlode, the humble tower of Birtsmereton, and the old Castle of Hanley, in the Severn vale by Upton.

Such were the scenes we gazed on that Midsummer morning, as we marked the distant landscapes and, to me, how fraught they were with the deeds and memories of the dead. What changes had elapsed since that morning when I looked out from the woolstapler's window at Gloucester and saw the young Edward of March ride by on his warhorse towards the Castle. Again the dingle at Kinsham came before me, and I saw the cruel face of Trollop as he dealt the blow, as he thought, of death.

Again I could hear the deep curses of Somerset, as he rode madly up the hill above Theocsbury and struck Lord Wenlock from his saddle; and saw once more the sorrow-stricken face of the Lady Anne of Warwick as she was borne senseless from the scene of her husband's murder. But while these sights and scenes again arose before my vivid fancy's view and as I related somewhat of the history, three bugle notes from the glens above the Holy Well, told us that the King and the hunters moving onwards towards our trysting place at Wind's Point.

We therefore left the bare hill summit and took our way downwards by the pass of the Wych. Bishop Alcock, who was learned in all local lore, as well as in all ecclesiastical research, again discoursed on the celestial wonders brought to mother earth, and instanced the example of St Catherine of Ledbury, the miraculous footsteps of her mare and colt, and how the bells of the church rung of their own accord as she rode with her maid Mabel into the town, and was saved from her pursuers.

As we listened to St Catherine's story, and how Bishop Foliot flouted Thomas a Becket, the Princess Elizabeth was searching for wild flowers, just at that spot near Wind's Point where great elm trees rise above a little spring. It is here, tradition says, the visions came to Will Longland, which he relates in the *Complaint* of Piers the Ploughman; and it was of this water, where grows the marsh violet[24] and the woolly grass, that he wrote, 'I was very forwandered and went me to rest under a broad bank by a burnside, and as I lay and looked in the water I slumbered in a sleeping it sweyved so merry'. Above and around this spring butterflies were hovering, and wild roses clustering with tangled stems; and here on a trailing briar the Princess Elizabeth found a cluster of roses both white and red. Little heeding the marvel of the mixture on one stem, the lighthearted girl wound them round her bodice and danced merrily down the hill.

Arrived at Wind's Point we were met by a forester sent by the King, bidding her Majesty not to wait for the hunting party, inasmuch as they were following a wounded stag. We therefore at once attacked the refection sent forward by the Prior, while Bishop Alcock discoursed on Ledbury cider, and told how 'crabs hot and hissing in the bowl' were good for hippocrass. He pointed out, too, where lay Bosbury, famous for orchards of the Bishops of Hereford, and once the home of that Thomas Brydges who was champion to Bishop Cantilupe. Of Cantilupe the Princess thought we had heard enough, and enquired where was the crab-tree under which King Edgas was reported to have slept after drinking too much cider?[25]

An hour passed away, the merry Princess asked to be conducted to the Hermit's Cave, which she had heard of as being at different times the refuge and hiding place of Sir John Oldcastle and Owen Glendower, when he had taken refuge in the wilds of Herefordshire. We now passed on from the little hostelrie by that wild hollow below the great British Gaer, near which nestles the ancient Priory of Malvern Parva. No rocks frown here from the mountain's brow, but green grass covers the hill slopes, where the coney burrows, and the whin-chat lays its blue eggs among the yellow gorse. With the exception of a cowled monk from the monastery, an occasional traveller, or a hind from the hostelrie, one may go for days without meeting a human being in these solitudes.

With wild forests all around, the camp above, once occupied by an armed multitude, is now a waste, the haunt of the eagle and the kite, save when some antlered stag seeks its solitude. Now its great trenches and deserted vallum are sole memorials of the past, where British bards and Roman legions have in turn looked forth on the surrounding regions, and beheld the Cotswolds on one horizon and the mountains of Wales on the other.

Taking our route below the Gaer we soon reached the Hermit's Cave above the Well of Waum. The refuge of Sir John Oldcastle and Owen Glendower furnished the Bishop with a theme on the subjects of heresy and heretics; magic and enchantments; for it is reported that Glendower, under the name of Jack of Kent, and by the aid of the Devil, built the bridge of Kenderchurch, in Herefordshire, in a single night. The Queen thought it was a pity the learned Bishop had not lived in those days, and I thought so too, for he was too good a man to be a persecutor with the brand and the faggot, and as regards good-will towards men, I would that there had been more like him.

Having well surveyed the haunt of the persecuted, and lately the den of robbers, we walked forward to the hill crest, and were standing upon the summit just above the Red Earl's dyke, when a tall figure in a flowing garb emerged from the woodlands of Waum's Well. I quickly recognized Mary Bolingbroke, who advanced towards us clad in a long cloak of Welsh serge, and with a steeple crowned hat, and with her now snow-white hair floating in the breeze.

The Queen seemed somewhat alarmed at this strange apparition on the wild hill side, until I told her that Mary was well known, and an innocent herbalist. Advancing to meet her, I told her into whose presence she had come, and gracefully, though somewhat sternly, she made her obeisance, for Mary had seen courts and royalty when her learned father was the guest of the good Duke Humphry. The Queen admired the wood vetch with which her hat was twined, and the oak balls she carried for my bonnie girls at home. While Mary's attention seemed concentrated on the briar with its red and white roses which the Princess Elizabeth had made into a girdle; Queen, Princess, and Bishop all seemed forgotten, as with clasped hands she stood gazing on that wreath of roses.

How long she would have continued thus I may not say, had not her trance been broken by the Queen waving her kerchief and saying, "There below us is the King and my noble Edward and truly in front of us, in the vale, but more to the westward, rode the King, the Prince of Wales, and Earl Rivers, their plumes dancing above their hunting caps as they galloped along the broad glade which reaches from the old Saxon mill at Castlemereton to the base of the Gullet pass. We could hear, too, the deep-mouthed baying of the hounds, and the shouts of the foresters and drivers, who were evidently on the track of a wounded stag. The Queen waved her kerchief again and again, the Bishop and I cheered heartily, and the Princess, joyous with glee, trolled forth with melodious voice,

Merrily ride the hunten,
And merrily sounds the horn.

when my own eyes were arrested by a sight which made my blood run cold. I saw the King, the Prince, and Earl Rivers ride from brilliant sunlight into Lethean darkness. I looked again, and *saw it was the Shadow of the Ragged Stone*. A glance at Mary told me she saw it too, as she stood with folded arms and her cheeks like a whited wall.

We said nothing to the wife and mother, and daughter, as they looked in ignorance upon this dread omen of the shadow of death, and were relieved when the Queen expressed a wish to return towards the village of Malvern, and rode back to the ancient Priory; but, in after years, we both remembered how little more than twelve months found the King in his grave at Windsor, the Prince of Wales and his young brother murdered, as was supposed by their uncle's commands, but without trace of their lonely grave,[26] and Earl Rivers a headless corpse at Pontefract. Nor did Mary forget to remind me of the wreath of roses gathered by Longland's water, when Elizabeth of York was happily married to our present noble Tudor King, and thus blended the red rose with the white.

Belief in witchcraft, conjurors, and necromancers, and accusations against others of dealing with the Devil, always haunted the family of the House of York Thus I ever consider that Mary Bolingbroke was a fortunate woman to escape the fate of her father, sooner or later, for we could never persuade her to give up pharmacies, herbments, and such like healings, whenever she knew any one was sick or sorry. Nevertheless, as Elsdune is a lonely spot among our border wilds, and she only visited us from time to time, she did not again acquire the dangerous notoriety for doing good, which arose when she was at Eldersfield; for doing good appears in certain circumstances to be far more dangerous than doing evil. She lived to be an old woman, much petted by us all, and now lies in our peaceful churchyard; her grave well planted with the herbs she loved so well.

Master Hasting is an esquire of no little renown. He fought his last battle on Bosworth Field, against Richard III, for he declares to the present hour that it was him, and no other, who foully spirited away the princely sons of Edward IV. He acquired a goodly property, and has exchanged his battle-axe and bow for the plough. He and his fair wife are ever welcome guests at all our feasts and festivals.

Robin of Elsdune, the noble-hearted archer, lived for several years at Castlemereton, and often received tokens of his royal master's affection and goodwill; but he never again frequented his Court or commanded his body-guard. My children know how we all esteemed his friendship, and how we lamented him when he died.

Sir Roger Calverley, like myself, is grey-haired, bald, and given to podagra; but Bessie is the bonniest and blithest dame in all our country side. Her husband and her children bless the very ground on which she treads. She still wears the red rose in her bodice on summer Sundays at church, but when she comes to see her old friends at our manor she wears a white one too. Dorothy Paunceforte married a learned knight, who, like Earl Rivers, was a friend of Master Caxton; and this was a happy marriage, for Dorothy had a shrewd wit, and much knowledge of the Bible. Silent John married in leap year, when a buxom damosel exercised the well-known privilege of saying "Will you?" and John replied in the one word "Aye".

My dear old mother passed away full of years, and we laid her by my father's side among the daffodils, the primroses, and the nodding star of Bethlehem. The Shadow of the Ragged Stone gave us no token as her death drew nigh, for her life smouldered away like the dying embers on the hearth. My daughter Tacinth is married to Sir Richard Nanfan,[27] a Cornish gentleman, who will succeed to the manor of Birtsmereton; and Amy is now Dame ap-Howell, and married to a descendant of the Welsh kings.

I have often, in past years, wandered among the clefts of the Ragged Stone in the gleaming of the summer evenings, and watched for the dark pillar thrown across the vale, but I never beheld it again.[28] Still, the old man needs no omen as a signal for his departure from this world to another; the grey hairs, the shrunken form, the feeble gait, and the blood which chills with the first frost; all tell him that death is casting his shadow before him as he advances with swift but noiseless steps.

Nor is this all. The companions of his youth are borne to the grave with every passing year, and drop like autumn leaves into their mother earth. But with all this, often, like Will Longland on the Malvern Hills, I have 'slumbered in a sleeping' as I rested 'under a broad bank by a burnside', and dear old faces have come back, and old familiar voices have been again eloquent; faces which are now dust, and voices which have long been silent. So, too, I have seen visions of another land, which lies beyond the deep and narrow stream we all must pass; a land where there is no persecution for religious opinions, no hellish fires, no death, no sin, but where – as says Master Wycliffe's Bible:

His yoke is soft and His charge is light.

Author's Notes

Chapter One
1. Pendyke (Pendock) is mentioned in King Edgar's Charter of AD 964.
2. A supposed portrait of Owen Glendower is still at Kentchurch Park. *Herefordshire Old Stones* p.106. new edition.
3. Bittern
4. Pike
5. Wood-pigeon
6. Male Peregrine Falcon
7. Hedge-sparrow
8. Hedgehog

Chapter Two
1. Bolts for crossbows.
2. Camden says that Edion, a powerful Saxon, gave Ledbury to the Church at Hereford.
3. Payne was chaplain to Sir John Oldcastle, and assisted in releasing him from the Tower.
4. Hippocrass was a spiced wine sweetened with honey. The name is from the filter *Manica Hippocratis* used in making it.
5. When the tomb at Hasfield was opened some years ago, a skeleton was seen with the right hand gone.
6. As late as the year 1649, Margaret Landis, Susan Cooke, Rebecca West, and Rose Holybred were tried and executed for witchcraft at Worcester.
7. *Comp. Hist. Eng.*, vol. i. p.617.
8. Goldsmith records the rubbing of a capon's heart with stinging nettles to make it hatch hens' eggs.

Chapter Three
1. Stow, writing in the time of Queen Elizabeth, says, 'York was prisoner and straighter would have been kept, but that it was noised that the Earl of March was coming'.
2. Hanley Castle, near Upton-on-Severn, was a stronghold of Earl Brithric at the time of the Norman Conquest; a hunting-seat of the Red Earl's in the time of Edward I; and afterwards the occasional resort of the Kingmaker's in the time of Edward IV
3. Mrs. Webb of Ledbury, aged 101, remembers the tradition of Oldcastle hiding. *Old Stones*. new ed. p.39.
4. *Sambucus nigra*, evidently.

Chapter Four
1. Shakespeare takes a poet's licence in the scene near Mortimer's Cross, *Henry VI*, Act ii Sc 1, where he introduces Richard on the battlefield.
2. About this time it was proposed that Henry VI should retire as a saint to the bosom of the Church.
3. See *Swinfield Roll*.
4. See an admirable description of Upton-on-Severn and its history by M. Lawson.

Chapter Five
1. Hosen consisted of breeches and stockings all in one.
2. Leland, who wrote in the time of Henry VIII, confirms this.
3. See the sermon in the *Harleian* MSS. The spelling only is modernised.
4. *Harleian* MSS.
5. See the dress for Satan in the Coventry Plays. In the churchwarden's book of accounts for Tewkesbury, AD 1578, is this entry: 'Pay'd for the Players' geers, six sheepskins for Christ's garments'. In 1585, 'And order eight heads of hair for the apostles, and ten beards, and a face or vizer for the devil.'
6. See *Comprehensive History of England*, vol.i p.683.

Chapter Six
1. Antiquarians believe this so-called tomb of Abbot Wakeman to be at least a century and a half older than Wakeman's time.
2. The arrest of Abbot Boulers was in 1452.
3. This cross was sixty-four feet high and was pulled down in 1749.
4. Bishop Boulers died in 1456.
5. Later on, Dame Digby, wife of Kenelm Digby, was said to be poisoned by the cosmetics of adder skins.
6. Abbot Sebroke died In 1451.
7. This was Abbot Boulers.

Chapter Seven
1. The 'lunar butter' is still believed in, in Russia and Bulgaria.
2. Later on the Witchfinder, Hopkins, was as great a scoundrel.
3. Dene was made Prior of the Gloucester and Welsh establishments in 1460.
4. This happened on July 2nd, 1460.

Chapter Eight
1. This was in 1308. *Comprehensive History of England*, vol.i. p.451
2. Roman coins have been found here.
3. The Danewort *sambucus ebulus* is still used for poultices for cattle.
4. Pendyke, now Pendock. At this church the stone stairs to the rood loft still exist.
5. As will appear, the period of the Wars of the Roses was a time of church restoration and ornamentation.
6. The will of Dorothy Stone is still in existence.
7. *Chenopodium bonus henricus.*
8. See *Swinfield Roll*, Camden Soc.
9. *ibid.*
10. McKay's *Herefordshire Beacon*
11. *Moreton Court* and Lees' *Scenery and Thought.*
12. The Shadow was seen still later in the times of Wolsey and Charles the First. See *Moreton Court.*
13. This battle was fought in 1460.
14. 'Lord Edward, Earl of March, received the news of the death of his father, brother, and friends at Gloucester.' *Comprehensive History of England,*

Chapter Nine
1 An interesting incised effigy of Sir John, in the armour of the period, may be seen in Elmore Church. He died in 1472.
2 See the *Guide* to Hereford Cathedral.
3 Leland, writing in the days of Henry VIII, says that 'it had been one of the fayrest, largest, and strongest castles in England'.
4 This is corroborated by Matthew of Westminster.
5 Dinmore hill was supposed to be the spot Prince Edward rode for, but it is not visible from Widemarsh, and Credenhill is.
6 *Lychinis viscaria* and *Scelanthus perennia* grow in the Devil's Garden still.
7 See the Works of Giraldus Cambrensis.
8 *Scenery and Thought*, p.231, by Edwin Lees.

Chapter Ten
1 See *Woolhope Transactions*, 1869,, p.164., for an interesting and accurate account of 'The ancient Forest of Deerfold' by Dr. Bull.
2 Since known as the battle of Mortimer's Cross.

Chapter Eleven
1 Towton was fought on the 4th of March 1461 and, according to the Paston letters, 40,000 men were slain.
2 See *Parliamentary Rolls*, quoted by Sharon Turner
3 King Edward heard mass at Great Malvern as he passed by.
4 Most of these trackway crosses were destroyed in 1571

Chapter Twelve
None

Chapter Thirteen
1 The portraits of these two celebrated men in the *Rous Roll* delineates them both of commanding stature.
2 It was he who, as Earl Rivers, introduced Caxton, the first English printer, to Edward IV.
3 Those who may feel astonished at the proceedings of these gallant knights, should consult the *Parliamentary Rolls* on the contempt of law at this period by persons of high rank and position.

Chapter Fourteen
1 'The gromes schall gadyi for the kinge's gowns and shetes, swete floures, herbis, rotes and thynes to make them breathe most holesomely and delectable.' *Manners and Household Expenses of Edaward VI*.
2 *Comprehensive History of England*.
3 *ibid*. These were choice dishes at the stately banquets of this period.

Chapter Fifteen
1 Shakespeare calls it Hamme Castle.
2 Called now Tewkesbury Park, and mentioned by Leland as the home of Lord Spenser.

3 A Mlle Angot is recorded as being the champion tennis player of France, 1426.
4 This is the present parish church of Winchcambe. See *Annals of Sudeley*, by Mrs Dent.
5 *ibid*. Abbot Kyderminster sent one to Cardinal Wolsey in 1520.
6 See Dyde's *History of Tewkesbury*, p.96.
7 In Henry the Eighth's time, according to Leland, only 'Ruines of the bottoms of waules appere'.
8 Fordington, now Forthampton, was called Fortemeltone in Domesday times.
9 This spire fell on Easter Day, 1559
10 Small baskets for catching eel fry.

Chapter Sixteen
1 See *Comprehensive History of England*, vol.i p.621.
2 'Scowles' are old mining shafts.
3 *The Great Berkeley Lawsuit*, J. H. Cooke, Trans. Brist, and Glou. Arch. Soc.
4 This window was destroyed by violent wind in February 1661
5 *Parliamentary Rolls*, 6. 232.
6 See de Comines' account of the Lancastrian sufferings in France.
7 Bury Mill is mentioned in Domesday, and Alice Shipside no doubt belonged to the family from whom was descended George Shipside, who was brother-in-law to Bishop Ridley, martyred at Oxford, and whose tomb is in Redmarley Church.
8 Destroyed by the order of Henry the Eighth.
9 Sir John Paston, who was in the battle, gives these numbers. Later writers made it 10,000. *Paston Letters*.
10 Holinshed.
11 *ibid*.
12 Now the residence of J. P. Sargeaunt, Esq. In Leland's time a house was built, 'yn this Theocsbyri Parke, wher the Lord Edward Spensar lay, and late my Lady Mary'. Leyland's *Itinerary*.

Chapter Seventeen
1 See *Swinfield Roll*, Camden Soc
2 See Holinshed's account
3 The Queen's Camp is pointed out to this day, but it is the opinion of soldiers and engineers that, if this was the spot, there were entrenchments, before Queen Margaret's occupation, of older date.
4 See Holinshed.
5 The church had to be re-consecrated, and this was afterwards done by the Bishop of Down and Connor.
6 See Holinshed.
7 *ibid*.
8 That the Princess was present, see Miss Strickland's *Queens of England*, and *Flemish Chronicle*.
9 *Cont. Hist. Croyl*. None of the earlier accounts implicate the nobles.
10 Fabyan's *Chronicle*.

11 Part of this pit was exposed, near the Cheltenham turnpike, during excavations for the new sewerage.
12 An old engraving at Ghent shows the King looking out from the window of a house in the exact position tradition assigns as that where Prince Edward was killed.
13 See list in Leland's *Itinerary*.
14 This tradition is well treated by the Rev. E.R. Dowdeswell, in the *Bushley Almanack* for 1877.
15 This alludes to a well-known Lancastrian scandal.
16 McKay, *Herefordshire Beacon*.
17 Dame Calverley seems to have been aware of Chaucer's description of the Daisy: 'Of all the flowers in the mede them love I most, those flowers white and redde, such as men call daisies in our town.'
18 *Paston Letters*. Queasy = uneasy.
19 Prior John de Malverne commenced the work of restoration in 1450.
20 Leland visited Malvern in the reign of Henry VIII, and noted St Werstan's chapel and death.
21 The glass in the great east window was probably the presentation of Edward IV or his Queen. The suns of Edward IV are still to be seen in the glass.
22 The Chapel of St Michael was situated a little below St Ann's Well. See *Antiquitates Prioratus* (Thomas), 1725
23 Wilement's *Heraldry*.
24 Probably *Pinguicula vulgaris*.
25 Lees on the Crab. *Herefordshire Pomona*, part iii
25 The bodies of the Princes were not found until the reign of Charles II.
27 Afterwards Governor of Calais, where Wolsey accompanied him.
28 Tradition, notwithstanding, connects the shadow with the duel in the Bloody Meadow, and before this with the last days of Cardinal Wolsey. See *Moreton Court*, by a Lady, and *The Camp of the Herefordshire Beacon*, by McKay.

Associated Works

GRINDROD, CHARLES F., *The Shadow of the Ragged Stone*: A novel. Elkin Matthew, London, 1909.

MCKAY, JAMES., Essays on the 'Lives of the Ancient Britons on British Camp and the Herefordshire Beacon'. 1875

GIBBON, VIOLET, *Malvern Chase*: A Pageant Play based on the novel, performed at Upton-on-Severn on 22nd, 23rd, 24th July, 1913. Malvern Library Local Collection.

Bibliography

W.S. SYMONDS

Personal Notebook of Natural History with illustrations. Malvern Library Local Collection.

Old Stones: 'Notes of Lectures on the Plutonic, Silurian, and Devonian rocks in the Neighbourhood of Malvern'. Malvern, 1855.

—New Edition: Simpkin, Marshal & Co., London, Malvern, 1880.

'Geology as it affects a Plurality of Worlds'. pp.94. An Essay reprinted from the *Edinburgh New Philosophical Journal* for 1855–6. London and Worcester, 1856.

Stones of the Valley: pp.xii. 270. 8 plates. Bentley, London, 1857.

'On the Passage Beds from the Upper Silurian Rocks into the Lower Old Red Sandstone at Ledbury, Herefordshire'. *Quarterly Journal of the Geological Society*, vol.xvi. pt2.no..2 May 1860.

Old Bones: or 'Notes for Young Naturalists', pp.viii 127. 10 plates. Worcester, 1860. London, 1861. 16mo.

—Second Edition: 'thoroughly revised', London, 1864.

—Third Edition: London, 1884.

'On the Sections of the Malvern and Ledbury tunnels and intervening line of Railroad'. illus. *Proceedings Geological Association*, 1861.

'On the Geology of the Railway from Worcester to Hereford', pp.34. Reprinted from the *Edinburgh New Philosophical Journal* for 1862. Harwick, London.

'Notes on the Geology of the Ross district'. 1863.

'Address on the enjoyment to be derived from the study of Natural Sciences'. London, 1863.

'Notes on a Ramble through Wales'. A Lecture delivered to the Worcester Natural History Society, etc. Worcester, Cheltenham, 1864.

'A Lecture of Progress and Development.' London, Gloucester, 1869.

Records of the Rocks: or 'Notes on the Geology, Natural History, and Antiquities of north and south Wales, Devon, and Cornwall.' pp.xx. 433. illus. London, 1872.

'The Geology and Archaeology of the South Malvern District'. pp.10. A paper read to the Cotswold Field Club, July 1875,

Malvern Chase: 'An Episode in the Wars of the Roses and the Battle of Tewkesbury.' pp.viii. 336. 8 illus. W. North, Tewkesbury, 1880.

—Second Edition: pp.viii. 336 8 illus. W. North, Tewkesbury, 1881.

—Third Edition: pp.viii. 336 frontis. W. North, Tewkesbury, 1883.

—Fourth Edition: pp.viii. 336 frontis. W. North, Tewkesbury, 1885.

—Fifth Edition: pp.viii. 336 frontis. W. North, Tewkesbury, 1887.

—Sixth Edition: pp.viii. 336 frontis. W. North, Tewkesbury, 1901.

—Seventh Edition: pp.viii. 336 frontis. W. North, Tewkesbury, ? 1907.

—Eighth Edition: pp.viii. 336 frontis. W. North, Tewkesbury, 1913.

—Reprinted Edition: Malvern Bookshop, 1974.

Hanley Castle: an Episode of the Civil Wars and Battle of Worcester, pp.xi. 347 W. North, Tewkesbury, 1883.

The Severn Straits: or 'Notes on Glacial Drifts, bone caverns, and old glaciers, etc., pp.65 W. North, Tewkesbury, 1883.

Biography

William Samuel Symonds was the son of William Symonds and Mary Anne Beale and was born at Elsdon in Herefordshire in December 1818. He graduated from Christ's College, Cambridge, in 1842, and in the following year was appointed as a curate at Offenham near Evesham.

He became Rector of Pendock in Worcestershire in 1845 and a few years later inherited Pendock Court from his mother. He devoted a great deal of energy to researches in archaeology, geology, and natural history, and made several visits to the Auvergne in a search for ancient glaciers. He was a member of the Worcester Natural History Society, the Woolhope and Cotteswold Field Clubs, and for eighteen years President of the Malvern Field Club.

William Symonds wrote forty-three papers on scientific subjects and edited two books by Hugh Miller. He compiled pamphlets on geology and natural history for younger readers and wrote *Malvern Chase* and *Hanley Castle*, the two historical romances for which he is best known.

He and his wife Hyacinth had three sons and a daughter, also called Hyacinth, who married Sir Joseph Hooker, the explorer, President of the Royal Society and supporter of Charles Darwin.

From 1877 onwards William Symonds' health declined and he lived with his daughter and son-in-law at Sunningdale. He died in Cheltenham on the 15th of September 1887 and is buried at Pendock.

Cappella Archive
Limited Editions

Cappella Archive provides a similar mastering service for writers that a recording studio does for musicians. The typeset book file is stored in a digital Archive and copies are printed individually on request as they are ordered; the Archive behaving as the printing equivalent of audio or video dubbing.

The Archive is application-independent and may be re-edited at any time or translated directly onto plates or film for quantity production.

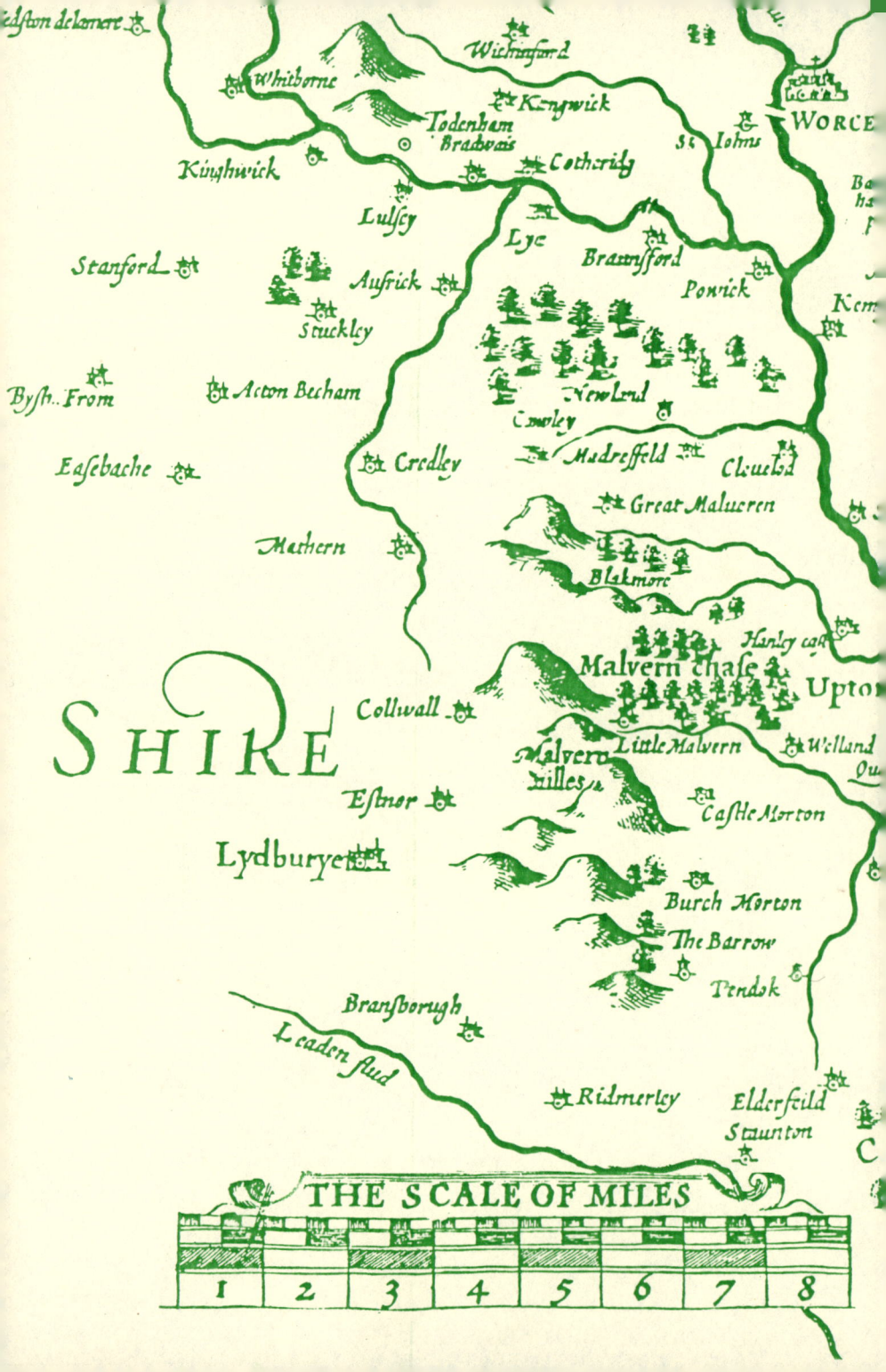

[Map of Worcestershire area]

- edston delamere
- Whitborne
- Wichinford
- Kingwick
- Todenham
- Bradwais
- Cothcridg
- St. Johns
- WORCE
- Kinghwick
- Lulsey
- Lye
- Bramsford
- Powick
- Ba ha
- Stanford
- Ausrick
- Kem
- Stuckley
- Bysh. From
- Acton Becham
- Newland
- Easebache
- Credley
- Cmoley
- Madresfeld
- Cluehd
- Great Malueren
- Mathern
- Blakmore
- Hanley cast
- Malvern chase
- Upto
- SHIRE
- Collwall
- Little Malvern
- Welland
- Malvern hilles
- Qu
- Estnor
- Castle Morton
- Lydburye
- Burch Morton
- The Barrow
- Pendok
- Bransborough
- Leaden flud
- Ridmerley
- Elderfeild
- Staunton
- C

THE SCALE OF MILES

| 1 | 2 | 3 | 4 | 5 | 6 | 7 | 8 |